Men, Women and Madness

Also by Joan Busfield

Thinking About Children: Sociology and Fertility in Post-War England (with Michael Paddon)

Managing Madness: Changing Ideas and Practice

Men, Women and Madness

Understanding Gender and Mental Disorder

JOAN BUSFIELD

Consultant Editor: Jo Campling

First published 1996 by
MACMILLAN PRESS LTD
Houndmills, Basingstoke, Hampshire RG21 6XS
and London
Companies and representatives
throughout the world

ISBN 0–333–46369–2 hardcover
ISBN 0–333–46370–6 paperback

A catalogue record for this book is available
from the British Library.

10   9   8   7   6   5   4   3   2   1
05 04 03 02 01 00 99 98 97 96

Printed in Malaysia

Contents

PART II   GENDER AND THE ORIGINS OF MENTAL
DISORDER

List of Tables and Figures

Tables

Figures

Acknowledgements

The author and publishers wish to thank the following for permission to use copyright material:

R. Cochrane for Table 6 from *The Social Creation of Mental Illness*, 1984, Longman, p. 91; The Controller of Her Majesty's Stationery Office for Tables 2, 4, 5, 10 from Crown copyright material; Royal College of General Practice for Tables 1, 3 from *Morbidity Statistics from General Practice, 1981–2*, 1986, Tables 8, 17; Tavistock Publications for Fig. 3 from G. W. Brown and T. Harris, *Social Origins of Depression: A Study of Psychiatric Disorder in Women*.

Every effort has been made to trace all the copyright holders but if any have been inadvertently overlooked the publishers will be pleased to make the necessary arrangement at the first opportunity.

Preface

The phenomena of mental illness or, to use a less medical term, mental disorder, attract enormous interest both lay and professional.[1] In lay understandings terms like mental illness and mental disorder frequently generate images of severe disturbance involving hallucinations and delusions – real madness – that often seem threatening, disturbing and dangerous, as well as difficult to comprehend. Equally the terms may conjure up images of people who face severe difficulties in their lives and become depressed or anxious, or resort to drugs or alcohol to deal with their problems. Such images, whether of the difficult and dangerous, or of the disturbed and tormented, conflict with the more detached, scientific language of illness and the formal characteristics of mental disorders provided by psychiatrists.

Yet, this detached, formal language hides a terrain that is highly contested both within psychiatry and between psychiatry and other mental health professions, and beneath the scientific language there is turbulence and controversy. There are contests over the precise boundaries of mental disorder and over what phenomena, if any, properly belong to the category, as well as over the language with which the phenomena should be described. There are also major debates about the identification of particular individuals as mentally disturbed, about the causes of mental disorder, and about the appropriate form of response to those who are deemed disordered.[2]

My aim in this book is not to try to settle all these key areas of debate. Rather it is to explore one controversial area: that concerning the relationship between gender and mental disorder. This will, however, require some examination of other disputed areas, especially that surrounding the category of mental disorder itself. Nonetheless, my overriding objective is to explore the interconnections between gender and mental disorder: to examine, for instance, the over-representation of women in present day patient populations and to see how far it remains once the data are disaggregated; to explore the extent to which gender is embedded in concepts of mental disorder; and to consider the extent to which the biological, psychological and social factors conducive to mental disorder differ between men and women.

It is feminist writers, such as Phyllis Chesler (1972), Barbara Ehrenreich and Deirdre English (1979), Dorothy Smith (Smith and David 1975), Ihsan Al-Issa (1980), Kim Chernin (1983, 1985), Susan Penfold and Gillian Walker (1984), Susie Orbach (1978, 1986), Elaine Showalter (1987), Susan Bordo (1985, 1990) and Jane Ussher (1991), who have largely opened up the terrain of gender and mental disorder to wider debate. Yet, significantly, very few of them are sociologists by training – they are psychologists (Chesler, Al-Issa and Ussher), literary scholars (Showalter), philosophers (Bordo), psychiatrists (Penfold), social workers (Walker) and psychotherapists (Orbach). Sociologists have been markedly absent from discussions of the terrain. One notable exception is Walter Gove (Gove 1972; Gove and Tudor 1972). However, his approach was epidemiological (see Chapter 10 for a fuller discussion of his work) and, while not uninfluenced by feminist writing, he was not a feminist. Feminist sociologists have made relatively little contribution to the field, apart from the important work of Dorothy Smith and the occasional, though significant, incursions by writers such as Carol Smart (1976) and Hilary Allen (1986); but the concern of the latter writers has been more with the criminal justice than the mental health system.

My own approach has its foundations both in sociology and in feminism (although my earlier training was in clinical psychology), and I have sought to locate an understanding of gender and mental disorder within a sociologically informed analysis that is sensitive to, and shaped by, feminist concerns. This book is not, however, intended for an exclusively sociological audience. I hope that it will be of interest to sociological colleagues, feminist or otherwise, who are interested in mental disorder; but I have also written it for those whose background is not in sociology – especially for a range of clinicians and practitioners, such as psychologists, psychiatrists and social workers, who have day-to-day contact with people with some mental disturbance. For this reason I have not assumed any great familiarity with sociological literature, feminist or otherwise. For the sociological cognoscenti this may at times mean that I am rehearsing ideas, concepts and arguments that could have been taken for granted. Yet if I detail some of the sociological arguments, this is not only because they are less familiar to those outside the discipline, but also because I think many repay further exploration.

The strategy I adopt in exploring this territory is both theoretical and empirical. On the one hand, I examine key concepts and theories which have been deployed in an effort to make sense of the field. This theoretical examination involves not only an exploration of the concepts of gender and mental disorder and of theoretical approaches to them, but also an examination of ideas about their interrelation, both those that focus on the impact of gender on the construction of categories of mental disorder, and those that focus on the origins of mental disorder and the way in which gender may make men or women more or less vulnerable to mental disorder as currently defined.

On the other hand, I draw on a range of empirical material in developing my own analysis and arguments. The data I consider are culled from a range of sources: from official statistics on the social distribution of mental disorder, from a diverse range of social surveys and qualitative interviews, from psychiatric textbooks, policy reports, and so forth – a diversity of documentary data that can help us to build up a detailed picture about the interconnections between gender and mental disorder.

In my view good sociology requires attention both to theory and to empirical data and there is a continuing danger of a split within the discipline, with fashionable theorists prone to build their exciting intellectual castles, which attract much of the academic attention, but are too often poorly grounded empirically, usually contain sweeping generalisations and are, at times, rather inaccessible. Against this there are empirical sociologists engaged in the difficult process of data collection, whose own work may be under-theorised, and is frequently dismissed as empiricist.[3] I have tried, therefore, to bring both theory and data together as far as possible, recognising that such an enterprise is far from easy and that in so doing one is likely to end up satisfying neither sociological camp.

My debts in writing this book are pervasive. A major debt is to feminist scholars over the past two and a half decades who made it impossible for issues of gender to be ignored within disciplines like sociology. In this it has been a tremendous advantage to be in a department of sociology like that at Essex, which has regularly had six or seven women members of the permanent full-time staff, most with varying interests in aspects of gender. Their presence has been an enormous support and inspiration, not least through the routine, fleeting and often apparently trivial interactions that make up the daily round of hard-pressed academic life. Indeed, I owe a debt to all members – students and staff – of the Department of Sociology at the University of Essex, which has provided a diverse, challenging and stimulating intellectual environment and a friendly and supportive community in which to work. I also owe a particular debt to Mary Girling, Julie Andrews, Brenda Corti, Sue Aylott and Diane Streeting who have all helped me in different ways to complete this work. I would also like to thank Colin Samson and an anonymous referee who have provided helpful comments on draft chapters.

Of course, the demands of Department and University have also frequently been a distraction from this study and the adverse impact of the Government's strategies for saving money has permeated all aspects of University life. The complex balancing act that is necessary in these circumstances to retain any residue of domestic or social life is regrettably invisible to those who see academics as leading protected lives in their ivory towers. Michael, Lindsay and Jeffrey have generally borne my absences from domestic affairs and my commitments to work with commendable tolerance. I would especially like to thank them for their support, as well as that of Delfina Dolza, Diana Gittins; my parents and friends.

JOAN BUSFIELD

Chapter 1

Introduction

> Psychiatry is both part of the ideological and coercive mechanisms of indus-
> trial society and at the same time is committed to the resolution of the very
> tensions and strains which that society and its institutions produce. It is from
> this central contradiction that many other difficulties stem and this makes it
> possible for psychiatry to take a part in the oppression of some of the very
> people it purports, and intends, to help (Penfold and Walker 1984: v).

Over the past twenty-five years feminist scholarship in all its diversity
has opened up the terrain of the relationship between gender, mental
disorder and the mental health services in an unprecedented way. In
previous centuries scholars and practitioners have, from time to time,
highlighted gender imbalances in patients with particular mental disorders and have also sometimes offered distinctively gendered accounts
of these disorders. Yet in the twentieth century it has only been with
the impact of second-wave feminism that gender has come into prominence as a major object of enquiry within the field of mental disorder.
The classic studies of psychiatric epidemiology – the study of the distribution of mental disorders – largely eschewed attention to gender
differences until the 1970s, and seemed to consider it a matter of little
significance whether patient populations were predominantly male or
female. For example, A.B. Hollingshead and F.C. Redlich's highly
influential study, *Social Class and Mental Illness* (1958), relegated data on
gender differences to an appendix and offered no interpretation of the
figures they provided.[1]

The varied feminist scholarship of writers such as Phyllis Chesler
(1972), Barbara Ehrenreich and Deirdre English (1974, 1976, 1979),
Dorothy Smith (Smith and David 1975), Ihsan Al-Issa (1980), Susie
Orbach (1978, 1986), Louise Eichenbaum and Susie Orbach (1982,

1984), Susan Penfold and Gillian Walker (1984), Kim Chernin (1983, 1985), Susan Bordo (1985, 1990) and Jane Ussher (1991) has helped to bring issues of gender centre stage. Much of their work, with a view to making women visible, has taken the over-representation of women in present-day (or past) psychiatric populations as a starting point and has then developed in one (or more) of three major directions.

First, some feminists have been keen to document, highlight and frequently condemn, the treatment (in its broadest sense) of women within the mental health system. Phyllis Chesler, for example, whose *Women and Madness* (1972) provided the path-breaking study in the field (it is discussed in detail in Chapter 6), not only highlights the fact that women are over-represented as psychiatric patients, but she also describes how gender influences the way women are treated by psychiatrists and mental health professionals. 'Clinicians', she asserts, 'most of whom are men all too often treat their patients, most of whom are women, as "wives" and "daughters", rather than as people: treat them as if female misery, by biological definition exists outside the realm, of what is considered human or adult' (1972: xxi).

Such claims about the way gender shapes the encounter between male professional, often a doctor, and female patient, were also emphasised by Ehrenreich and English in various publications (1974, 1976, 1979). They argued that female dependence and female sickness were actually advantageous to the interests of medical men, not only providing them with patients, and thereby helping to secure their expertise and professional standing in the competition with other healers (often women), but also increasing women's compliance as patients:

> The general theory which guided doctors' practice as well as their public pronouncements was that women were, by nature, weak, dependent, and diseased. Thus would the doctors attempt to secure their victory over the female healer: with the 'scientific' evidence that women's essential nature was not to be a strong, competent, help-giver but to be a *patient* (1979: 92).

Women were encouraged to be *The Patient Patients* (Roberts 1985).

Chesler, however, in documenting women's experiences as psychiatric patients, took the argument one step further and pointed not just to the creation of compliant patients but also to the direct sexual exploitation of women patients by male therapists. In *Women and Madness* (1972), she devoted a chapter to 'Sex Between Patient and Therapist'. In it she provided evidence that the sexual exploitation of vulnerable patients was not uncommon and pointed to the way in which some therapists actually claim that sexual intercourse with patients is therapeutic for the patients and is to be recommended. Not surprisingly, given the major ethical issues such practices raise, the matter has been taken up by others, including some professional associations. For example, in 1974 the American Psychological Association established a Task Force to explore sexism in psychotherapeutic practice. Its report contended that 'The percentage of therapists engaging in sexual relations with their patients is unknown but *believed* to be small' (American Psychological Association Task Force 1975, my italics). It noted that almost all complaints were from female patients regarding male therapists, but did not proceed to make a clear recommendation on the issue, though it noted that 'sexual intimacy makes it difficult if not impossible for the therapist to remain objective and to conduct the course of therapy in a manner beneficial to the patient's interests' (ibid). Certainly, although it is difficult to quantify its occurrence, there is considerable evidence that some male therapists do exploit their position of power and sexually abuse their female patients (see Masson 1990: Chapter 6; Ussher 1991: 179–83).

Less extreme, but quantitatively more significant, is the use of psychotropic drugs to control female patients. Psychotropic drugs are, of course, widely used within the mental health services, both for inpatients and out-patients, and within primary care settings. Feminists have, however, pointed to the fact that women patients are far more likely to be prescribed some form of psychotropic medication than men, the standard ratios being something in the order of two to one (see, for instance, Cooperstock 1981; Penfold and Walker 1984: Chapter 9; Ettoré and Riska 1993).[2] And women have also been active as users in identifying the problems of drug dependence associated with tranquilliser use. Other feminists have pointed to the greater use of ECT on women patients and to the biases against women in family therapy where women tend to be blamed for any problems within the family.[3]

In documenting these phenomena, feminists point to the way in which gender permeates professional thinking about patients and this, in turn, influences the types of treatment offered and the nature of the professional–patient interaction. In particular, as the quotations above from Chesler and from Ehrenreich and English indicate, some feminists have emphasised and explored the way in which differences between men and women are attributed to 'nature', and are held to have a fixed, biological basis (such ideas are discussed more fully in Chapter 8). A number of feminist social historians have, for example, examined the character of biological thinking about women in the eighteenth and nineteenth centuries (see, for instance, the influential work of Carol Smith-Rosenberg 1974). Others have focused their attention on twentieth-century ideas (see Penfold and Walker 1984: Chapter 6), pointing to the way in which such theories regulate and control women and are a crucial feature of gender biases in mental health practice.

However, feminists have also sought to move beyond documenting the injustices perpetrated on women within the mental health system as part of the supposedly therapeutic process – the contradiction Penfold and Walker term 'the psychiatric paradox' (1984) – and have endeavoured to explain their over-representation in psychiatric patient populations. The focus has been on one of two broad approaches. One approach, which constitutes the second main direction of feminist scholarship, has been on the way in which categories of mental disorder are themselves constituted. Here the work often draws on the intellectual foundations of 1960s anti-psychiatry (see Chapter 4 below). Chesler's *Women and Madness* (1972), has also been especially influential in exploring this particular direction. Her claim is that gender is embedded in the concept of mental disorder itself and that there is a double standard of mental health, with the result that women are more likely than men to be defined as mentally disordered.

Chesler's claims, which are analysed in Chapter 6, have also been affirmed by other feminists. Elaine Showalter in *The Female Malady*, which deals with the period 1830 to 1970, identifies a strong cultural association between conceptions of madness and femininity throughout this period. Contemporary feminists she asserts:

> have been the first to call attention to the existence of a fundamental alliance between 'woman' and 'madness'. They have shown how women, within our dualistic systems of language and representation, are typically situated on the side of irrationality, silence, nature and body, while men are situated on the side of reason, discourse, culture and mind (1987: 3–4).[4]

The task, she suggests, is to show 'how, in a particular cultural context, notions of gender influence the definition and, consequently, the treatment of mental disorder' (1987: 5). Similar ideas about the link between women and madness are also put forward by Jane Ussher in *Women's Madness* when she argues, albeit from a rather different theoretical perspective, that women tend to be positioned as mad and sees this as a product of misogyny which silences women and renders them powerless (1991: 7).[5]

Finally, the task of explaining the female over-representation in psychiatric patient populations has also been explored by feminists through an examination of the ways in which women's position in society may be particularly conducive to madness and mental disorder (as they are defined at particular times and places). This third direction of feminist scholarship, which often involves a rejection of biological explanations of difference, is the most diverse and has been explored both in relation to specific mental disorders and in relation to mental disorders in general. Notable in the first group is the work of writers such as Susie Orbach (1986, 1993), Kim Chernin (1983, 1985) and Susan Bordo (1985, 1990) on anorexia nervosa (see Chapter 9). Notable in the second group is the work of feminist authors on female and male psychology such as that of Juliet Mitchell (1975), Nancy Chodorow (1978, 1989) and Jean Baker Miller (1988), some of which is also discussed in Chapter 9. Also relevant here is the work of those who have linked mental disorder in women to their oppression (see Oakley 1982).[6]

Some writers have contended, however, that in pursuing both of these directions – that of an emphasis on mental disorder as a social construct and the emphasis on mental disorder as a social product – the feminist stance is contradictory: that it is illogical both to wish to call the category of mental disorder into question and at the same time to wish to argue that women are more likely to be driven to madness and mental disorder by virtue of their oppression (see Sedgwick 1982: 236–7). However, as I have argued elsewhere (Busfield 1988), these two basic approaches to the task of explaining gender differences are not in fact inconsistent. It is not at all contradictory both to analyse critically concepts of mental disorder and point to the way gender is embedded within them, whilst also examining the factors that may lead women (and men) to feel and act in ways that place them within the boundaries of mental disorder as currently constituted.

Nonetheless, despite the invaluable contribution of this varied feminist scholarship over the past twenty-five years, there are limitations and weaknesses in some of the feminist arguments and analyses and there are areas that require further study and development. First, as the title of many of the books mentioned so far, and others, indicate – *Women and Madness* (Chesler 1972); *Women Look at Psychiatry* (Smith and David 1975); *For Their Own Good: 150 Year of the Experts' Advice to Women* (Ehrenreich and English 1979); *The Psychopathology of Women* (Al-Issa 1980); *Women and the Psychiatric Paradox* (Penfold and Walker 1984); *The Female Malady* (Showalter 1987); *Women's Madness* (Ussher 1991) – most have primarily focused on women. This strategy has been vital in bringing women into the framework of analysis when they have too frequently been ignored. As Ussher, talking of psychology, puts its: 'psychology has developed as a singularly male enterprise, with men studying men and applying the findings to all of humanity; hence it is time to redress the balance' (1991: 9).

Yet, in my view (see Chapter 3), there is a danger in trying to redress the balance through a simple reversal of the previous masculine vision, as many feminists have been prone to do. Women certainly need to be made visible and their experiences described and explored. But if we are to move beyond documenting their experiences and treatment within the mental health services, the experiences and treatment of men do need to be explicitly and regularly kept in the frame. And this means attention not just to male professionals but also to male patients. Hence, though taking feminism as its starting point and building on feminist scholarship, this book focuses on gender – that is, on differences between men and women – and on gender relations, not just on women.

Second, apart from a few significant exceptions (a paper by Dorothy Smith (1975) is especially notable), feminist scholars have seemed rather reluctant to examine the epidemiological data on gender and mental disorder in any detailed or systematic way, to disaggregate them in terms of diagnosis, age, marital status, social class, ethnicity and so on, and to consider the inferences that can be drawn from them. I believe this is unfortunate. I argue that a fuller exploration of the epidemiological data – both in terms of the findings and the way the data is produced – can help to illuminate the interrelationships between gender and mental disorder. This is not least (although not solely) because the concept of mental disorder as formally constituted is given meaning through the specification of distinctive mental disorders (the so-called categorical model of mental disorder – see Chapter 4), which are themselves linked to gender. Chesler, for example, while she emphasises 'a large female involvement with psychiatric facilities' (1972: 118) and provides some quantitative data, does not attempt to examine them very systematically. And this reluctance to give much attention to the quantitative picture or to attempt any disaggregation applies even more to Showalter's *The Female Malady* (see Busfield 1994), although in an earlier article (1980) Showalter does consider some patient statistics.[7]

Third, while some feminists have claimed, controversially, that gender is embedded in the concepts of madness and mental disorder, they have had rather little to say about how we can best theorise the concepts themselves. Most have operated with the assumption, fashionable in the 1960s, that mental disorder is best viewed as a form of deviance, but have made little attempt to develop the theorisation of the concept in ways that would facilitate our understanding of gender differences. One objective of this book is, consequently, to advance the debate about theorisations of mental disorder in a way that can inform our understanding of gender and mental disorder. To this end I argue (see Chapter 4) that neither the medical conceptualisation of mental disorder as illness or the sociological conceptualisation of mental disorder as deviance is entirely satisfactory for theoretical purposes. Instead, drawing on Foucault (1967), I advocate a conceptualisation of mental disorder in terms of irrationality and unreason, arguing that this offers a range of advantages, including that of providing clues as to the way in which conceptions of mental disorder interact with gender.[8]

Fourth, with the significant exception of Chesler's analysis in *Women and Madness* (1972) and Hilary Allen's (1986) critique of her argument, feminists have given relatively little attention to the precise *mechanisms* that link gender to the construction of categories of mental disorder. The significance of this issue is suggested by Beverley Brown's interesting discussion of biologism – the tendency to attribute the characteristics of women to biology – in the context of criminology and criminal justice settings. She argues that we cannot simply assume that biologism has particular consequences for practice. Rather we need to raise questions about 'how such ideological beliefs are in fact supposed to produce the claimed effects' (1990: 48). This is because we can readily hypothesise alternative consequences from the same beliefs. The same argument applies not only to the relation between biologism in mental health professionals' beliefs and their actual practice, but also to the issue of the ways in which gender relates to categories of mental disorder (see Chapter 6). It is essential, therefore, to consider precisely *how* gender is linked to constructs of mental disorder.

Feminist scholarship has arguably not only been most diverse, but also most successful, in its accounts of why women may become mentally disturbed. This particularly applies to some of the work on specific mental disorders; it is perhaps less true of the more general accounts which tend to focus on either female (and male) psychology, or on the pressures women face in contemporary society. Whilst the feminist psychologies tend to be constructed in rather too universal terms and expose themselves to the dangers of essentialism (see Chapter 9), accounts structured in terms of female oppression, tend to be grounded in epidemiological work on stress and suffer from the deficiencies of this approach (see Chapter 10). There is also a need, therefore, for further examination of possible gender differences in the origins of mental disorder. I shall argue that, although the evidence of the impact of social factors in generating mental disorder (as currently constituted) is very strong, a focus on the specific structural features of men's and women's lives, and the meanings attached to them, is more fruitful than more generalised claims about quantities of stress or levels of oppression or, indeed, about fundamental differences in the psychological needs of men and women. However, as some of the best work on specific disorders indicates, a satisfactory analysis requires us to range across matters of biology, psychology, social structure, material resources and culture.

These issues form the focus of the chapters that follow. Part I of the book deals with gender, constructs of disorder and services. My starting point is, as it has been for many other authors in the field, with the over-representation of women in patient statistics. In Chapter 2, I analyse this over-representation in some detail, disaggregating the data across a range of dimensions – diagnosis, age, marital status, social class, ethnicity and historical period – to show a complex, gendered landscape of patient populations. This provides an essential preliminary to further consideration of the interrelationships between gender and mental disorder. So, too, do Chapters 3 and 4 in which I examine concepts and theories concerning first gender and then mental disorder. I believe it is important to have some awareness of approaches to the analysis of both gender and mental disorder independently of one another before we can properly analyse their interrelationships. In Chapter 4, I develop the conceptualisation of mental disorder as unreason and irrationality.

Chapter 5 returns to the epidemiological data and asks, in the light of the examination of the discussion of the concept of mental disorder, what inferences can be drawn from the data on gender differences. In particular, it considers whether it is possible on the basis of the data, to make any claims that women are – either in aggregate, or within particular sub-groups – more likely to become mentally disordered than men. This entails some consideration of gender biases in diagnosis and willingness to report symptoms. These issues are then further explored through a consideration of one disorder – depression. Here I touch on the question of whether depression and alcoholism are in certain respects psychological equivalents, which also raises important issues about gender differences in emotional expression that I examine. I conclude by arguing that any claims about gender differences in levels of disorder must necessarily be highly qualified and restrictive and are always *construct specific*. I also note that the epidemiological data often tell us more about psychiatric practices and the mental health services than they do about gender differences in mental health problems.

In Chapter 6, I turn to the specific issue of whether gender is embedded in constructs of mental disorder as Chesler and others have claimed. I contend that the evidence does support this claim, and I examine the precise mechanisms through which the two are connected paying particular attention to issues of agency and rationality. Chapter 7 brings the threads of the earlier arguments together through an analysis of the history of psychiatric ideas, practices and institutions in Britain, primarily covering the nineteenth and the twentieth centuries, indicating the ways in which they have been linked to changes in the gender balance of patient populations.

In Part II of the book, the emphasis shifts from constructs and services to the origins of mental disorder. Chapter 8 examines biological theorising about gender and the origins of mental disorder. In it I argue that while consideration of biological processes is relevant to understanding the causes of mental disorder, twentieth-century ideas manifest the types of biologism and gender bias found in nineteenth-century ideas. Assumptions about the nature of women still help to shape the way professionals think about the patients with whom they deal, the categories of disorder that are constructed (such as pre-menstrual disorder) and the treatments that are provided. In Chapter 9 the focus is on feminist accounts of the psychological development of men and women. I argue that, though these accounts have important strengths and help us to understand gender differences in emotional expression, they also have, as I have already noted, a number of limitations. The way in which such ideas can be deployed more effectively in theories which combine some concern with psychology, but move beyond that to emphasise social and cultural factors, are then examined through a discussion of feminist theories of anorexia nervosa.

In Chapter 10, I consider a different explanatory tradition and examine epidemiological accounts that link features of the individual's social situation to mental disorder via the notion of stress. I argue that while the notion of stress has some heuristic value in explanations of mental disorder, it is not possible to make satisfactory quantitative comparisons between the different levels of stress men and women experience. Instead, a focus on specific structural features of men's and women's situations is likely to generate more explanatory insights. Two of these features – the domestic division of labour and women's employment outside the home are explored in the remainder of the Chapter. Another feature of men's and women's situations – violence – is the focus of Chapter 11 which examines first the specific trauma of war, via the concept of shell-shock, and then the important issue of sexual violence. In the final chapter, Chapter 12, I draw the arguments of the book together and briefly consider the policy implications.

Part I

Gender, Constructs and Services

Chapter 2

The Gendered Landscape

It should seem that no chronic disease occurs so frequently as this [hysteria]; and that, as fevers with their attendants constitute two thirds of the diseases to which mankind are liable upon comparing them with the whole tribe of chronic distempers, so hysteric disorders, or at least such as are so called make up half the remaining third part, that is they constitute one moiety of chronic distempers. For few women, (which sex makes one half of the grown persons) excepting such as work and fare hardly, are quite free from every species of this disorder, several men also, who lead a sedentary life and study hard, are afflicted with the same ... But it must be own'd that women are oftner attack'd with these disorders than men' (Thomas Sydenham, ... *de affectione hysteria*, 1682).[1]

The claim that mental disorder is a distinctively, though not exclusively, female malady is, as we have seen, common. Elaine Showalter in *The Female Malady* (1987), for instance, argues that whereas in the eighteenth century madness had a masculine face – the typical representation of the lunatic was of a wild, frenzied beast – from the beginning of the nineteenth century it was increasingly domesticated and transformed into more feminine forms and images. The new image was typified by the Romantics' vision of suicidal Ophelia. While Showalter's claim of a feminisation of madness in the nineteenth century can be contested (Scull 1989: 267–79; Busfield 1994), in this century a belief in a close association between women and the broader category of mental disturbance has been widespread.[2] Indeed, the belief that mental disorder is more common amongst women than men is itself both a reflection of, and a justification for, further assumptions about male–female differences. For many, it is linked either to the assumption that women are biologically and psychologically inferior to men and are more

13

emotional, volatile and irrational, or to the assumption that they are, by nature, more vulnerable to the various strains and stresses of daily life and are, consequently, more likely to become mentally disturbed.

It is easy enough to see how the idea that mental disorder is primarily a female condition should have developed and flourished in recent decades, consistent as it is both with stereotypical images of women as neurotic and irrational, as well as with a range of data which show that women are over-represented in psychiatric patient populations. In postwar Britain more women than men have been admitted to mental hospitals, and service data show women's episode rates for mental disorders based on consultations with GPs in recent years to be double those of men (Royal College of General Practitioners, 1986: Table 8). Moreover, with one or two significant exceptions (see Myers et al. 1984), surveys in the US and the UK of the prevalence of psychiatric disorder in the community in postwar decades usually show a similar two to one ratio (Goldberg and Huxley 1980: 23–4, 1992: 18).

Yet, once we look beneath the surface and disaggregate the patient data, it is clear that the picture is far more. complex, and the actual female predominance is far from monolithic. Showalter herself, although at times she talks of a general link between women and mental disorder, also points to historical changes in the association when she asserts a feminisation of madness in the nineteenth century. Elsewhere, the data show enormous variations, with men predominating in certain sectors of the terrain, women in others. The object of this chapter is to explore these gender differences in the landscape of identified mental disorder.[3]

Gender and Diagnosis

The most striking and most significant finding to emerge in any detailed examination of male–female differences in identified mental disorder is a distinctive patterning of diagnosed disorder by gender. The term mental disorder embraces a diversity of phenomena from the brain deterioration of senile dementia through to states of misery, fear and anxiety, as well as drug and alcohol addiction, And it is not so much that mental disorder overall is a female malady even in the twentieth century, but that some mental disorders appear to be more distinctively female, whilst others have a more masculine face, and yet others are more or less gender-neutral. This pattern can be seen in data from community surveys – studies which screen for 'untreated' as well as 'treated' cases – as well as in patient data.[4] Indeed, the linkages between gender and type of mental disorder are some of the most consistent findings of psychiatric epidemiology.

The eating disorder of anorexia nervosa, characterised by a refusal to eat, loss of body weight and disturbances of body image, is the prime candidate for designation as a distinctively female mental disorder in patient populations in advanced industrial societies in the late twentieth century. Although it is a far less common condition than depression or anxiety, its very high degree of gender specificity amongst patients makes it of especial interest in the analysis of gender and mental disorder. First formally identified in the 1870s, it has replaced hysteria as the women's disorder *par excellence*, with studies indicating that in clinical contexts more than 90 per cent of cases occur in women (American Psychiatric Association 1994: 543). However, epidemiological data on anorexia from general populations are limited and these figures need to be treated with some caution, not least because we cannot assume stability over time in the size of the gender difference in identified cases.[5] Some feminist theorists analyse anorexia as if it is almost by definition a female malady and does not occur in men (see, for instance, Lawrence 1987). However, male cases are not infrequently identified in clinical contexts. Bulimia nervosa, another eating disorder, characterised by alternative bingeing and vomiting, is a relatively new addition to the psychiatric lexicon and was initially viewed as a variant of anorexia (Russell 1979). It is also a predominantly female condition according to patient statistics. Both disorders are more frequently diagnosed in middle-class rather than working-class women (Dally and Gomez 1979), and also typically occur in adolescence or early adulthood (World Health Organisation 1992: 176,178), so that age and social class are built into the construction, though not definition, of the disorders (see Chapters 5 and 6).

In contrast, in the eighteenth and nineteenth centuries, hysteria was the paradigmatic female mental disorder in patient populations, and the condition was quite widely diagnosed. The final decades of the nineteenth century have been called the 'golden age' of hysteria, a period when the condition apparently flourished throughout Europe and the United States (Goldstein 1987: 322), and when what once had been a distinctively upper-class complaint was held to be quite common even in the working class (ibid: 335).[6] The term, with its etymological roots in the Greek term 'hysteron', meaning the womb, had distinctive gender connotations and the condition was initially thought to be caused by a movement of the womb. Even when these ideas had long been rejected, hysteria was still considered a primarily female condition and was more frequently diagnosed in women than in men, many medical men believing that it only occurred in women (Veith 1965). However, by the second half of the nineteenth century, an increasing number of practitioners asserted the existence of male hysteria. Freud, for instance, followed Charcot in rejecting the view that it was an exclusively female malady; yet it still continued to be primarily associated with women, and the terms 'hysterical' and 'feminine' were almost interchangeable (Showalter 1987: 125).

In the early decades of this century, hysteria continued to be an important diagnostic category with patients largely treated outside the confines of the asylum, but its central position as the major female malady began to be replaced by anxiety (anxiety neurosis) and depression.[7] By mid-century these two sets of disorders were of increasing importance in the psychiatric spectrum and are now by far the most commonly identified mental disorders. Table 2.1 provides data showing the incidence of identified cases in general practice in England and Wales.[8]

The data show overall episode rates for anxiety disorders in general practice of 19.3 per 1,000 in 1981–2, and for neurotic depression 16.9 per 1000 across all age groups, the highest for any mental disorder. In contrast, the rates were only 0.9 per 1,000 for senile and pre-senile dementia (11.3 amongst those aged 75 and over) and only 0.4 for schizophrenia. (Unfortunately, anorexia does not feature as a separate category in the data.) Significantly, as the same table shows, the rates for anxiety and depression were only surpassed by those for a relatively limited number of physical problems, such as back pain and conjunctivitis and a range of respiratory conditions, where the highest episode rates of all are to be found.

The data in Table 2.1 also indicate that, like anorexia, anxiety and depression are predominantly female diagnoses in the landscape of identified mental disorder, although the gender difference is not as large as that usually cited for anorexia. The observed gender differentials for various types of depression in patient populations (which I discuss more fully in Chapter 5), are commonly in the order of at least two to one and sometimes over three to one, as they are in these general practice figures. Community surveys of symptoms of anxiety and depression have generally indicated a two to one ratio (Weissman

TABLE 2.1 *Episodes of Illness in General Practice for Selected Diagnoses by Gender, England and Wales, 1981–82*

Diagnostic group†	Persons*	Male*	Female*
Mental disorders			
Anxiety disorder	19.3	11.3	26.6
Neurotic depression	16.9	8.1	25.0
Senile and pre-senile			
organic conditions	0.9	0.5	1.2
Schizophrenia	0.4	0.3	0.4
Chronic abuse of alcohol	0.7	0.9	0.5
Other drug abuse	0.3	0.3	0.2
Psychogenic disorder of			
sexual function	1.2	1.3	1.1
Acute alcohol intoxication	0.4	0.6	0.3
Other common disorders			
Coughs	24.5	23.1	25.7
Bronchitis	60.4	59.8	60.9
Tonsillitis	44.5	40.8	47.9
Upper respiratory infection			
(non-febrile)	103.0	93.4	111.7
Catarrh	18.8	17.1	20.4
Back pain	24.8	23.6	26.0
Conjunctivitis	28.0	23.7	31.9

* Incidence rates per 1,000 persons at risk.
† The data were classified using the College Diagnostic Code.

SOURCE *Morbidity Statistics from General Practice, 1981–2*, Royal College of General Practitioners 1986, Table 8.

and Klerman 1977; Goldberg and Huxley 1980: 25), a finding also supported by the large-scale Epidemiological Catchment Area (ECA) survey carried out in the United States in the early 1980s, which yielded a ratio in six-month prevalence rates for the broader category of affective disorders of close to two to one (Myers et al. 1984).[9] The picture for anxiety disorders – including panic disorders, phobias and obsessive–compulsive disorders – is not dissimilar, although the observed gender differences are often not quite as large (ibid). Arguably, the similarity is to be expected, given the high correlation between depression and anxiety and the attendant difficulties of diagnostic differentiation.[10]

Patient statistics like those in Table 2.1 also show senile dementias, such as Alzheimer's disease, are more frequently diagnosed among women than men, even when allowance is made for gender differences in mortality, although the gap is not as marked as for anorexia or even for depression. The 1981–2 GP morbidity survey yielded episode rates for senile dementia of 12.6 per 1,000 amongst women aged 75 and over, compared with 8.7 per 1,000 amongst men of the same age (Royal College of General Practitioners 1986: Table 8). Significantly, however, the ECA community survey found little difference between men and women in levels of cognitive impairment (Myers et al. 1984).[11]

There are, however, some mental disorders more commonly diagnosed in men. In the seventeenth, eighteenth and nineteenth centuries, for instance, hypochondriasis, a much broader disorder then than it is now, was typically considered a male mental disorder. The disorder, characterised by 'low spirits, apprehensiveness, diffuse physical malaise, languor, irritability and even pain' (Oppenheim 1991: 142), was seen as enfeebling the will and rendering the individual passive and helpless. Men were considered to be especially prone to the disorder; Sydenham for one viewing it as the counterpart to female hysteria (ibid). In the nineteenth century, however, an even more important male malady was the condition eventually identified as general paresis or general paralysis of the insane (GPI) – a quite commonly diagnosed disorder in nineteenth–century asylums (Lowe and Garrett 1959). GPI is a form of dementia arising from syphilitic infection of the brain, and was severe, progressive and led to institutionalisation. It was predominantly a male disorder in the nineteenth century (ibid; Showalter 1987: 111), and had an important impact on the gender composition of the asylum inmates of the time.[12] Nowadays syphilis can be treated quite successfully and GPI is extremely rare.

In the twentieth century, the introduction of the category of shell-shock (see Chapter 11) in the First World War introduced a new male mental disorder, especially interesting because it was located in the emergent terrain of the psycho-neuroses which Freudian ideas did so much to shape. Numerically more significant this century as mental disorders more commonly diagnosed in men, are the 'substance use disorders' of alcoholism and drug addiction. As Table 2.1 indicates, male cases of alcohol-related disorders identified by GPs are around twice as high as female cases (see also Heather and Robertson 1989: 110). The ECA survey in the US using screening interviews yielded a roughly similar ratio (Myers et al. 1984). These disorders, though far less common diagnoses in general practice than anxiety and depression (partly because alcohol problems are less likely to be brought to doctors), have played a prominent part in admissions to psychiatric beds over recent decades. However, since their symptoms relate to behaviour rather than mental processes, their status as mental disorders has been widely contested – an issue to which I return in Chapter 4.

The group of conditions more frequently detected in men than women also includes sexual disorders such as paedophilia and transvestism, and other personality disorders such as the psychopathic or anti-social personality – a category with antecedents in the nineteenth-century diagnosis of moral insanity (Ramon 1986).[13] Again these are relatively uncommon diagnoses in general practice but are of far more importance amongst psychiatric in-patients. The diagnosis of psychopathic personality is of especial interest, not only because it is separately identified in British mental health legislation, but also because it is often assigned to those within the criminal justice system who are identified as having psychiatric problems. Both child abuse and domestic violence, which are typically male crimes, if and when they are treated as symptomatic of psychological difficulties, usually generate diagnoses within this grouping of personality or behaviour disorders.

In between are a range of disorders where the gender differences in identified cases are less clear cut. These include schizophrenia (Goldstein 1992), paranoid states and mania – much more the paradigm of real madness than the conditions we have considered so far – suggesting that it is less 'madness' that is identified as the female malady than the broader territory of more 'minor' psychiatric conditions.[14]

The association between gender and diagnosis found in service statistics and community surveys should not be regarded as static or fixed, just as we cannot view any association between aggregate levels of detected mental disorder and gender as unchanging. The reasons for this gendered landscape of diagnosed disorder are, of course, contentious and are explored in subsequent chapters, and we need to examine the construction of the disease categories themselves, biases in psychiatric assessment, as well as differences in how appropriate male and female behaviour is constructed and how men and women respond to pressures and difficulties. It is, for instance, clear that diagnosis is not a very precise art and is also subject to changes in fashion, a point to which I return below. It is equally clear that social and cultural factors can modify the associations between gender and particular pathological behaviours. An obvious case is that of the substance use disorders. For example, as men's and women's patterns of 'normal' alcohol consumption change with changing access to resources and changing social expectations, so do the gender differences in patients identified as having alcohol problems.

Significantly, however, certain associations between gender and broad types of identified psychological difficulty, if not with specific medical diagnoses, seem to be long-standing. Michael MacDonald's (1981) fascinating study of Richard Napier's case notes (a physician who practised during the early decades of the seventeenth century), shows that more women than men visited him because they were considered distressed as the result of some misfortune. The ratio for these particular cases (cases where no social misfortune was at issue were excluded from this analysis), was in the order of roughly two to one (ibid: 36). This figure echoes the current gender differences in psychological disorder detected in community surveys using screening instruments which are considered more fully in Chapter 5. It also echoes the gender differentials for diagnoses of depression and anxiety noted above – conditions perhaps closest to the distress with which Napier dealt.[15]

These marked and sometimes changing linkages between gender and diagnosed disorder have profound implications for understanding the gender differences detected in a range of empirical studies, since it is clear that the size and nature of any gender difference in the aggregate level of mental disorder is affected by the spectrum of psychiatric conditions under consideration. Change the psychiatric spectrum and you change the size and sometimes even the direction of the gender difference. Exclude cases of anxiety and depression and you are likely to diminish the female predominance considerably.[16] Conversely, exclude behavioural, substance use and personality disorders and you increase the female predominance.

The impact of the association between gender and diagnosed disorder, on the gender differences observed, can be seen very clearly if we compare figures for the overall gender differences in levels of identified mental disorder of in-patients with those from the GP data. Data on gender differences in admissions to psychiatric beds are given in Table 2.2 and on GP consultations in Table 2.3.

The GP data show a larger gender difference than the in-patient data. This is because they derive from services dealing with very differ-

TABLE 2.2   *All Admissions to Mental Illness Hospitals and Units, England, 1986*

Age	Female*	Male*	Female–Male Ratio
0–9	8	16	0.5
10–14	33	38	0.87
15–19	144	142	1.01
20–24	310	358	0.87
25–34	441	469	0.94
35–44	504	454	1.11
45–54	539	390	1.38
55–64	565	388	1.46
65–74	756	529	1.43
75–84	1,221	1,156	1.06
85 and over	1,559	1,733	0.90
All ages	468	364	1.29

*Rates per 100,000 population.

SOURCE   *Mental Health Statistics for England, 1986*, Tables A2.2 and A2.3, Department of Health and Social Security.

ent patient populations and a very different spectrum of psychiatric diagnoses. In-patient mental health services in England and Wales deal primarily with persons assigned diagnoses such as schizophrenia, senile dementia and psychotic depression, and there is a high proportion of the elderly amongst those admitted. These are precisely the disorders where gender differences in identified cases tend to be smaller, although gender differences in mortality, as well as in discharge rates, ensure that there are often more women than men residents at any one time. In contrast, GP services cover a different spectrum of psychiatric disorders – the bulk of patients having rather less severe complaints, diagnosed as neurotic depression, anxiety states and phobias as well as some behavioural problems. Except for some of the behavioural problems, these are conditions where there is generally a female predominance in identified cases. As a result, the aggregate gender difference is far greater.

Where provision is even more selective, as with mental health services for highly targeted client groups, the gender differences may be even more marked. Not surprisingly, given the gender imbalance in criminal

TABLE 2.3 *Patients Consulting General Practitioners for Mental Disorders by Gender,
England and Wales, 1981–82*

Age	Female*	Male*	Female–Male Ratio
0–4	26.6	36.6	0.73
5–14	16.9	17.5	0.97
15–24	87.7	37.9	2.31
25–44	142.7	64.8	2.20
45–64	152.2	77.7	1.96
65–74	143.7	69.7	2.07
75 and over	148.3	91.2	1.63
All Ages	112.7	55.4	2.03

* Rates per 1,000 at risk.

SOURCE *Morbidity Statistics from General Practice, 1981–2: Third National Study*,
Table 17, Royal College of General Practitioners 1986.

populations, hospitals for the criminally insane tend to have more male
than female inmates, whereas special services for anorexics deal with
more female than male patients. These are very basic points yet they are
central to understanding the gender balance of patient populations.

The linkage between gender and diagnosed disorder is further com-
plicated by a range of other factors – age, marital status, social class
and ethnicity – which we also need to consider.

Gender, Age and Mental Disorder

The patterning of diagnosed mental disorder relates to age as well as to
gender, and gender differences in the balance of patient populations
vary over the life-cycle. There are few psychiatric disorders where age
is itself *formally* a defining characteristic. Senile and pre-senile dementias
are examples – dementia is categorised as senile for those aged 65 and
over and as pre-senile for persons under 65. In many other cases,
however, age, like gender, is seen as closely associated with certain
categories of mental disorder and is, in effect, part of their construction.
For example, as we have seen, anorexia nervosa is described as commonly occurring in young girls (and rarely if ever in women who have

passed the menopause), just as schizophrenia, with its roots in the old label *dementia praecox* (precocious dementia), is still regarded as typically a disease of adolescence or early adulthood (American Psychiatric Association 1994: 281).[17]

The way in which age and gender intersect over the life-cycle is manifest in the in-patient and GP data presented in Tables 2.2 and 2.3 above. For example, the GP data in Table 2.3 indicate that the marked female predominance in identified disorder is reversed for the under 15s – an age range when consultation levels for psychiatric complaints are generally low – although the gender difference is not very large. By the 15–24 age group, when consultation levels are rather higher, the gender difference takes on its more familiar present-day form of a definite female predominance and is greater than at any other point in the life cycle. Amongst those aged 25 and over, the gender difference does not vary much from one age band to another, although it declines amongst the over 85s.

The admissions data in Table 2.2 also show that amongst the under 15s, male rates tend to be higher than female, and the difference is actually rather larger than in the GP consultations, even though admission levels are low. They also indicate that a marked female predominance in admissions does not emerge until the 35 to 44 age group, and then peaks amongst those aged 55 to 64. However, the emergence of a definite female predominance in admissions only rather late in the life cycle is a relatively recent phenomenon in England. In the 1970s, for instance, it was visible from the 15 to 19 age group onwards (see Busfield 1983: 112–3), and in that respect the pattern was rather closer to that noted for GP consultations at the beginning of the 1980s. Undoubtedly the shift is primarily a result of changing policies over the use of psychiatric beds. Policies of community care have changed the character of the in-patient admissions, and have, in particular, reduced the numbers admitted with severe neurotic complaints. It is important to note, however, that we have been considering admissions. If we turn instead to data on residence rates, the picture looks somewhat different. Table 2.4 gives figures on the residents of psychiatric beds by gender and age.

The data indicate that a female predominance in residence rates does not emerge until we reach the group aged 65 and over. The difference between the two sets of data is due to the differing length of stay of patients and the associated issue of differences in mortality. At younger ages women patients tend to have shorter stays than men. At older ages

TABLE 2.4   *Residents of Psychiatric Beds, England, 1972–76*

Age	Male*	Female*	Female–Male Ratio
0–9	4.8	1.8	0.38
10–14	12.2	8.8	0.72
15–19	32.8	38.0	1.16
20–24	71.8	65.2	0.91
25–34	103.4	80.4	0.78
35–44	157.4	119.2	0.76
45–54	278.0	201.6	0.73
55–64	364.6	303.6	0.83
65–74	448.8	541.2	1.21
75+	650.2	1100.0	1.69
All Ages	173.8	218.2	1.26

*Rates per 100,000 population.

SOURCE   *In-patient Statistics from the Mental Health Enquiry, 1976*, Table A5, Department of Health and Social Security 1979.

their enhanced survival rates tend to mean they stay longer than men once admitted. In absolute numbers the discrepancy is even larger.

The male predominance in identified childhood mental disorders found in the GP and admissions data in recent decades has also been noted in other patient statistics and is not specific to this country. Walter Gove noted a similar male predominance in psychiatric patients amongst the under 20s in the United States (Gove and Herb 1974). He suggested that the male predominance in childhood and the subsequent reversal to a female predominance in adulthood (which he identified from his data as occurring around the time of late adolescence), is linked with the greater stress which boys, for a range of physiological and psychological reasons, experience in childhood (indeed the higher rates of treated mental disorder amongst boys are for him the consequence of, and evidence for, that higher stress). However, Gove ignores the differences by age in the types of disorder that come under medical scrutiny which are clearly of vital importance.

Data from the 1981–2 GP morbidity survey show that the type of mental health problems receiving medical attention differ markedly according to age. In childhood the most commonly diagnosed psychological problems are personality and behavioural problems, which include psychopathic tendencies, enuresis (bed-wetting), sleep disorders and the relatively new disorder of hyperactivity (Box 1981; Taylor 1986). In adults of working age the predominant disorders diagnosed belong either to the neurotic or, to a far lesser extent, the psychotic group – disorders such as depression, anxiety and schizophrenia. Amongst the over 65s conditions associated with ageing, such as the various forms of senile dementia, play a much more important role. Consequently, consideration of health service statistics by age reinforces the claim that it is essential to examine the pattern of diagnosed disorders when analysing gender differences. The increasing emphasis in psychiatry on childhood disorders may increase the significance of the male predominance in this stage of life to the overall psychiatric picture. However, the increasing emphasis may broaden the spectrum of complaints that receive attention, which could well, in turn, modify the extent and even direction of the gender imbalance in identified childhood disorders.

Marital Status, Social Class and Ethnicity

Three other sources of variation in the gender balance of patient populations are perhaps less striking but nonetheless merit attention. The first is marital status. Marital status affects not only the overall level of service use, with the married having lower rates of service use than the unmarried; it also affects gender differences. Indeed, in the US and Britain, amongst the unmarried, whose rates of mental disorder as measured by service use are considerably higher than amongst the married, male rates are higher than female (Gove 1972). In contrast, amongst the married, who generally make far less use of mental health services, the situation is reversed and female rates are higher than male rates (ibid). The divorced and single fall somewhere in between, with intermediate levels of psychiatric disorder and women's rates higher than men's, but the difference is rather smaller than for the married. However, since the married are numerically the more important group their rates dominate the aggregate picture. A typical set of figures derived from a survey of residents of psychiatric beds in England and Wales in 1971 is given in Table 2.5.[18]

Data from community surveys, which are only available for recent decades, do not, however, reveal the same large differences in levels of

TABLE 2.5   *Patients Resident in Mental Illness Hospitals and Units by Sex and Marital Status, England and Wales, 31 December 1971*

Marital Status	Male*	Female*
Single	704	685
Married†	91	127
Widowed	535	647
Divorced	835	780
All	272	322

*Rates per 100,000.
† Includes 1,562 'separated' males, and 1,898 'separated' females.

SOURCE   *Census of Patients in Mental Illness Hospitals and Units in England and Wales at the end of 1971*, Table 3, Department of Health and Social Security 1975.

identified mental disorder according to marital status, the differences being either considerably reduced or disappearing altogether (Cochrane 1984: 53). The impact of marital status on mental health is a matter of some controversy and is discussed further in Chapter 10.

Regrettably, social class and ethnicity have received rather little attention in the context of discussions of gender differentials. A range of data indicate a marked association between social class and levels of mental disorder as measured in patient statistics and community surveys (with the lower social classes generally having higher levels of disorder), as well as of major differences in treatment patterns by social class (see Hollingshead and Redlich 1958; Dohrenwend and Dohren-wend 1969). But there is much less evidence on the interaction of gender and social class. Hollingshead and Redlich's study, *Social Class and Mental Illness* (1958), showed marginally higher patient rates for men than women. The male over-representation was especially marked in the lowest social class, whereas the gender differences in classes I and II and class IV were insignificant; in class III women were over-repre-sented (see Busfield, 1983: 116–7). Again the distribution of diagnosed complaints by social class is likely to be one factor accounting for this variation. The study showed that in classes I and II some 65 per cent of the patients were diagnosed as neurotic, and 35 per cent psychotic, but that the percentage of neurotic patients declined as you moved down the social scale, with only 10 per cent of those in class V diagnosed as neurotic (Hollingshead and Redlich 1958: 222). This must surely be relevant to the fact that the male predominance was greatest in the lowest social class, although the data do not present the clear linear picture we might expect.

A range of data suggest a linkage between ethnicity and levels of identified mental disorder although, as with social class, there is considerable controversy as to the reason for the observed relationships. The data are of considerable interest since they point to important cultural differences in patterns of mental disorder. Within Britain there are striking differences in levels of compulsory admission to psychiatric beds with Afro-Caribbeans heavily over-represented in formal admissions (Carpenter and Brockington 1980; McGovern and Cope 1987). Differences in rates of identified schizophrenia are also very high (Harrison et al. 1984). But there is considerable variation between ethnic groups.

One study compared the admission rates to mental hospitals in Britain of two groups, native born and immigrants, and found admission rates were almost double in the latter group (Cochrane 1984: 90). However, once the data were broken down further it emerged that admission rates were only higher amongst Irish and, to a lesser extent, West Indian immigrants. Admission rates were lower for immigrants from India and Pakistan than amongst the native born (Cochrane 1984: 90). There were also marked variations in the size of the gender difference by country of birth. The data are given in Table 2.6.

They show that the overall gender difference in admissions was smallest for those born in Scotland and Ireland (there was actually a slight male predominance for those born in Scotland). Significantly, as the figures also indicate, these are the two groups with very high rates of identified alcohol-related problems, the male bias being very marked for such problems in both cases, and this undoubtedly contributes to the overall male predominance in these two groups. Community surveys show a somewhat different picture, with Irish immigrants having generally low levels of identified psychiatric problems (Cochrane 1984: 95). Cochrane suggests this indicates that those admitted to psychiatric beds are a very selected group, not typical of the community as a whole. Another factor, however, is that the general screening instruments used for detecting mental disorder in the community are not usually designed to identify alcohol-related problems (see Chapter 5).

These variations according to diagnosis, age, class and other factors in the observed gender balance of patient populations are also visible if

TABLE 2.6   *Sex Specific Rates of Mental Hospital Admissions in England and Wales by Selected Diagnoses and Country of Birth, 1971*

Country of birth	All diagnoses*		Alcohol related*		Schizophrenia and related*	
	Male	Female	Male	Female	Male	Female
England and Wales	434	551	28	8	87	7
Scotland	712	679	218	46	90	97
Republic of Ireland	1065	1153	265	54	153	254
India	368	436	34	9	141	140
Pakistan	294	374	10	14	158	103
West Indies	449	621	14	7	290	323

*Rates per 100,000 population.

SOURCE   Cochrane (1984: 91).

we examine historical changes. Up until now, although some reference has been made to historical changes, especially in categories of mental disorder, the examination of patient populations has been primarily cross-sectional.

Historical Changes

Both the marked, though not fixed, associations between gender and diagnosed disorder, and the selective character of mental health services, need to be borne in mind in any examination of variations in gender differences in patient populations observed over time. According to Elaine Showalter mental disorder became a distinctively female condition during the first half of the nineteenth century. She backs up this claim by a brief discussion of the gender distribution of asylum inmates in the nineteenth century, and a more detailed analysis of the cultural representations of madness in art, literature, photography and psychiatric texts. Her analysis, both of the statistical data and of the cultural representations is, however, selective (see Busfield 1994). Although there were, as Showalter notes, marginally more women than men asylum inmates during the second half of the nineteenth century (see Chapter 7), much of this difference was due to the higher mortality of male inmates. Moreover, while there were marked changes in the portrayal of madness between the eighteenth and nineteenth centuries, from an image of the wild, uncontrolled rage of the beast to a more regulated, human face, men no less than women were portrayed according to the new conventions. Madness may have been tamed, but men as well as women were part of the new landscape of madness and of nervous complaints: the criminal lunatic, the maniac and the hypochondriac were typically represented as male rather than female, and need to be counterposed to the female melancholic or hysteric.

As we shall see in Chapter 7, a more careful analysis of the epidemiological data suggests that a female predominance in psychiatric admissions is primarily a feature of the second half of the twentieth not the nineteenth century. This can be seen very clearly in the data presented in Table 2.7 on admissions to mental hospitals over the period 1884 to 1951.

Since 1951 the female predominance has remained, although as Table 2.2 above showed, having increased to a female–male ratio of 1.38 to 1 in the mid-1970s (Busfield 1983: 113), it has declined somewhat and was 1.29 to 1 in 1986. Similarly, data from the US from community surveys which screen for mental disorder and include

TABLE 2.7 *Admission Rates to Mental Hospitals in England and Wales by Age and Gender, 1884–1957*

Year	Age (male)*							Age (female)*						
	15	25	35	45	55	65+	All ages 15+	15	25	35	45	55	65+	All ages 15+
1884	46	91	115	111	107	107	87	44	88	111	107	98	90	83
1891	42	83	112	112	111	116	85	42	86	105	114	100	102	82
1901	45	88	118	122	128	149	93	42	84	111	125	116	130	89
1911	44	76	98	111	128	135	85	42	78	101	123	117	117	86
1921	39	70	87	94	111	128	79	41	74	96	115	107	106	82
1931	38	65	77	87	103	106	76	35	70	89	113	110	93	82
1939	64	86	90	97	111	115	91	46	85	108	136	137	110	100
1951	105	169	133	137	171	230	153	103	172	191	214	222	268	196

*Rates per 100,000 population.

SOURCE Lowe and Garratt (1959).

untreated as well as treated cases, show some diminution in the observed gender difference over the 1960s and 1970s (see Kessler and McRae 1981).

It is tempting to tie these historical changes to changes in the underlying levels of psychological disorder in men and women. For example, we can suggest, as Gove and Tudor (1972) have done, that the changes in women's domestic role in the postwar period generated the new female predominance (see Chapter 10). However, claims about changes and differences in underlying levels of disorder derived from patient statistics are of doubtful value (see Chapter 5). Instead, it is essential to consider the way in which changes in the character of the mental health services have themselves played a key role in changing the social character and, thereby, the gender balance of patient populations. This is the task of Chapter 7. However, before we do this we need to examine both the ways in which gender and mental disorder are best theorised and the way gender is embedded in categories of mental disorder.

Conclusion

This examination of epidemiological data on gender differences in identified mental disorder shows there is no simple, consistent, female predominance amongst identified cases and casts doubt on any general claim that mental disorder is a female malady. Whilst women are over-represented in patient populations, once the data are disaggregated what emerges is a gendered landscape in which some diagnoses are linked to women, some to men, and others do not have very marked gender associations – a landscape in which gender also intersects with other social characteristics such as age, marital status, social class and ethnicity. Moreover, the data show that far from being a long-standing feature, the aggregate female predominance in admissions is relatively new. In subsequent chapters I explore how this complex picture is produced. In the next two chapters I consider the concepts of gender and mental disorder.

Chapter 3

Gender and Feminist Theorising

'Gender' means practice organised in terms of, or in relation to, the reproductive division of people into male and female (Connell 1987: 140).

The term gender entered sociological discourse as a way of conceptualising male–female differences at the end of the 1960s (Stoller 1968), a product of the rise of the women's liberation movement – feminism's second wave. Since then the value and meaning of the concept has been widely contested amongst feminists, sociologists and other academics. Some feminists have, for instance, argued that attention to gender and gender relations can lead to a denial of women's oppression and 'excludes and silences many women' (Jackson 1992: 31). The category of gender, they contend, is more neutral and academically acceptable than that of woman, for which it often serves as a substitute (see Scott 1986: 1056). Its use depoliticises the feminist project. In the mental health field, therefore, the need is for studies of women and mental disorder, not of gender and mental disorder. Similarly the burgeoning work on men and masculinity during the last five to ten years (Hearn 1987; Hearn and Morgan 1990; Segal 1990; Morgan 1992), might equally be taken to require separate studies of men and mental disorder. Furthermore, even those who argue that any adequate analysis must incorporate both women and men, do not agree that gender is the most appropriate concept to employ, some preferring the older concept of sex, rather than the more recent term gender.

This chapter explores debates both about the concept of gender and about how gender divisions and gender relations can best be

31

theorised.[1] I argue that an analysis in terms of gender does offer the most fruitful way of enhancing our understanding of mental disorder in women as well as men, and that such an approach allows, indeed requires, an examination of women's oppression – an examination that can be used to facilitate political action. Gender must be analysed at the level of social structure and material relations as well as of the individual and individual meanings. I begin by examining the concept of gender.

The Concept of Gender

Gender, as an analytical category designed to refer to and aid the understanding of the social and cultural origins of male–female differences in personal characteristics and behaviour, was introduced as a challenge to biological determinism. Biological sex was to be contrasted with social 'gender' – the former denoting bodily differences between men and women in the reproductive organs, the latter differences in male and female qualities and behaviour which were held to be a product of social factors and could not be reduced to matters of biology. In British sociology, Ann Oakley's text *Sex, Gender and Society*, first published in 1972, heralded the new linguistic and analytic precision that allowed feminists not only to distinguish the social from the biological when considering male and female behaviour, but also to avoid the old ambiguity in meaning between sex as sexuality and sex as the broader corpus of male–female differences. As a result, the old language of sex roles and sexual divisions was, by the middle of the 1970s, being replaced by the language of gender roles and gender divisions. And instead of an assumption of natural differences between men and women, there was a growing emphasis on the way in which gender differences are socially constructed and vary across time and place.

The precise definition of the term gender varies. Stoller in *Sex and Gender* (1968), the book said to have introduced the new terminological contrast, linked gender with notions of masculinity and femininity – that is, the characteristics or qualities regarded as appropriate to men and women:

> Gender is a term that has psychological and cultural rather than biological connotations; if the proper terms for sex are 'male' and 'female', the corre-

sponding terms for gender are 'masculine' and 'feminine', these latter being quite independent of (biological) sex. Gender is the amount of masculinity and femininity found in a person, and obviously, while there are mixtures of both in many humans, the normal male has a preponderance of masculinity and the normal female a preponderance of femininity (quoted in Plumwood 1989: 2).[2]

Here the opposition between biological sex and psychological or cultural gender leads to the assertion that gender is 'independent of sex', although this is implicitly negated a moment later by the assertion that the normal male (presumably biologically defined) has a preponderance of masculinity, the normal female a preponderance of femininity.

Oakley, referring to Stoller's work, posits a similar opposition between sex and gender, 'Sex is a biological term; "gender" is a psychological and cultural one' (1972: 158), and she puts the same emphasis on their independence. More recently, R. W. Connell in his book *Gender and Power*, attempts to clarify the relation between sex and gender contending that 'social relations of gender are not determined by biological difference but deal with it' (1987: 139–40). In his view ' "Gender" means practice organised in terms of, or in relation to, the reproductive division of people into male and female' (ibid: 140). Val Plumwood elaborates Connell's focus on practice (see the quotation at the beginning the chapter). Arguing that gender is 'the social meaning of sex as embedded in social practices', she comments:

> Perhaps we can say instead that gender is what the society or culture *makes* of the reproductive aspects of the body where this includes both material treatment and practices, and especially, how the sexual aspects of the body are given social meaning and significance, as well as how they are conceived to be. Gender thus incorporates a theory, or a story, of how the body is, and how the person is, as well as material treatment... (1989: 8).

What both Connell's and Plumwood's definitions retain is the relation of gender to biological sex. If instead, gender is viewed as independent of sex and conceptualised exclusively in terms of masculinity and femininity, then femininity can reasonably be studied independently of biological sex – an approach that permits women to be included in the masculine category and men in the feminine. For some purposes, such an analysis may be useful and from this perspective masculinity and femininity can be viewed as distributed along some linear dimension rather than as a binary categorisation (see Annandale and Hunt 1990). Yet the linkage with the binary categorisation embedded in the standard conceptualisation of biological sex is crucial and the idea of 'dealing with' or 'making of' biological differences is important. In many contexts it is the constructions of, and attribution of, maleness and femaleness, masculinity and femininity, to men and women differentiated on grounds of biology that is central.

We can help to clarify the concept of gender further by highlighting some of its key features. First there is the assumption, already mentioned, that gender differences are, at least in part, a social product rather than a biological given and that they vary across time and place. There is no necessary historical constancy about what is expected of women or of men, about what is constructed as 'masculine' or as 'feminine', or about what it means to be a woman or a man at a particular historical moment. Class, age and ethnic differences between women and between men are important. To say this does not commit us to the postmodernist view, which I consider later in this chapter, that the category woman – or man – is, by virtue of this variation, so problematic that it needs to be rejected. Rather it requires us not only to examine differences between men and women as groups, but also to attend to differences between men, or between women, and to examine the varying ways in which the requirements of being male or being female are constructed and developed.[3] Nor does it commit us to the view that biological factors play no part in accounting for male–female differences.

Second, as we have seen, the concept of gender commonly suggests a binary categorisation of male and female, masculinity and femininity. It is a concept that, like sex, categorises and divides the human world into a duality of men and women. Gender can, as I have already suggested, be viewed as a dimension or continuum of degrees of maleness and femaleness, with the most extreme forms placed at either end, and there are clearly contexts in which this conceptualisation is useful.[4] However, when it comes to gender identity – at its simplest the recognition of a person as male or female – either in self attribution and subjectivity (that is self-awareness and individuality (Henriques et al. 1984: 3)), or in the attribution of gender to others, then the initial categorisation is likely to be binary, and such attributions of gender identity are central to, and the starting point of, the salience of gender in social relations.[5]

Third, and linked to this, gender is a relational concept whose meaning is generated through opposition. Put another way, it is a concept of social difference founded on comparison and contrast, and the meaning of one component, whether masculinity or femininity, cannot be fully understood without reference, explicit or implicit, to the other. It is because of this that studies either of men or of women on their own, whilst they have considerable value in making specificities visible – including oppression and exploitation – cannot provide the basis for a full understanding of the situation of either group alone.[6] Feminist scholars who have sought to make women visible because they have long been 'hidden from history' (Rowbotham 1973) have been invaluable. Nonetheless, an effective analysis of women's position requires an analysis of that of men and, hence, of gender relations. A feminist approach does not require an exclusive concentration on women, even though it involves looking at the world from the perspective of women's lives.

Fourth, the concept of gender typically, though not universally, connotes structural relations of inequality, including inequalities of power. Men and women stand not only in a relation of difference but also in a structural relation characterised by both asymmetry and hierarchy. Asymmetry is evidenced in the way that men have typically been treated as the norm and women and their characteristics as somehow abnormal – a deviation from the general standard and as persons who, if and when they are given attention, have to be problematised. Freud's analysis of femininity (1973) in which femininity, on the rare occasions when it is discussed, is viewed as problematic and has to be differentiated from normal, implicitly masculine, personality development, provides but one example. This asymmetry is also conveyed in sexist language in which the male gender is used to stand for both male and female, whereas the female is always gender specific. These asymmetries reflect the underlying structural inequalities in power between men and women that the term gender also usually connotes. Male power and domination, which are such a pervasive feature of social structures and social relations, account for much of the feminist concern about studies both of gender and of men and masculinity which appear to threaten to draw attention away from women. However, if women's oppression is to be contested, we need to examine the ways in which, and the social structures through which, power operates – the ways in which women's work is demeaned and diminished; the ways in which a range of exclusionary practices operate, and so forth – and this requires us to study male power as well as women's subordination.

Finally, gender is what Connell calls a 'linking' concept – one that links practice surrounding male–female difference to other areas of activity (1987: 140). Gender relations are not an autonomous sphere of activity, but permeate social life. This means not only that we cannot study gender independently of other spheres of activity, but equally that we should not study other spheres of social activity independently of gender. Gender is, however, a more salient dimension in some spheres than in others (see Chodorow 1989: 196, 217–8). As Connell puts it 'There are times and places where the links are more extensive and compelling, where (to change the metaphor) a greater percentage of the social landscape is covered by gender relations; and times and places where they are less' (1987: 40). However, we should not simply assume the unimportance of gender in any particular sphere. As feminists have shown, the invisibility of gender in many spheres is not a measure of its actual salience. Indeed, many have argued that gender is a more fundamental feature of social life than class or ethnicity. Ludmilla Jordanova in her study *Sexual Visions* asserts its fundamental (though not always overriding) importance:

> there are some aspects of human life that touch people more deeply than others, because these vary in the extent to which they inform social relations. Gender is one of these profound dimensions, since for all children, as for all societies, it is constitutive of basic identity (1989: 3).

This link with identity is stressed by other authors who point to the fact that our knowledge of whether we are male or female is basic to our sense of who we are. Gender it is frequently, and surely correctly, noted, is a pervasive feature of social relations.

Jordanova, however, seems somewhat uncertain about the status of her claim that gender is a basic dimension of social life. Initially she comments 'I see no way in which such a claim can be "proved"; rather it is an indisputable starting point for the historical study of masculinity and femininity' (ibid), so putting the claim beyond the framework of empirical observation. However, a moment later she emphasises diversity across time and place in gender differences: 'Anthropologists have stressed the cross-cultural diversity with respect to sexual difference in theory and in practice; historians similarly, can show how a recurrent preoccupation with an issue takes on a myriad of forms' (ibid), thereby suggesting the diversity of gender difference is open to empirical observation. The same surely applies to the importance of gender as a basic division of social relations, whether at the level of social structure, consciousness or action. We should not assume, but have to establish, the importance of gender both in general, and in relation to a particular aspect of social life. Its salience in relation to mental disorder has already been established by the data presented in Chapter 2 which showed a clearly gendered landscape.

Some feminists have, however, argued that the distinction between sex and gender, which has been widely employed over the past two decades and now extends well beyond academic circles, is problematic and should be abandoned (see Edwards 1989). A number of problems have been identified and the arguments are examined by Plumwood (1989). The first is that the sex–gender distinction assumes, falsely, a clear distinction between the biological and the social. Biological difference, it is contended, is itself culturally constructed in that, for instance, we have to read a polarisation of sexual difference into natural biological diversity as cases of hermaphroditism attest (Birke 1986). Such a view is given especial emphasis within postmodernist theorisations which are discussed later in the chapter, with their belief in the relativity of all categories and all understandings. However, recognition that the contrast between the biological and the social is itself a social construct which orders a more complex natural diversity, does not, I would argue, require us to abandon the distinction between sex and gender. On the one hand, we can accept that the male–female polarisation usually assumed in the concept of biological sex, is a heuristic simplification imposed on biological diversity, that has both pragmatic and analytical value. On the other hand, to argue that the realm of the biological is itself socially constructed, in that it is socially interpreted and mediated, does not require us to accept that the biological–social contrast has no analytic value, or that a sex–gender opposition founded on that contrast must be rejected. Clearly there is a dualism here that has its limitations, but to collapse the distinction is to abandon the gains that can be, and are, secured by the differentiation.[7]

Second, it has been suggested that 'the sex/gender distinction assumes the connection between the body (sex) and gender is *arbitrary*' (Plumwood 1989: 5). By this is meant that the distinction assumes that gender is independent of sex. However, as Plumwood points out, no such assumption is required. Those who use the distinction have varying views about the relations between biological sex and social gender, but none in practice view gender as entirely independent of biological sex, notwithstanding the comments of writers such as Stoller quoted above.

Finally, it is claimed that the sex–gender distinction implicitly involves 'a body-consciousness distinction of a rationalist or Cartesian type, with the body assumed to be neutral and passive' (ibid). But again the sex–gender distinction does not require such a polarity of conceptualisation. The argument, if it has any force, constitutes a critique of particular ways of understanding the opposition rather than of all uses of it. Rather than abandoning the distinction, we need to be aware of how we are using it, making appropriate not ill-founded assumptions and claims about the relation of sex and gender. Let us consider, therefore, some of the ways in which gender has been theorised.

Theorising Gender

As is already apparent from the discussion of the concept of gender, a major issue in theorising gender and gender divisions has been to challenge the key role frequently attributed to biology in the determination of gender differences. However, although the concept of gender itself, and the sociological analysis of gender divisions, involves a rejection of any simple biological determinism, the issue of how best to theorise gender is not solved so readily. I want to distinguish four different approaches to theorising gender, although the approaches overlap and intersect and many theorists draw on more than one of them.

Sex and Gender Roles

The concept of social role has played an important part in twentieth-century Anglo-American sociology. Role analysis was a significant feature of the structural functionalism which was the most influential theoretical paradigm in sociology in the 1950s.[8] Talcot Parsons, a key exponent of the perspective, developed an analysis of the social system in which the concept of role – the set of expectations governing a particular position in the social system – was central (see Parsons 1951).[9] He not only introduced the concept of sick role as a way of understanding the social dimension of sickness (see Chapter 4), but also analysed male–female differences in terms of social roles. In the 1960s, the sociological orthodoxy of structural functionalism was successfully challenged by interactionist ideas amongst others, but the notion of role still remained central to interactionist thought, albeit that the concept was often used in more dynamic ways – role making and the negotiation of roles replaced role taking (Turner 1963).

This intellectual context helped to shape feminist writing in the late 1960s and early 1970s (and later), such as that of Chesler, and a range of feminists deployed the concepts first of sex roles and then of gender roles. In so doing they appropriated a language and form of analysis of the positions of men and women in society that was widespread within sociology and anthropology, but gave it a distinctively feminist character by focusing on male power and the oppression of women. In Parsons's formulation certain roles are allocated on the basis of biological sex, and this sex role allocation is deemed functional to social order. Men are engaged in the public realm of paid employment and are socialised into instrumentality; women are located within the private realm of the family and are socialised into the expressivity necessary for their activities in this realm – the rearing of children and emotional support for their husbands – what would now be called emotional work (Hochschild 1984: 7). In its feminist form (see Rosaldo and Lamphère 1974) the emphasis is placed on the inequalities of this sexual (gender) division of labour: the exclusion of women from the labour market or their concentration in secondary labour markets; the burden of work they carry in the household; the low status and stereotyping they face, and so forth. The feminist political project is, from this point of view, primarily one of securing emancipation from this oppression, and the liberal political associations are usually clear.

Theorising gender differences in terms of sex roles raises major problems, and a range of writers have questioned the appropriateness of this conceptualisation (see Connell 1987: 47–54). The key argument is that neither sex nor gender are themselves roles. As Thorne puts it 'the problem with the term "sex role" is that there is no such thing' (Lopata and Thorne 1978: 720). She continues:

> It seems to me that being a woman is not a social role but a pervasive identity and a set of feelings which lead to the selection or the assignment to others of social roles and to the performance by women of common roles in some ways differently from men (ibid: 721).

Yet, as the passage suggests, the terms sex or gender role(s) are ambiguous. On the one hand, they can be used to imply that being a man or a woman is itself a social role – a claim that Thorne, rightly, views as problematic. Sex or gender are better viewed as statuses, positions or social identities rather than as roles; just as social class, age and ethnicity are much more statuses (or positions or identities) than roles. On the other hand, the term sex or gender roles can be used as a shorthand for roles selected or assigned on the basis of gender – a social phenomenon that Thorne acknowledges – roles which for women may include that of wife, mother, sister, nurse, teacher, domestic servant or whatever. This usage of the terms sex or gender roles, although perhaps somewhat loose, is more legitimate than the first, but always requires the plural 'roles' not 'role' (i.e., not 'the female role' but 'female roles'). It might be desirable to avoid even the second usage because of the danger that the phrase may be misinterpreted, but its convenience as a shorthand means it is unlikely to disappear. Moreover, it also needs to be remembered that even when roles are not allocated primarily on the basis of gender, the expectations of occupants may be gendered.

A second problem with the concept of role is 'the passivity and infinite malleability it attributes to human social behaviour' (Segal 1987: 120). In the words of Dennis Wrong (1963) it too often suggests – at least in its structural functionalist forms – an 'oversocialised' conception of the individual in which there is little room for inner conflicts and tensions, or for resistance and struggle. A further, related problem is that the language of role and the theoretical approaches in which the concept is typically located, tend to draw attention away from the structural differences in power between men and women which are such a central feature of gender relations. This is true in both usages of the terms sex or gender role(s). Role analysis too readily suggests a fixed picture of complementary roles, usually deemed to be working to the benefit of the social system, with power, conflict and negotiation excluded from the analysis.

The concept of gender identity, along with the terms masculinity and femininity, provides one alternative to the language of sex or gender role. The notion of gender identity refers to a sense of maleness or femaleness: 'the sameness, unity and persistence of one's individuality as male or female as experienced in self-awareness and behaviour' (Money, quoted in Penfold and Walker 1984: 96). While it should be noted that gender identity and biological sex do not necessarily coincide, the concept of gender identity has the advantage of drawing attention both to the social status of a person and to the individual's subjective awareness of that status. However, it has rather fewer structural connotations than the concept of role.

Patriarchy

In contrast to role analysis, power is at the centrepoint of the highly controversial concept of patriarchy – a concept invoked by a range of feminists writing at the end of the 1960s and early 1970s and subsequently, including Chesler, Ehrenreich and English and Showalter (see also Millett 1972), but whose standing has continued to be highly contested. The concept of patriarchy, meaning either specifically the rule of the father, or more generally the rule of men, places power squarely on the theoretical and political agenda. This accounts for much of its attraction to feminists, some seeing patriarchy as having primacy in relation to all other aspects of social life. Whereas the concept of gender suggests not only differences but also asymmetries and inequalities in the relation between men and women, the concept of patriarchy is used to characterise the wider social structure in which men and women are located, whether it be the family with the focus on the power of the father, or the wider society where it is the power of men more generally that is emphasised. The concept consequently clearly moves beyond concepts like sex or gender, to the level of social structure and social institutions. This is captured quite explicitly in Sylvia Walby's definition of patriarchy as 'a system of social structures, and practices in which men dominate, oppress and exploit women' (1989: 214).

The problems with the concept of patriarchy are well known. Whilst some feminists have tended to emphasise the universality of patriarchy, 'our society, like all other historical civilizations, is a patriarchy' (Millett 1972: 25), critics have argued that analytically the concept cannot readily deal with historical specificity (see Beechey 1979). Yet this objection is not decisive. It has equally been applied to the concept of social class and does not in itself constitute an adequate reason for its abandonment. What the concept does is to draw attention to certain common characteristics of social structures which then need to be examined in their historical specificity. Walby, for one, has proposed a framework in which the patriarchal system is analysed in terms of six main structures: household production, employment, the state, sexuality, violence and culture (1989, 1990). With or without this particular framework there is little difficulty in allowing for historical specificity in the precise mechanisms and structures through which patriarchy operates.

More problematic is the responsibility the concept appears to attribute to men as the source of women's oppression, whether within the family or outside; a feature we find, for instance, in Ehrenreich and English's work (see 1979). Male domination is invoked as the problem

– something that has made the concept particularly attractive to radical feminists with their call for a radical separation of women from the sphere of male activity – and if male domination is the problem then it is men or particular groups of men (such as doctors) who are to blame for women's oppression. There is a double shift in the argument here: first from a descriptive use of the concept of patriarchy to characterise male power at a structural level, to its use to *explain* that power (male power is caused by the actions of men); and second a simultaneous shift from male-dominated structures to male agency. For many, such a view is not only politically but also theoretically unacceptable, either because they see women's oppression as having other origins (such as capitalism), or because they believe that men cannot be blamed for the fact that they have more power (patriarchy is a structural feature of society and not a matter of individual agency), or because they do not believe there is a simple fault-line between men and women, with men always having more power, women less so. However, the concept of patriarchy is arguably more valuable for its descriptive power then its explanatory connotations (except in directing explanatory attention to structures of domination). Indeed, the concept is deployed in a variety of theoretical contexts and its use does not commit us to any one particular theorisation.

There is a further related criticism: that the concept of patriarchy, like the concept of gender, emphasises the similarities between men as a collectivity and women as a collectivity rather than the differences between men and between women – such as diversities of class, age, ethnicity and culture. It operates, it is argued, with essentialist notions of male and female – that is, the tendency to assume differences 'in essence' between men and women. Put another way, the concept is often used to suggest that there are underlying biological differences between men and women which are the source of patriarchal relations. Precisely how this is theorised varies, but a range of theorists attach considerable importance to women's reproductive capacity as crucial to their oppression (see Firestone 1971). It is the control of women's reproduction, they suggest, that legitimates and occasions male dominance.

A parallel psychic essentialism (see Segal 1987: Chapter 4) is found in the writings of some feminists who, influenced by psychoanalytic theorising, link biologically based reproductive capacity to mothering – a mothering for which women are deemed especially suited and which is held up as a source of celebration, as in Nancy Chodorow's highly influential *The Reproduction of Mothering* (1978), which is discussed in Chapter 8. However, it is important to note that, whilst there may be essentialist tendencies in this type of thinking, they do not necessarily preclude an attention to differences *between* women (or between men) (see Harding 1991: Chapter 2).

An alternative conceptualisation to that of patriarchy, which also draws attention to the dimension of power in the relations between men and women, is that of 'gender order' (see Matthews 1984; Stacey 1988: 7–8; Connell 1987: 98–9). Connell uses the concept to refer 'to the structural inventory of an entire society' (ibid), that is, the list of structures within a particular society that characterises its gender relations. The term is used to suggest the structural, institutionalised dimension of gender relations. It is arguably a more neutral concept than patriarchy, but beyond that does not seem to have any strong advantages over it; like patriarchy it is grounded in a structural analysis of social relations. In my view the concept of patriarchy still has some utility as a descriptive term for structural differences between men and women and, in the absence of more suitable alternatives, should not be abandoned.

Capitalism and Dual Systems Theory

Marxist feminists in their early theorisations tended to see the source of women's oppression as lying not in male power in general, but in the capitalist class. Capitalists, they suggested, have an interest in subordinating women into domestic labour, for domestic labour supports and sustains capitalism through the reproduction of labour power ensuring a continuing healthy labour force over the generations. Consequently, whereas men's activities relate primarily to the realm of production, women's relate primarily to reproduction – both biological reproduction and social reproduction (the domestic mode of production) – and are located in the private sphere of the family. In addition, women also play a part in paid employment (production) serving as the reserve army of labour, typically restricted to the secondary labour market, with insecure, often part-time jobs with low pay and so forth. In this account gender tends to be secondary to social class which is held to be the key division within society.

The criticisms of Marxist-feminist analyses are also well known. It is not at all clear why women rather than men or some other social group should constitute the domestic labour force (Molyneux 1979).

Nor, indeed, is it obvious why the reproduction of labour power should be carried out on a domestic basis within the sphere of the family (ibid). Equally, as others have pointed out, gender inequalities are not specific to capitalist societies. This suggests that capitalism cannot serve as an explanation of gender divisions within society. Consequently, some Marxist feminists have developed what is known as the dual systems approach postulating the existence of two separate systems – the class relations of capitalism and the gender relations of patriarchy; one system focusing on production, the other on reproduction – which are assumed to interact. Theorists vary in their precise assumptions as to the independence of the two systems, some assuming two very independent systems (see Hartmann 1979), others a high degree of interdependence (Eisenstein 1979). The problem, however, with a dual systems approach is the assumption of two separate systems that need to be separately analysed and have then to be articulated. It is preferable to try to develop a more unified theory which can encompass both gender and class relations within a more complex framework. Glucksmann (1990), for example, in her study of women factory workers, develops a materialist theory in which the focus is still, as in Marx, on the relations of production but 'primacy is not accorded to paid employment in the public economy, as constitutive of class relations as such' (ibid: 18). Instead, the framework is broadened to embrace 'the much wider sexual division of labour between the spheres of production and reproduction' (ibid: 17). A dual systems approach encourages a separation in the analysis of gender relations from other analyses, whereas an integration, in which the potential salience of gender relations as well as class relations are always considered, is required.

Such an integrated approach need not, of course, be Marxist. However, even though Marxist theorising of gender relations has not been especially successful, there are features of the Marxist approach to the analysis of gender relations that need to be retained and have been effectively deployed in considering gender and mental disorder. The prime example is Penfold and Walker's *Woman and the Psychiatric Paradox* (1984). The first and most obvious feature, is the importance attached to the material conditions of people's lives and the control over material resources as a source of power. The second feature is the recognition of possible discrepancies between individual consciousness and material reality and interests that is captured by the Marxist notion of ideology. The notion of ideology has been of particular importance in the analysis of gender (see, for instance, Barrett 1980). Indeed, 'there is a strong tendency to make ideology the site of sexual politics' (Connell 1987: 241). Ideology has been an effective analytic tool because of the way it embodies notions of social interest and power, and links ideas to material situations. In this respect it has advantages over Michel Foucault's notion of discourse which, though it is linked to ideas of power – indeed, to the inseparability of power and knowledge – and though it incorporates both ideas and practices, does not link these to an analysis of material conditions and is, consequently, more prone to the dangers of idealist analysis (see Harré 1986).

This view of the value of the concept of ideology would be rejected by some feminists, who attach great weight to the value and truth of women's experience, and are reluctant to move beyond subjectivity, seeing all claims to objectivity as but an attempt to impose a male view of the world. In my view, however, any understanding of women's situation requires us to move beyond that conscious experience and to theorise it. Sandra Harding puts the argument like this:

> But it cannot be that women's experiences in themselves or the things women say provide reliable grounds for knowledge claims about nature and social relations. After all, experience itself is shaped by social relations; for example, women have had to *learn* to define as rape those sexual assaults that occur within marriages. Women had experienced these assaults not as something that could be called rape but only as part of the range of hetero-sexual sex that wives should expect (1991: 123).

Instead she advocates a move to what she calls 'strong objectivity', which recognises historical and cultural relativism (the diversity of meaning and experience), but rejects judgemental or epistemological relativism allowing for shared standards of scientific knowledge. Any such science would need to encompass systematic examination of the assumptions and beliefs that underpin its own practices (ibid: Chapter 6). Harding's case for 'strong objectivity' is at least in part a response to and critique of postmodernist tendencies that constitute a fashionable alternative approach to the analysis of gender.

Texts, Language and Deconstruction

Postmodernist theory is grounded in the work of writers such as Jacques Derrida and his idea of deconstruction, and Michel Foucault and the concept of discourse.[10] The closest exemplar in analyses of gender and mental disorder is to be found in Jane Ussher's study

Women's Madness, which calls for a deconstruction of madness (1991: 11–14). In this approach, language, meaning and subjectivity are the focus. What we take to be social reality is constituted only through language and its social meanings – meanings which are necessarily socially and historically specific and highly variable. Different languages, with their attendant sets of meanings and related practices, constitute discourses which mediate our perceptions of the world. Thus far the approach is not especially contentious. The controversial belief lies in the inference made from this focus on language and meanings: that there is no reality independent of our apprehensions of it – that language is constitutive of reality and differences in language and meaning are of equal status and validity – a position of extreme epistemological relativism not unfamiliar in previous philosophical writings (for example, Berkeley or Winch), as well as sociology (for example, ethnomethodology). Consequently, the search for causal explanations is misguided, for there can be no satisfactory criteria for choosing between alternative causal accounts. Instead what we have are narratives or stories (the fictional connotations of the terms are surely intended), and those theorists such as Marx who attempt to construct overarching grand theory simply provide us with what are now to be called metanarratives. From this perspective the object of academic endeavour is simply to deconstruct these narratives or texts – that is, to unearth the diversity and complexity of meanings in a particular text, whether this is a particular piece of literature, medical text, an autobiographical account, or whatever. Nothing is privileged except, of course, the text and the analysis of texts.

The main merit of the approach is the attention that is given to the way in which language and meanings shape our consciousness and subjectivity and are both varied and changing, and postmodernist analyses of texts and representations can be very valuable (a good example of work inspired by, though critical of, postmodernism is provided by Susan Bordo's (1990) illuminating analysis of cultural representations of thinness – see Chapter 9 below). However, the focus on the diversity of meanings is a strongly established tradition within sociology and does not depend on postmodernist theorisation. The idea of social construction is, for instance, integral to symbolic interactionism, as is the idea of the flexibility, variety and negotiability of meanings. Likewise, Weberian sociology attaches central importance to *verstehen* or understanding – a process in which the objective is to identify and understand actors' meanings.

The mistake of postmodernism as a theoretical approach, as opposed to a characterisation of society or of aesthetic movements, is a dual one.[11] First, there is its tendency, stronger in some authors than others, to epistemological relativism. Whilst it is true that there is a plurality of languages, meanings and interpretations and, consequently, of explanatory accounts, this does not mean that we cannot have satisfactory criteria for choosing between them and determining which are more adequate and closer to the 'facts' than others. For, even though we cannot apprehend the material world directly – our apprehension is always mediated through language and meaning – this does not mean that there is only a world of multiple languages and meanings and no independent material reality. Since meanings can be and are shared (as the notion of culture implies), there can be a world of agreed fact within the framework of those shared meanings. It is perfectly reasonable since we have a shared (though not totally unchanging) notion of sickness, to ask whether an individual is sick or not. Equally, since we have a category of rape (whose exact boundaries are of course contested), we can legitimately ask if a woman has been raped or not. To say this, does not commit us to the view that the meaning of such categories are invariant, or that the boundaries can be easily settled, or that the identification of individual cases is never problematic (is a person sick or malingering?) But it does mean that a woman's claim that she has been raped should not be treated primarily as a narrative. We have a range of criteria that can be applied to determine the facticity of such claims, and the reality, brutality and trauma should not be rendered insignificant or bracketed off by fascination with narratives. Judgemental relativism does not, as Harding (1991) argues, have to go hand in hand with a recognition of cultural relativism. What is needed is a realist philosophy of science (Bhaskar 1978, 1989).

Second, and related to this, postmodernism directs our attention to the realm of language, meaning, culture and discourse at the expense of the analysis of social structures and material resources – of inequalities in economic and political power, whether between social classes, ethnic groups or between men and women. Its concern with texts and representations blinds it to political, social and economic structures that constitute the fabric of society and generate social inequalities. Bordo, for instance, criticising a postmodernist analysis of how viewers read television programmes, points to:

a characteristically postmodern flattening of the terrain of power relations, a lack of differentiation between, for example, the 'power' involved in creative *reading* in the isolation of one's own home and the 'power' held by those who control the material production of television shows, or the 'power' involved in public protest and action against the conditions of that production, or the dominant meanings – e.g. racist and sexist images and messages – therein produced (1993: 277).

Not surprisingly, given postmodernism's epistemological relativism and its lack of interest in material conditions and economic and political power, many critics of postmodernism have argued that its underlying assumptions destroy the basis for political action and intervention and constitute a highly conservative framework. Stevi Jackson contends:

> when 'women', 'experience' and 'knowledge' all become problematic concepts, we can find ourselves with no place from which to speak as women and from which to make political demands or to challenge patriarchal structures (which themselves are held to have no existence except within feminist discourse) (1992: 29).

Postmodernists, she suggests, are all too ready to contend that any use of the categories of man–woman, male–female commits us to essentialism. Yet without such categories political action is impossible. Postmodernist theorising has, therefore, to be rejected.

The Foundations for a Theory of Gender

If no existing theory of gender relations is entirely satisfactory, what is the alternative? It is beyond the scope of this book to attempt to develop a new theory of gender relations. We can, however, set out some of the foundations for satisfactory theorising that indicate the assumptions on which the argument in this book is based. There are six underlying assumptions.

First, that an adequate theory of gender must be based on feminist foundations. By this I mean simply that it must take women's lives seriously and, indeed, take a concern for women's lives as its starting point. It does not and cannot mean, as I have already indicated, that the analysis should focus exclusively on women. Whether this feminist standpoint requires a distinctive feminist epistemology as well as a distinctive sociology is a matter of debate which goes beyond the confines of this book (see Harding 1987, 1992).[12] Nonetheless, given the history of women's oppression, I regard a feminist standpoint as an essential foundation for the analysis of gender.

Second, an adequate theory must reject epistemological relativism along with its abandonment of the search for causal explanations. Instead it should adopt a realist philosophy of social science (see Bhaskhar 1978, 1989; Harré 1986). The extreme relativism of post modernism must be eschewed. This does not mean a return to a simple positivism, but an approach to knowledge that accepts the existence of a real world that is potentially knowable, and accepts the superiority of some claims over others.

Third, and related to this, an adequate theory of gender relations must give proper attention to economic and material conditions as well as to the realm of meanings, symbols and culture – a material realm that includes social structures and social and economic institutions, such as the way work is organised, the way wealth and resources are distributed and so forth. An emphasis on the importance of the material does not commit us to a specifically Marxist approach to theorising, and we have already seen how Marxist accounts attempting to link gender relations to capitalism are far from satisfactory. Nevertheless, a range of Marxist concepts such as social class (defined in terms of its economic basis), social interest and ideology, as well as the attention to social and economic conflicts and struggles, are invaluable to any material analysis of gender relations.

Fourth, and also related to this, an adequate theory of gender relations requires a systematic examination of the sources of power and of power relations. Such an analysis should not be restricted to the ideological and cultural as postmodernists often assume. Rather, not only should the economic and material bases of power be recognised (e.g. the importance of women's exclusion from the labour force, if and when it occurs, or their concentration in lower-paid jobs), but so, too, should the political and military bases (see Mann 1986).

Fifth, an adequate analysis of gender relations requires proper attention to historical and cultural specificity, without sliding into the trap of epistemological relativism into which postmodernists have fallen. What is needed is both a theoretical and conceptual sensitivity and a recognition of material and cultural specificities – a combination that is most obviously visible in the work of the best Marxist historians, such as E. P. Thompson and Eric Hobsbawm, who have used Marxist conceptual tools to facilitate their understanding of particular historical developments. This combination is also visible in the writings of some of the best feminist historians (see, for instance, Leonore Davidoff and Catherine Hall's *Family Fortunes*, 1987).

Sixth, and finally, an adequate analysis of gender relations should not treat gender as a separate system which interacts with other systems, but as an all-pervasive dimension of social relations and social institutions, which is more or less salient in particular situations. A unitary, integrated rather than a dual systems approach is necessary. This applies to the analysis of gender and mental disorder just as much as to the analysis of gender and social class. In order to explore this area further I now consider the concept of mental disorder.

Chapter 4

Mental Disorder, Medicine and the Regulation of Rationality

The Reason–Madness nexus constitutes for Western culture one of the dimensions of its originality (Foucault 1967: xiii).

If we go back to first principles, what the 'mentally ill' have lost is not their bodily health, nor their virtue, but their *reason*: their conduct simply does not 'make sense'. Insanity ascriptions, on this view, are made when behaviour does not seem accountable by any plausible motive, or when belief seems to be quite unfounded: they may be ruled out simply by providing a credible motive for action or a reasonable ground for belief (Ingleby 1982: 128).

Psychiatrists, as medical specialists, still have prime responsibility for the care and treatment of the mentally disturbed, although in the world of community care other professionals compete with them for influence and power. As such, psychiatrists formally construct the dominant social discourse through which mental disorder is constituted and given meaning. From a medical point of view, mental disorder is viewed as a distinctive type of illness to be understood, as with other types of illness, first and foremost in physical terms, and is commonly to be treated by physical means. The task of the sociologist is, however, not only to explore medical conceptualisations of mental disorder, but to move beyond them and to offer new ways of thinking about mental disorder, locating it within a broader social context and an analysis of social relations. In later chapters I examine, through the prism of gender differences, a range of ideas about the social causes of mental disorder. In this chapter and in Chapter 6 my concern is with the category of mental disorder itself. Precisely what phenomena are constituted as mental disorder? Where are the boundaries of mental disorder set? How can we account for the way in which mental disorder is constituted as a category? In what ways, if at all, is gender embedded in constructs of mental disorder? I argue in this chapter that the phenomena of mental disorder occupy a bounded, highly contested and changing terrain that falls between physical illness, deviance and normality. I further argue that at a societal level we can best theorise the way its boundaries are set in terms of the regulation of rationality and irrationality. In Chapter 6, I look at gender and the construction of mental disorder.

The Terrain of Mental Disorder

Medical and societal thought and practice are nowadays largely at one in viewing mental disorder as belonging to the realm of illness and in regarding mental disorder, like physical illness, as a generic term that embraces a diverse range of specific disorders, many of which were discussed in Chapter 1: schizophrenia, manic-depression (now frequently termed bi-polar depression), anorexia nervosa, drug addiction and so forth. As such, the formal meaning of the concept is given by an elaboration, more or less detailed, of specific mental disorders, and little attempt is made to specify the nature of mental disorder as a general category.[1] Put another way, psychiatry has adopted a categorical model in which specific mental disorders (categories of disorder) constitute the building blocks from which the generic term is constructed.[2] As with physical illnesses, the range of mental disorders is large and diverse, extending from conditions known to involve some physical malfunction, such as the broad group of dementias, through the so-called 'thought disorders' of which schizophrenia is the best known, through the 'affective disorders', including the various types of depression, to anxieties, phobias and the substance use disorders, such as alcoholism and anorexia nervosa. Apart from the fact that, as the term 'mental illness' indicates, all are deemed suitable objects of psychiatric attention, the one shared characteristic of the disorders is that they all involve, or are presumed to involve, some disturbance of *mental* functioning, be it intellectual capacities, thought processes, emotions, or underlying motivations.

It is this presumed disorder of mental functioning, and the attendant behaviour. with which it is associated, that provides the rationale for treating these disorders as a distinctive grouping to be differentiated not only from physical illness but also from social deviance − that is, the breaking of social rules. Yet mental disorder stands in a difficult, precarious position between bodily illness and social deviance, and there has been an ongoing struggle between various professionals, social theorists and others as to where its boundaries should be set and whether it can, or should, be demarcated from its neighbours. On the one hand, many medical professionals, including psychiatrists as specialists in mental disorder, argue that for most practical purposes mental disorders are like other illnesses. And, with the primacy given to physical processes in contemporary medicine, they often focus on the physical causes of mental disorders, rather than on psychological and social causes, and on physical treatments − a stance given credence by the discovery of the organic basis of conditions such as general paresis of the insane (GP1), and by the impact of physical treatments on psychological states. In so doing they frequently imply that mental disorder can be assimilated to physical illness. On the other hand, a range of sociologists along with the 1960s anti-psychiatrists, have tended to assimilate the phenomena of mental disorder to models of deviant action. In this they have followed ideas frequently articulated within the criminal justice system, when lawyers reject claims that criminal actions can be accounted for by mental disorder. Figure 4.1 portrays this ongoing pressure to assimilate mental disorder to the realms of either physical illness or social deviance.

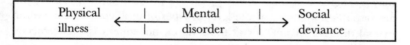

FIGURE 4.1   *The Assimilation of Mental Disorder*

Yet, notwithstanding these assimilatory pressures, we can readily locate a distinctive terrain of mental disorder at least analytically. The analytical destination between the three lies in their different referents: mind, body and behaviour. The difference between mental disorder and physical illness is not that one has mental, the other physical causes, but that one involves judgements *of* mental functioning, the other *of* physical functioning. It is the *referent* that is at issue, not the mental or physical processes that may be involved in producing the phenomena in question. The notion of mental disorder consequently embodies a clear dualism of mind and body. This dualism has been widely contested, but remains a fundamental feature of medical and lay discourse.[3] It is important to note, however, that physical illness, mental disorder and deviance are not mutually exclusive categories. A particular condition may, for instance, be deemed a physical illness or a mental disorder according to the situation in question. In part this will be a matter of the specific constellation of symptoms; in part a matter of the interests and expertise of the professionals and lay people involved. Similarly, certain behaviour may be viewed both as socially deviant *and* as indicative of mental disorder. It is this potential choice over where and how we locate what is problematic that leads to so many of the debates and difficulties over the proper terrain of mental disorder.

While, therefore, it is relatively easy to point to an *analytic* difference between the concepts of mental disorder, physical illness and deviance, this does not mean that the boundaries between the phenomena so identified are uncontested. This is primarily because of the evaluative, prescriptive nature of the three concepts, all of which imply some form of pathology, whether of body, mind or behaviour.[4] This evaluative character is a vital feature and creates major disputes over their use. We may agree that the term mental disorder refers specifically to problems of mind rather than of body or behaviour, but faced with a particular problem or difficulty we may not agree that the 'real' problem – that is, the one that merits our attention and possible intervention – is a problem of mind not body or behaviour; or, equally importantly, we may not agree that there is any significant problem at all. Such boundary disputes may occur at the level of types of problem (is alcoholism a mental disorder or not?) or at the level of individual cases (is someone physically sick or mentally disturbed?)

In examining these disputes it is useful to identify three contested, changing boundaries – the two discussed so far between mental disorder and physical illness, and between mental disorder and social deviance (madness and badness); and a third between mental disorder and mental health (madness and normality). We can then portray the terrain of mental disorder and the respective boundary disputes in diagrammatic form, as in Figure 4.2, the broken lines representing the disputed, changing nature of the boundaries.

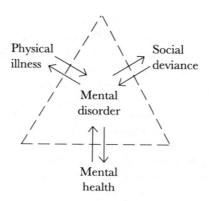

FIGURE 4.2 *The Contested Boundaries of Mental Disorder*

The location of the boundary between physical illness and mental disorder has long been contested, both within the medical profession, and outside. Significantly, whilst I have suggested until now that medicine has been the source of the main pressure to assimilate the terrain of mental disorder to that of physical illness, the position of psychiatry itself has been far more contradictory. Certainly the strong, though varying, emphasis within psychiatry on the physical causes and physical treatments of mental disorder is indicative of assimilatory tendencies. But, psychiatry also emerged and survived in the nineteenth century on the assumption of the distinctiveness of the terrain of mental disorder. Indeed, as an emergent speciality it faced competition from neurology (see Rosenberg 1968; Blustein 1981) – a specialisation within the general hospital focused on the brain and the nervous system which had far stronger links with the rest of medicine. In this struggle psychiatry, with its empire of the asylum, had some success in its territorial claims and in maintaining its distinctiveness as a medical speciality both in the second half of the nineteenth century – a period that has been termed the 'golden age' of psychiatry (Castel 1988: 7) – and in the first half of the twentieth century. However, with the shift to community care (see Chapter 7) and psychiatry's loss of a clearly demarcated empire, and with major developments in neuroscience in recent decades which threaten to outflank psychiatry's own biomedical biases, neurology is now once more encroaching on the terrain of mental disorder at the expense of psychiatry.

While disputes over the boundary between mental disorder and physical illness have been dominated by professional rivalries *within* medicine, the boundary between mental disorder and social deviance, the latter roughly co-terminous with the lay category of wrongdoing, has often been a matter of rivalry between the medical profession and the law (see Smith 1981; Walker 1968), as well as between medicine and the wider public. The division relates to assumptions about human action; about whether the phenomena in question are to be viewed as a product of human agency and as ones for which the individual is to be held responsible, or are instead to be considered outside the individual's control who is not to be deemed responsible – a position that can be presented as more humane (Flew 1973).

The division also relates to whether it is action or the underlying mental processes that are deemed problematic. As such it is probably the most indeterminate and highly contested of the three boundaries. This is not least because, although we may be willing to allow, even emphasise, the co-presence of mental disorder and physical illness – and accept, for example, that Alzheimer's disease can be viewed as both a mental and a physical disorder – madness and badness do persistently remain mutually exclusive categories in our everyday understandings (see Wootton 1959: Chapter 7). Analytically, the basis of the distinction may be clear – if we evaluate an aspect of *mental* functioning unfavourably, it is a matter of mental disorder; if of *behaviour* it is a matter of delinquency. But this does not determine which evaluation is the most appropriate, as the uncertainties surrounding legal cases like the 'Yorkshire Ripper' attest. Psychiatrists provided evidence of the defendant's diminished responsibility: the jury convicted him of murder and rape.[5]

Decisions on cases of this nature are not just a matter of the power and potential of competing discourses and attendant values; they are also linked to service provisions. The reduction of residential provision for the mentally disordered has ensured that some individuals, such as those with alcohol or drug related problems, who might have been treated as disturbed in mind, have instead ended up in prisons within the purview of the criminal justice system (Reed 1992). With fewer and fewer psychiatric beds, the difficult, disruptive and troublesome are treated as wrongdoers rather than as disturbed. The difficulties of drawing a clear boundary between mental disorder and wrongdoing are not, however, restricted to cases where the criminal law has been broken. There are a range of behavioural problems now frequently treated as mental disorders, such as sexual deviations like transvestism, and the range of eating disorders, alcoholism and drug addiction, where actions are deemed socially unacceptable, though not criminal, but they may equally be viewed as symptomatic of underlying psychological difficulties.[6]

Finally, there is the boundary between mental disorder and normality – an imprecise and ill-defined distinction. Indeed, whilst the categorical thinking usually involved in medical classifications presumes a boundary between sickness and health, many have argued for a dimensional view in which there are gradations of health and sickness and, consequently, only an arbitrary cut-off point between the two (see, for instance, Eysenck 1960: Chapter 1; Goldberg and Huxley 1992: Chapter 5).[7] In a similar vein, Freudian theorising emphasises the continuity of mental health and pathology and in so doing facilitates an expansion of therapeutic intervention across the range of mental functioning. In practice, however, some boundary between mental health and disorder is usually made. But frequently it is not based solely on assessments of the inner world of thoughts, motivations and feelings; it is also a matter of the way in which we judge behaviour and attribute agency. If we deem behaviour problematic, if for some reason duties or obligations are not fulfilled, we are more likely to consider whether they are the result of some physical or mental incapacity (where agency is not assumed). Put differently, socially deviant behaviour may lead to assumptions of psychological pathology (see Wootton 1959: Chapter 5) and the denial of agency either at the individual or social level. The developing categories of domestic violence and child abuse are examples of emergent social problems where what was often viewed as normal, or seemed invisible, is not only made visible but also deemed unacceptable. And, in consequence, the question of underlying psychological disorder becomes an issue. The pathway is from the normal to the unacceptable to the disturbed. An example of a reverse trajectory is that of homosexuality, which having been assigned the status of a mental disorder in the 1950s and 1960s, was then deemed no longer a psychiatric disorder in itself and is now viewed by some, though by no means all, as normal (Spector 1972).

What is clear, therefore, is that while psychiatrists may find it relatively straightforward to offer a formal definition of the concept of mental disorder via their listing of specific types of disorder, determining the precise boundaries of the terrain of mental disorder is far from easy in practice. For example, the inclusion of alcoholism, drug addiction or bulimia nervosa in the list of mental disorders may appear to settle the boundaries at least in relation to these problems. However, official recognition does not ensure there is widespread acceptance outside the profession that they are to be treated as mental disorders (or even that this is accepted across the whole profession). Moreover, even if it is widely agreed that it is appropriate to constitute say alcoholism as a mental disorder (for some of the counter-arguments, see Heather and Robertson 1989: Chapter 5), there will still be debates about the allocation of individual cases, the outcome of which will themselves contribute to the determination of the boundary. Matching individuals to formal delineations is no easy task – an issue discussed more fully in Chapters 5 and 6.

Categories of mental disorder and the psychiatric classifications that elaborate, group and formalise them, constitute in effect, therefore, practical devices constructed primarily by the medical and psychiatric professions to arrange and order the diversity of mental and nervous problems with which, for whatever reason, they deal. They serve as intellectual lenses, attempting to impose clarity and order on the complexity of human mental states, structuring thought and practice and providing recipes for action. Put another way, they facilitate decisions about what precisely is wrong and what is to be done about it – decisions that are essential to clinical practice.[8]

However, as is already very clear, the intellectual constructions of psychiatrists and other mental health professionals develop and change. Professionals are actively engaged in trying to improve and develop their skills, expertise and knowledge to provide a more secure basis for their practice, with potential gains to them in effectiveness and status. In addition, the demands they face may also change as what is considered problematic in the wider society changes, as well as what, if any, are deemed the appropriate sources of help (a process to which, of course, they contribute). As a result, what constitutes psychiatric knowledge is always under negotiation and subject to revision and transformation.

One important feature of these historical changes is the elaboration of new categories of disorder to embrace phenomena formerly largely outside medical nosologies, though not necessarily previously considered either unproblematic within the society or beyond the scope of medical attention. In the nineteenth century moral insanity, monomania and masturbatory insanity were added to the psychiatric lexicon. More recently psychiatric attention has focused, for a number of reasons, on problems of childhood, and disorders such as hyperactivity (Schrag and Divoky 1981) and dyslexia have entered the psychiatric repertory. Eating disorders are also a territory with intense activity, with conditions like bulimia nervosa (Russell 1979) joining anorexia nervosa in the list of eating disorders. What we observe is a formalisation and theorisation, both by medical practitioners and other mental health professionals, of a domain that had formerly received much less medical attention. In some cases problems widely recognised, but not viewed as medical or health matters, come to be 'medicalised' – that is, they become subject to the medical gaze. In other cases, such as neurasthenia and hysteria, conditions virtually disappear from the psychiatric lexicon and are declassified; in yet others one medical problem is transformed into another, both being seen as suitable for professional attention. A generation of difficult delinquent children are replaced by a generation of hyperactives – a case of madness replacing badness. A generation of patients with anxiety neurosis is replaced by a generation of patients suffering from depression – one form of mental disorder replacing another.[9]

Not surprisingly, given this fluidity, there is, despite considerable endeavour, no single universally accepted classificatory schema of mental disorder (see Kendell 1975). The proponents of the *International Statistical Classification of Diseases* (ICD), attempt to secure world-wide acceptance for the framework, but have not fully succeeded even for statistical purposes, let alone in relation to the diagnoses used in clinical contexts. Moreover, as psychiatric ideas and practices change, the classification is subject to not infrequent revision – the ninth revision of 1985 was replaced by the tenth revision in 1992 (World Health Organisation 1992). So, too, is its major contender, the American Psychiatric Association's *Diagnostic and Statistical Manual* (DSM), first published in 1952 and now in its fourth edition – the DSM-IV (American Psychiatric Association 1994).[10]

We have to recognise, therefore, that mental disorder is a culturally and socially relative category whose precise boundaries and meanings vary over time and place and are highly contested. It is, to use the sociological phrase, a 'social construct'. I shall consider the implications of these points for an examination of gender differences in subsequent chapters. For the moment, however, I want to touch on one question: that of whether the claim as to the social and cultural relativity of the category – of the way it is shaped by social processes – involves a denial of the material reality of mental disorder as 1960s ethnometodologists and 1980s postmodernists, as well as the defenders of psychiatric orthodoxy, have tended to assume. Does the claim involve a denial of the reality of the sufferings of the mentally disturbed and a total rejection of the idea of the physiological basis of some, if not all, mental disorder? I would contend that it does not. My position here, as indicated in the previous chapter, is that of the philosophical realist (Sayers 1982; Harré 1986; Bhaskar 1978, 1989). I do not wish to deny the existence of the pain, sufferings and confusions of the disturbed. However, I do assume that our cognitive mappings of that material reality vary and change and mediate our apprehension of it. We need, as I argued in the last chapter, to distinguish an awareness of social and cultural relativism from judgemental or epistemological relativism.

Mental disorder is, then, a 'label' in the sense that it is, like all words, a social construct; but it is not 'merely' a label. It has a referent that has an ontological reality, and although that reality is mediated through diverse constructions or discourses which give it meaning, we can still test these constructions empirically against material reality. There is a reality of structures, interests and power beyond the multiplicity of 'voices' to which we must attend.

Theorising Mental Disorder

I have argued that there is a terrain of mental disorder, whose boundaries are contested and changing. It is a terrain which is primarily mapped by psychiatrists, although during the twentieth century other mental health professionals, including psychologists and non-medical psychotherapists, have played an increasing role in its intellectual construction. However, while these professionals map the terrain and, indeed as we have seen, help to shape its boundaries through their struggles with other professionals, medicine does not attempt, nor is it necessarily reasonable to expect it to attempt, given its professional concerns, to ask broader questions about why we have the category of mental disorder, or the place of mental disorder in the wider society, or even about how the boundaries of mental disorder come to be set in particular ways in particular times and places. These are questions for sociologists, social theorists and social historians. I want, therefore, to explore some of the ways of approaching these questions. My concern here is not to settle the now rather tired debate about whether mental disorder is or is not best treated in practice as a form of illness or, indeed, whether it should be treated in practice as social deviance. Rather it is to consider how we can most usefully characterise and theorise mental disorder as a social phenomenon and to place it in a wider social context. While psychiatrists and other mental health professionals play a key role in constituting the language and concepts through which we apprehend mental disorder, they do not do so in a vacuum. They are responsive to external demands and pressures.[11] I begin by considering the ideas of two influential sociologists, Émile Durkheim and Talcot Parsons, both of whom tend, like many sociologists, to appropriate mental disorder to models of deviance.

Durkheim and Parsons

Durkheim's classic discussion of crime in his *Rules of Sociological Method* (1964 [1885]), has been a key influence on sociological thinking about social deviance, and can be readily extended to mental disorder. Central to Durkheim's argument is the assumption of the need in any society for the existence and application of standards of conduct for its members – for morality and law – if it is to function effectively. Society, he contends, cannot exist without rules defining what is acceptable and unacceptable behaviour; deviance – that is, rule breaking – is a corollary of the social regulation necessary for social order. For even if individuals closely adhere to a set of rules, deviance does not disappear; instead the standards themselves become stricter. Durkheim illuminates this point in a familiar passage:

> Imagine a society of saints, a perfect cloister of exemplary individuals. Crimes, properly so called, will there be unknown; but faults which appear venial to the layman will create there the same scandal that the ordinary offense does in ordinary consciousnesses. If, then, this society has the power to judge and punish, it will define these acts as criminal and will treat them as such. For the same reason, the perfect and upright man judges his smallest failings with a severity that the majority reserve for acts more truly in the nature of an offense (ibid: 68–9).

Durkheim was, of course, talking about rules of behaviour and about crime and wrongdoing, but his insights can be readily used to suggest there are also standards governing mental functioning – thought and emotion – and these depend on the social context. Indeed, the example of a society of saints readily lends itself to such an extension, since in such a community a concern with appropriate thought and feeling would be as likely to emerge as with behaviour. However, we need to distinguish a concern with the appropriateness of the *content* of thought and ideas (what is in today's jargon called 'political correctness'), from a concern with the appropriateness or normality of *processes* of mental functioning, since psychiatrists assert, not entirely incorrectly, that mental disorder is to be judged by the latter not the former.[12] Using Durkheim's framework it is far easier to see why there should be a concern with the content of thought and feeling than with the character of mental activity *per se*, and although we need to be sceptical of psychiatrists' claims that content is irrelevant (see Chapter 6 below), there can be little doubt that the assessment of mental processes is central to definitions of mental disorder. How then can we account for such societal concerns?

Talcot Parsons, writing at the beginning of the 1950s, developed and explicitly extended Durkheim's functionalist ideas to the domain of illness in ways that can help to illuminate the category of mental disorder. Parsons, best known in this field for his concept of the sick role (1951), developed two distinct though interrelated models of illness (Gerhardt 1989). In the first 'capacity model', the starting point is health, which is defined from a sociological perspective as the capacity for 'the effective performance of social roles' (ibid: 43). Consequently, illness is to be viewed sociologically not simply as some physiological disorder, though the existence of physical diseases is recognised, but as 'the failure to fulfil one's role' (ibid: 16). The roles that Parsons had in mind are the individual's everyday social roles, and in this model the failure to fulfil them is viewed as involuntary – a view in line with everyday understandings about illness. However, according to Parsons, individuals who cannot fulfil their customary roles are themselves placed in a special situation – a situation governed by social expectations and so itself also a social role. Parsons terms this the sick role, which Uta Gerhardt describes as a kind of 'niche in the social system where the incapacitated may withdraw while attempting to mend their fences, with the help of the medical profession' (ibid: 15). The key expectations of this role are: that sick individuals be exempted from their normal social responsibilities; that it be accepted that they cannot help being ill; that they should want to get well; and that they should seek, where appropriate, medically competent help in so doing (Parsons 1951: 436–7). Through these expectations, the sick role provides a mechanism by means of which sickness is regulated, thereby contributing to the smooth functioning of the social system.

Parsons's capacity model offers, therefore, a way of thinking about disorder, mental or physical, that specifies very clearly the reason why certain phenomena are identified as illnesses: *they are incapacities that prevent satisfactory role performance.* The distinction between physical illness and mental disorder is then simply a matter of whether it is the body or mind that leads to the incapacities of role performance. The analysis allows both for variations in the boundaries of illness across time and place, since the requirements of role performance vary, and also for high levels of consensus over certain illnesses, such as those that are very life-threatening. Moreover, it can embrace physical and mental handicap (long-term disability) as well as illness.[13]

Parsons's second model is more controversial, and the Durkheimian influence more patent. In this model, illness, rather than being juxtaposed to deviance as societal beliefs typically assume, is itself viewed as a form of deviance. Here the stress is on the motivational elements in illness and the model is much more voluntaristic and highly influenced by Freudian theorising. Parsons contends that illness often, if not always, involves motivational factors – the very motivational factors suggested in his formulation of the sick role, such as the desire to get well or, less obviously and usually unconsciously, the possible gains from being ill arising from the exemption from social responsibility. And, he argues, in as far as illness is motivated it can be considered a form of deviance, since it fulfils the two key criteria of deviance. It involves deviation from social norms in that there is a non-performance of social roles; and, since the behaviour is motivated, we can assume agency (albeit that the motivation may be unconscious).

At first sight Parsons's conceptualisation of illness as deviance rather than incapacity seems a very relevant way of thinking about mental disorder if not about physical illness, since the role of psychological motivations in generating the behaviours considered symptomatic of mental sickness has, under the influence of Freud, been widely accepted. Moreover, in its emphasis on motivation, the conceptualisation differs in significant ways from the simple extension of Durkheim's ideas considered earlier: it is the motivations that underlie role performance that are at issue, not conformity in the content of thoughts, ideas and beliefs. This means that if role performance is adequate, mental functioning is unlikely to be called into question. It also means that the emphasis on any scrutiny of mental states is more on motives and desires and less on beliefs (though the separation of these may in practice be difficult).

However, there are serious problems with the deviance formulation. I would contend that neither of the two basic requirements of deviance is met – that is, that the behaviour breaks some socially accepted rule (the rule-breaking requirement), and that there is agency (the agency requirement). First, since the withdrawal from social obligations associated with illness is socially sanctioned, it cannot itself be properly described as rule-breaking. It is, as Parsons's sick role analysis indicates, more a form of normatively governed incapacity, short or long-term, than of deviance. Second, to recognise that there can be *some* motivational elements in illness is not sufficient to establish that the illness itself is willed and that there is agency. There is a slippage in Parsons's analysis from his claims – surely correct – about the common presence of motivational elements, especially once someone is already ill or disturbed, to the requirements of agency of a deviance model – a slippage that is not justified either empirically or theoretically. This assumption of agency is precisely the aspect of the deviance formulation that offends so many psychiatrists, who argue that the sufferings of the mentally disturbed are denied and diminished by the idea that mental disorder is a type of deviance, with its suggestion that the difficulties experienced by the individual are willed.

Neither the flaws of Parsons's deviancy model nor the functionalist character of his approach should, however, blind us to the insights of his analysis of the sick role and his incapacity model. Although the extent to which the norms governing the sick role are applied universally in the way that Parsons's suggests can be questioned (see Turner 1987: 48–9), the analysis has two major strengths. First, it suggests, as we have already noted, that the boundaries of sickness and health are drawn in terms of the capacity to meet the social obligations of role performance – the social obligations of paid work, family life and so on – a phenomenon that is, for example, visible when soldiers attempt to plead sickness to exempt themselves from military duties (Daniels 1970), and is also often visible when any failure or inability to perform everyday tasks is seen as a possible sign of sickness. This linkage between illness and social obligations accounts for the controversy surrounding the issue of malingering, a concept that embodies the idea of wilful and false attempts to occupy the sick role (see Szasz 1961).

Second, Parsons's analysis illuminates the linkages between illness and social control, indicating how and why control is exerted. Here, although part of the inspiration comes from analysing illness as deviance, the conceptualisation of illness as simultaneously a failure by virtue of incapacity to meet normal social obligations and as itself a social role are key elements. Satisfactory role performance is necessary to the social system (the functionalist element of the theory is strong). Consequently, those who are sick have to be controlled and brought back into the system as quickly as possible. Motivational factors may be important in this (some may wish to evade social responsibilities) but do not require a deviancy formulation. Doctors play a key part in this process acting as the agents of regulation in the interests of the wider society, and their own conduct is also governed by social expectations. However, the fact that, viewed in terms of the social system, doctors play a regulatory role does not mean that they may not be genuinely concerned to help such individuals. From a sociological perspective care and control are not necessarily incompatible.

Parsons's analysis of illness clearly has potential value in helping us to understand the development of categories of mental disorder. However his vision of society as a smoothly functioning system operating in the interests of all is problematic and has been challenged both within sociology and outside.

The Anti-Psychiatrists

A range of authors, including some psychiatrists, have taken up the theme of social regulation in their consideration of mental disorder but, focusing on the interests and perspective of the patients rather than the wider society, have stressed the oppressive nature of such control for those deemed disturbed. In the 1960s the diverse group of theorists, known as anti-psychiatrists, argued that the notion of mental illness acted as a hidden mechanism of social control that serves to mystify moral, legal and ethical judgements of human behaviour under the guise of scientific objectivity and the ideology of care associated with medicine. In so doing they followed Parsons in viewing illness as a form of deviance, but differed from him in treating illness and deviance as mutually exclusive categories and in juxtaposing care and control. Mental disorders, they contended, are not illnesses at all. According to the US psychiatrist and libertarian, Thomas Szasz, the notion of mental illness is but a metaphor and the phenomena so labelled should, more properly, be termed 'problems in living' (Szasz 1960).[14] To call these problems illnesses and see them as part of the province of medicine (unless they have clear organic causes in which case they are brain diseases), is to mystify the social control that is involved, since the ideology of medicine is of voluntaristic care not regulation and compulsion (Szasz does not object to social control as long as it is explicit). Szasz does not, however, consider how and why these processes of oppressive regulation operate in the way that they do, simply arguing that we persecute and harass the mentally disturbed just as we persecuted witches in the past because all societies need their scapegoats (Szasz 1971).

According to R.D. Laing (1967), the British anti-psychiatrist whose ideas were influenced by existentialism, the use of labels of sanity and madness equally involves the evaluation, judgement and condemnation of human behaviour. Indeed, the starting point for Laing, as for Szasz, is the existence of a clear division between the natural world and the realm of human action – and, consequently, between physical illness and mental disorder. It is because the label of mental disorder involves judgements of human action not physical functioning that it is problematic. These judgements, he contends, are not objective and value-neutral as medicine tends to assume, rather they are evaluative, and what counts as sanity and insanity is largely a question of adjustment and conformity to social norms. Whilst, however, Laing makes it clear that a person may be deemed mad because their independent, autonomous actions seem to threaten society and do not conform to the statistical norm, like Szasz he offers little in the way of an analysis of the factors underpinning these processes of control. We are offered a rich portrayal of the internal conflicts of the disturbed individual and of the complex dynamics of their family relationships (Laing and Esterson 1964), but no wider analysis of how or why sanity and madness developed as categories in particular ways in particular times and places.

A more explicit attempt to deal with this question is provided by another 1960s author, often grouped amongst the anti-psychiatrists, Thomas Scheff. As a sociologist, Scheff (1966) explicitly theorises mental disorder in terms of deviance. He accepts, however, that mental disorder differs from other forms of deviance, and raises the question of which rules the person identified as mentally disturbed has broken that distinguish this type of rule-breaking from others. In this respect he explicitly tackles a further major problem raised by sociological analyses, such as Parsons's, which view mental disorder as deviance: that of differentiating this form of deviance from those that lead to labels of wrongdoing rather than sickness. Scheff's answer is that persons labelled mentally disturbed have broken 'residual' rules, that is rules that are 'left over' when other forms of rules have been excluded, such as the rules whose infraction leads to the identification of criminal behaviour, bad manners and so forth (ibid: 33–4). He also suggests that the rules at issue, which he contends are widely broken, are 'taken for granted'. They are rules of which we are not normally aware – rules about the distance at which you stand from someone, about looking at them when they speak, and so forth. Moreover, according to Scheff, the societal reaction to rule-breaking behaviour is crucial. Only if it receives some response will the rule-breaker begin to be pressured into entering the role of the mentally disturbed person. Whether the action is identified as deviant or not depends on a number of factors, such as the visibility of the infraction, the power of the rule-breaker, the frequency of rule breaking, etc. Such a model, like that of Szasz and Laing, sees the concept of mental disorder as linked to issues of control and power and to pressures to maintain conformity. Regrettably it is least satisfactory in the endeavour, via the concept of residual rule-breaking, to specify why certain behaviour is deemed symptomatic of mental disorder, primarily because of the vagueness and imprecision of the concept of residual rules (see Busfield 1989a: 92).[15]

Marxist and Weberian Theorising

In the 1970s, a number of writers influenced by Marxist ideas offered perhaps the most detailed attempts to account for the social regulation involved in setting the boundaries both of illness in general, and of mental disorder in particular. One of the most interesting was provided by Joel Kovel in his paper 'The American Mental Health Industry' (1978). Significantly Kovel, a psychologist, does not theorise mental disorder in terms of behavioural deviance; instead he locates it squarely in the mental realm by talking of the regulation of 'subjectivities' – an increasingly fashionable term in Marxist theorising in this period, which was used to refer an individual's thoughts, feelings and psychological experiences – their inner world (see Henriques et al. 1984: Introduction). Taking as a case study the mental hygiene movement in the US in the early decades of the twentieth century, Kovel claims that capitalism – or more particularly late or monopoly capitalism – requires a regulation of our 'structures of experience' in order to make us good producers and good consumers, so as to satisfy the capitalist imperatives of production and consumption. The regulation is effected by what he calls a 'psychologization' of our daily lives, which is evidenced by the considerable growth of experts in the mental health field – psychologists, psychotherapists, psychiatric social workers, psychiatric nurses, as well as psychiatrists. Again the functionalist character of the argument, this time a Marxist functionalism giving primacy to the interests of capitalism and capitalists, is clear. The problem is that, as with a simple extension of the Durkheimian framework to the mental realm, the focus is, via the notion of subjectivity, more on the *content* of ideas and beliefs and less on mental processes. Another is the assumption that developments such as psychologization are necessarily functional for capital (see Busfield 1989a: 136).

Kovel's theorisation in terms of subjectivities is not employed by other Marxist writers. Vicente Navarro (1976), building on Parsons's analysis of the distinctive character of illness as a form of deviance (Parsons suggests it is more individual and solitary and less threatening to the social system), sees ill-health, whether mental or physical, as a way in which the tensions and problems of the capitalist order are channelled. It is a way in which the worker's alienation can be expressed, most obviously in stress-related disorders, without disrupting the social order, and the analysis fits well with data suggesting that ill-health, both mental and physical, is more common at the bottom of the social structure (see Townsend and Davidson 1988). Medicine plays an important ideological role in this process, for, in its emphasis on the physical causes of illness and its lack of attention to the social origins of sickness, it individualises and depoliticises illness. For Navarro, the smooth running of the capitalist system is the determining factor, but he stresses less the 'correct' construction of subjectivities than the harmless (to capitalism) expression of tensions and conflicts. Navarro's analysis, like Kovel's, arguably involves an over-simple economic determinism and an overly simple functionalism (see Busfield 1989a: 130–9). Yet, the attention to the interests of capitalists, and to the changing nature of the processes of production and consumption, is surely appropriate. Though their values and their models of society differ, Parsons's concern with role performance is not that far removed from either Navarro's or Kovel's concern with the conditions that ensure individuals are good producers and good consumers.

A similar focus on sectional interests is to be found in the work of a range of Weberian theorists who have analysed the activities of the medical profession (see, for instance, Freidson 1970, 1994) and have argued that the profession tends to act in its own interests rather than those of patients. Such theorists, unlike Marxists who tend to see doctors as administrators of a health system that serves the interests of the ruling class, stress the power and authority of the medical profession and its role in shaping the character of health services (see Busfield 1989a: Chapter 4). For them 'medicalisation', the process in which the territory occupied by medicine is extended, is often not just the product of external forces acting on medicine, but a process in which they as professionals play an active, even imperialist, role, keen to extend their own domain, to legitimate their own activities and to see themselves as offering the most objective knowledge, ideas and treatments. Again, there can be no doubt that attention to professional interests is invaluable and can be applied very effectively in understanding certain changes within psychiatry and the terrain of mental disorder (see, for instance, Goldstein 1987); however, an exclusive focus on professionals and their ideas and interests is not sufficient.

The Regulation of Rationality

I want to argue that a theorisation of mental disorder in terms of the regulation of 'reason' and rationality provides the most useful conceptualisation for analysing the boundaries of mental disorder, its regulation and its relation to gender. In so doing I want to draw on the theorisation of madness formulated by Michel Foucault, which develops Durkheim's and Parsons's insights linking crime and illness very fruitfully. Foucault's analysis has the advantage of focusing squarely on disturbances of mind rather than body or behaviour, and makes no attempt to appropriate mental disorder either to medical models of illness or to sociological models of deviance; instead, juxtaposing reason and madness, he analyses madness as a form of unreason. This conceptualisation, as we shall see in Chapter 6, also provides a valuable foundation for the analysis of gender and mental disorder.

Foucault's theorisation of madness as unreason is developed in his book *Madness and Civilization* (1967). This offers a study of madness (a narrower category than mental disorder), which examines the changing opposition between madness and reason. The study primarily covers the period from the mid-seventeenth century through to the end of the eighteenth century – the so-called Classical Age. Its starting point is the Middle Ages, a period in which he suggests reason was engaged in a dialogue with madness, a dialogue shaped by religious ideas and religious imagery:

In the Middle Ages and until the Renaissance man's dispute with madness was a dramatic debate in which he confronted the secret powers of the world; the experience of madness was clouded by images of the Fall and the Will of God, of the Beast and the Metamorphosis, and of all the marvellous secrets of Knowledge (ibid: xiv).

With the development of the Classical Age and the Enlightenment a new value was placed on reason. Unreason in all its forms – madness, poverty, crime and disease – was banished in a 'great confinement', a space in which 'reason reigned in the pure state, in a triumph arranged for it in advance over a frenzied unreason' (ibid: 61). The Enlightenment's exaltation of reason required the demarcation of unreason (the affinities with Durkheim's argument are clear). However, madness differed from other forms of unreason in showing humanity's links with animality, an animality that related not to nature but to unreason. Madness he suggests was unreason's empirical form:

> the madman, tracing the course of human degradation to the frenzied nadir of animality, disclosed the underlying realm of unreason which threatens man and envelops – at a tremendous distance – all the forms of his natural existence. It was not a question of tending towards a determinism, but of being swallowed up by a darkness. More effectively than any other kind of rationalism, better in any case than our positivism, classical rationalism could watch out for and guard against the subterranean danger of unreason, that threatening space of an absolute freedom (ibid: 83–4).

However, with the second half of the eighteenth century the meanings of madness begin to change once more: 'The evil which men had attempted to exclude by confinement reappeared, to the horror of the public, in a fantastic guise' (ibid: 203) – as an indifferentiated image of 'rottenness', as an image of disease. The mad, it began to be argued, needed special places of confinement, both to protect others from their dangers and to give them the special help they needed. The result was 'the birth of the asylum' – places where the medical profession came to acquire new powers and status *vis-à-vis* the mad, and where the relations between madness and reason were reorganised:

> In the severe world of mental illness, modern man no longer communicates with the madman: on one hand, the man of reason delegates the physician to madness, thereby authorizing only through the abstract universality of disease; on the other, the man of madness communicates with society only by the intermediary of an equally abstract reason which is order, physical and moral constraint, the anonymous pressure of the group, the require-

ments of conformity. As for a common language there is no such thing (ibid: xii).

Foucault offers a powerful reading of madness in which its complex meanings are analysed and placed in their historical context. This reading is, however, thematic, fragmentary and at times inaccurate (Midelfort 1980) and does not, nor is it intended to, provide either a more explanatory analysis of the changes in meanings, transitions and transformations (indeed, causal analysis is explicitly rejected), or a precise analysis of the shifting boundaries of the term. The task is to portray differences in meaning over time and to relate them to cultural changes, not to link them to economic and structural changes within society. Durkheimian, Weberian and Marxist theorisations have had more to offer in these directions.

Nonetheless, Foucault's theorisation of an opposition between madness and reason offers vital insights which can be extended to the analysis of the broader category of mental disorder and to its linkages with gender. Above all we can see the identification of unreason and irrationality through constructs of mental disorder as an affirmation of reason. Significantly, a range of writers in addition to Foucault have pointed to the way in which issues of reason and 'unreason' or irrationality are bound up with judgements of madness and mental disorder.[16] Karl Jaspers (1963) in his classic phenomenological study of psychopathodology describes the psychic life of the schizophrenic as 'ununderstandable'. And R.D. Laing (1960, 1967), in his influential analysis of schizophrenia, talks of the schizophrenic's lack of intelligibility (though arguing that this is a failure of apprehension and that we could understand the behaviour if only we bothered).[17] Similarly, Dorothy Smith (1967, 1978), examining the way in which the label mental illness is ascribed, talks of incomprehensibility as a key criterion in judgements of mental disorder. 'I suggest' she argues:

> that the behaviour of persons who come to be labelled as mentally ill fails to confirm that they share the same version of reality as does the observer. What they do and say indicates that they do not construct reality in a way that the observer can understand and which he also believes to be how it is understood by other members of the cultural community of which they are both members. Mental illness thus bears an analogous relation to social reality as that which nonsense has to sense in language. Behaviour is recognised as odd, funny, bizarre, etc. because it does not make sense in terms of the rules for producing intelligible behaviour in a given cultural community (1967: 11).

The issue, however, is not the content of the beliefs, thoughts and actions, although if the content is unusual this may occasion questions about their rationality. Rather it is the *reasoning* that underlies beliefs and behaviour that is crucial.[18] As Jennifer Radden puts it, the point is that 'The way a belief is formed and held, not its truth or falsity, determines its irrationality or unreasonableness' (1985: 58). Judgements of rationality concern the grounding of beliefs and behaviour, not their content *per se*.

Although these writers provide support for the central place of rationality and irrationality in notions of mental disorder, it might be argued that notions of unreason, rationality and intelligibility are only relevant to the domain formerly covered by the term madness and now occupied by its twentieth-century equivalent: psychosis. This is the domain where, in the standard psychiatric parlance echoed by Smith, the individual is 'out of contact with reality'. Such notions of unreason and irrationality are surely not relevant to the wider domain of disorders such as anxiety, phobias, anorexia nervosa, drug addiction, and so forth, where there is instead in the standard phraseology an 'exaggerated response to reality' and psychic life is to use Jaspers's terms, 'meaningful and *allows empathy*' (1963: 577). This is the realm where the individual may be 'troubled in mind' (MacDonald 1981), but is not mad. I would contend, however, (*contra* my earlier view – see Busfield 1989a: 100–101) that rationality and 'unreason' are still at stake in the new psychiatric categories as they were in the old.

For example, anorexia nervosa is identified as a mental disorder, not simply in terms of low body weight and its physical sequelae such as amenorrhoea, or in terms of behaviour such as dieting, but in terms of the relation between these bodily conditions and behaviours and the *intentions* and *motivations* of the individual, such as the fear of eating and putting on weight, that are held to underlie them. It is acceptance of the legitimacy or illegitimacy of the *reasons* for action and of the rationality of the individual's thoughts and perceptions that are at the core of the identification of the condition. It is refusing to eat when you are already thin, believing you are fat when your weight is well below average and so forth, that lead to judgements of mental disturbance.

Similarly, an individual may be deemed depressed if their sadness and 'low spirits' appear out of proportion to the possible causes: the misery is 'unreasonable', that is, it cannot be satisfactorily explained by what has happened to them.[19] Of course, with greater exploration of the social causes of depression the reasons for a person's depression may become visible, just as the schizophrenic's behaviour may start to become intelligible with considerable knowledge of their biography. But this does not mean that the judgement of whether they are depressed or not, is not made in terms of 'reasonable', appropriate feelings. Of course, unreasonable is a looser, broader notion than irrational, and not all that is unreasonable or, indeed, irrational leads to judgements of mental disorder (there are issues of severity, persistence etc). Yet, they share a focus on reason and reasoning which is central to judgements of mental disorder.

Reason, rationality and what is reasonable are complex notions and there is, notwithstanding Enlightenment aspirations, arguably no single rationality, but rather a set of traditions of rationality that are normatively governed and whose influence varies across time and place (see MacIntyre 1988). And since both the value attached to reason and rationality and their precise character vary, so do the boundaries of mental disorder. Weber, for instance, differentiating types of rationality, has argued that legal rationality is an essential component of the bureaucracies that increasingly characterise modern society. In such societies we might expect a stronger and more extensive regulation of rationality and hence of its antithesis, madness. Moreover, as we shall see in Chapter 6, what is constituted as rationality is also in practice gendered. It is also clearly linked with behaviour and role performance. Indeed, in my view, a theorisation of mental disorder in terms of rationality complements Parsons's formulation of illness (including mental disorder), in terms of incapacities of role or task performance. Where role performance is adequate, then rationality is less likely to be called into question. However, if and when it is, then assessments of the individual's rationality may well be made.

A key advantage of the focus on rationality is that, as I have noted, it allows us to concentrate our attention on mental processes and reasoning and to examine the social processes that underpin their regulation through the setting of the boundaries of mental disorder. The writers we have considered so far have pointed to a number of motivations that can underlie the categorisation of some state or action as in some way unacceptable or undesirable as part of the process of regulation: apart from the affirmation of rationality (Foucault), there is the need to emphasise a society's rules, standards and values in order to maintain social order, the societal need for satisfactory task and role performance and the consequent need to identify incapacity (Parsons); the capitalists' needs for 'good' consumers and producers (Kovel); the capitalists' needs to deflect tensions and conflicts (Navarro); and men's needs within a patriarchal social order for women to be compliant and subordinate (Chesler). Such insights can help us to understand why refusal to eat, being miserable, listless and unable to cope, or hearing voices that threaten you, can come to be categorised as some form of mental problem. However, the precise processes, mechanisms and factors involved will vary and require detailed examination in specific historical contexts – one such analysis is outlined in the discussion of shell-shock in Chapter 11.

The theme of regulation which extends, as we have seen, well beyond Foucault and is also deployed by many feminist writers (see, for instance, Showalter 1987, who also views madness in terms of irrationality), can be criticised as overly pessimistic, conspiratorial in its assumptions and as denying individual freedom and agency. In *Madness and Civilization* Foucault argues, for instance, that the apparently more humane regimes, symbolised by the liberation of the mad from their chains at Bicêtre and developed in accordance with the principles of moral treatment, were just as repressive as the earlier physical coercion they replaced (1967: Chapter 9). Similarly Kovel, although he follows Althusser (1971) in distinguishing between repressive (using physical coercion) and ideological forms of control, argues that the regulation of subjectivities takes ideological not repressive forms; he nonetheless suggests such a strong regulation that he appears to deny the individual all freedom and capacity for resistance.[20] However, two points need to be made. First, an emphasis on regulatory power does not require an assumption that those who are regulated are merely passive victims. Even those who are apparently quite powerless may find means of resistance and subversion, as Goffman's (1961) influential study of the informal culture developed by asylum inmates shows so graphically. Second, an emphasis on social regulation does not commit us to the postmodernist position that notions of progress have to be abandoned entirely. Criticism of simplistic Whiggish assumptions of historical progress does not necessitate the abandonment of all belief in progress and all optimism.

Theoretically, some subsequent writers (see Castel 1988; Miller and Rose 1986), influenced by Foucault's later writings and asserting the interdependency of power and knowledge (with power operating through discourses – sets of ideas and practices), have emphasised the enabling as well as repressive aspects of regulation as, for instance, in the wider understandings that can be generated through new discourses. New ideas and ways of thinking, they contend, not only control but they may also empower. Regrettably however, in practice the analyses, their theoretical stance notwithstanding, all too frequently stress regulation, control and repression, not facilitation and empowerment, and there is considerable attention to the pervasiveness of regulation through what are referred to as 'soft' techniques of control (Castel 1988). Arguably, however, such debates about repression and empowerment are, at least in part, empirical matters and cannot be settled solely by theoretical discussion. We need to examine the social and economic context in which the regulation of rationality and irrationality are operating, the powers that are being used, over whom and to what purpose. In analysing the regulation of reason we cannot, for instance, ignore the social characteristics of those who are identified as mentally disturbed, including the dimension of gender. However, before turning to the question of gender and the regulation of rationality, I want to look at the important issue of the inferences we can draw from epidemiological data in the light of this discussion of concepts and theories of disorder.

Chapter 5

Measuring Mental Disorder

It is a cardinal principle of epidemiology that investigations are only as good as the techniques used in case-identification (Mechanic 1970: 4).

The epidemiological data examined in Chapter 2 revealed a gendered landscape of identified mental disorder with the gender differences varying according to diagnosis, age, social class, marital status and ethnicity as well as historical period. However, in the light of the examination of constructs of mental disorder in the last chapter, we need to consider precisely what weight can be attached to the data. Certainly they show some marked associations, such as those between gender and diagnosis. But do they reveal any more than this? Can we make any inferences about gender differences in the distribution of medically defined mental disorder from them? Can we say that overall more women than men are disordered in mind as the patient statistics might seem to imply. How does the fact that psychiatric categories vary across time and place affect the conclusions we can draw from epidemiological studies? In this chapter I argue that the social and cultural specificity of medical categories of mental disorder, which are embedded in the epidemiological data, severely restricts the inferences we can make. Even associations supported by a range of empirical data are *construct specific*, and claims about the social distribution of disorder, even when they recognise that specificity, have to be treated with great caution because of the limitations of the data on which they are based.

In order to explore these questions further, we have to examine the two main types of epidemiological data: patient statistics and community surveys. Many of the issues I cover in this chapter will be familiar to social scientists interested in health and illness, and especially to social epidemiologists; some may seem overly technical to those concerned with feminist politics or with understanding the social origins of psychiatric disturbance. Yet they cannot be ignored if our analysis of gender differences is to be properly grounded. Moreover, they rapidly raise very interesting questions about the impact of gender on the evaluation of mental disorder – questions which I examine in more detail in the following chapter. The focus throughout the discussion is on determining the value and limitations of epidemiological data as potential measures of medically defined and constructed mental disorder, rather than on calling that framework into question. However, the data I consider do raise questions about the categorical model of mental disorder.[1]

Patient Statistics

As will already be apparent, patient statistics, usually generated for purposes of public policy, provide the most common basis for claims about gender differences in levels of medically defined mental disorder and are the only data available for earlier periods before community surveys were developed around the middle of this century. Considerations of cost and availability ensure they are widely used as a basis for epidemiological claims, even though they are far from comprehensive. In the UK they often exclude information on marital status and occupation and recent estimates of residents in psychiatric beds in England do not even include a breakdown by gender.[2] Data on activity outside hospitals and in the private sector are even more scanty. This has become an especial problem with the shift away from hospital-based services that characterises the move to community care, and we do not have a very precise picture of many of the services and activities which constitute the health service component of community care.[3] To some extent official statistics can be complemented by data collected by other organisations, such as voluntary bodies and private companies, and by special patient surveys – such as Hollingshead and Redlich's study reported in *Social Class and Mental Illness* (1958). But such data are often fragmentary and the cost of special patient surveys is frequently prohibitive.

The greatest advantage of patient statistics as potential measures of *medically* defined mental disorder, is that they do incorporate medical conceptualisations of disorder and are usually based on medical assessments of individual cases. On the one hand, the statistics are constructed and presented within the framework of the official psychiatric classifications developed for diagnostic and statistical purposes. On the other hand, the cases included in the statistics have normally been assigned a diagnosis by qualified medical practitioners or other qualified clinicians. In both respects they meet the criteria for being proper cases of medically defined mental disorder and so constitute a potentially good foundation for claims about gender differences in the distribution of disorder.

Against this significant advantage must be set important, oft-cited, limitations. These are summed up in the phrase that the statistics cover only 'treated' cases, that is, they include only persons who have some contact with the service in question. Consequently, as measures of mental disorder in the wider population they are severely defective since 'untreated' cases are excluded.[4] In order to explore the significance of this point, and its relevance to the gendered landscape of mental disorder, we need to examine the ways in which individuals may be excluded from the statistics. I shall consider three issues: mental health policies; illness behaviour; and the reliability and validity of medical assessments, relating each to the issue of gender differences.

Clearly mental health policies shape patient statistics. We do not have to agree with Ivan Illich that professionals 'gain legal power to create the need that, by law, they alone will be allowed to satisfy' (1977: 16), to accept that decisions concerning service provision inevitably structure patient statistics, so that changes in patient numbers are often likely to be more a product of service developments than of any changes in levels of mental disorder (as defined at that moment in time) in the population. The point is not new; it was, for instance, debated in a *Special Report on the Alleged Increase of Insanity* published in 1897. The Commissioners in Lunacy had initially assumed that:

> the hurry and restless movement, the keen competition and struggle, the growth and corresponding evils of large cities, must of necessity have conspired to produce a larger and increasing ratio of incident mental disorder in the population (Commissioners in Lunacy 1897: 2).

However, after examining the data more carefully, they concluded that the very marked increase in identified cases of lunacy in the Victorian period did not provide evidence of an actual rise in lunacy, noting that amongst other factors the opening of new asylums was important in increasing patient numbers. In London in 1892 and 1893, for example:

> on a large provision of beds becoming available, such cases were poured into the Asylum wards at last ready to receive them, and so swelled the list of the officially known and enumerated insane (ibid: 18).

Service arrangements affect the 'pathways into treatment' (Goldberg and Huxley 1980) and so structure patient statistics.

Moreover, services are structured in ways that are not in practice independent of gender (or of class or race), even though the policy underpinning the development may well be blind to these social characteristics. In Britain, for example, services dealing with male pathologies such as sexual abuse, psychopathy, alcoholism, drug addiction or the 'new' male problems of child abuse and domestic violence have not been very widely developed. Mental health services for alcoholism and drug addiction, which increased during the 1970s and early 1980s, have seen something of a retrenchment since then. There have also been cut-backs in psychiatric beds which, as I noted earlier, deflected some individuals towards the criminal justice system; yet psychiatric services within prisons have also been reduced (Reed 1992). In contrast, 'drop-in' services for those with psychiatric problems, such as depression and anxiety – typically female problems – tended to increase in the 1980s with the accelerated move to community care and the opening of non-residential community mental health centres (CMHCs) (Brown 1985; Sayce et al. 1991).

Second, there is the issue of individuals' perceptions, actions and practices *vis-à-vis* their disorder, whether mental or physical – so-called illness behaviour (Mechanic 1978: Chapter 9) – which affect whether they use a service or not, so structuring patient statistics and diminishing their value as measures of disorder in the population. It is factors such as the individual's decision as to whether or not to visit a doctor, lay perceptions of mental disorder, the extent of family support, the degree of family intervention, and the ease of access to services that determine the levels of disorder, not just the extent of medically defined disorder in a given population (lay definitions are shaped by cultural factors and are influenced by, though not coterminous with, medical definitions). In this respect it is lay individuals as well as mental health personnel who set the boundaries of mental disorder as measured by patient statistics. To take but one example, the high rates of disorder identified amongst the single as measured by hospital admissions (see Chapter 2), are just as much a product of the lack of available informal care for the single from an immediate family member in times of severe disturbance (Robertson 1974), as of differences in the level of mental disorder by marital status.

The impact of illness behaviour on measures of mental disorder derived from service statistics would not matter when making comparisons between social groups, were there no systematic differences in illness behaviour between the groups being compared. But the evidence indicates that, at least in the case of gender, there are differences in relation to mental disorder. For example, there is evidence that in Western societies women are more likely than men to admit to psychiatric problems, to seek medical help for them and to do so at an earlier stage of their disorder (Phillips and Segal 1969; Horwitz 1977; Padesky and Hammen 1981). These findings are particularly interesting in the light of two other widely-supported observations. First, that self-referral tends to be more common with the less severe mental disorders, such as anxiety and depression, where women predominate, than with the more severe psychoses where gender differences are often insignificant (Hollingshead and Redlich 1958: 183–5). Second, that according to estimates from community surveys, the proportion of treated cases is, as we might expect, considerably lower for the less severe neuroses than for the more disabling psychoses (that is, the more severe the disorder the more likely the individual is to feature as a treated case (Goldberg and Huxley 1992: 34)). Taken together, these observations suggest that at least part of the observed gender difference in the distribution of the more common mental disorders is attributable to the greater willingness of women to identify these problems and to seek help for them – a conclusion in line with Nathanson's (1977) general observation that the more subjective the measure of illness the greater the gender difference detected, and the more objective the measure the smaller the difference.

Third, though patient statistics incorporate medical concepts and assessments of mental disorders, they are made by practitioners whose skills, expertise, theoretical orientations and constructs of disorder vary, and are not standardised across time and place even if they operate with the same formal classificatory schema. Indeed, not surprisingly, studies of diagnostic reliability under clinical conditions have long provided clear evidence of the lack of exact diagnostic agreement between practitioners (see, for instance, Beck et al. 1962; Kreitman et al. 1961,

Kendell 1975: Chapter 3), especially in relation to the more specific psychiatric labels. Furthermore, most of these studies compare the diagnostic judgements of qualified psychiatrists. Agreement is likely to be even lower if we include a wider range of professionals – GPs, psychiatrists and social workers – who often have far less diagnostic training and often have very different patterns of referral. It is true that there is now quite a strong pressure towards greater standardisation of the diagnostic schema and the criteria used by clinicians, as well as in the conduct of diagnostic interviews. However, while this may enhance agreement, especially under research conditions, it is not at present enough to ensure uniformity in clinical contexts, nor is it likely to be sufficient in the future, not least because of the frequent modifications to psychiatric classifications.[5] Indeed, both the expansion of community care and the proliferation of mental health professionals are likely to increase the diversity of concepts, assessment practices and referral patterns embedded in mental health service statistics, just as they are likely to diminish their comprehensiveness.

It might be argued, nonetheless, that when comparing social groups, variations in concepts, assessments and referral practices affect each group roughly equally and can be assumed to more or less cancel themselves out. However, there is evidence of systematic biases in the evaluative process which calls this assumption into question. Biases arise even in the assessments of specialist clinicians employing relatively standardised diagnostic criteria. For example, a study of 290 psychiatrists in the United States employing the DSM-III found evidence that the gender (as well as the race) of the patient influenced the psychiatrists' diagnostic judgements, even when clear-cut diagnostic criteria were presented (Loring and Powell 1988). The precise extent of the biases is a matter of debate. Reviewing the data towards the end of the 1970s, Zeldow concluded that the results of studies were 'sufficiently diverse and ambiguous as to be interpretable both as strong and weak evidence for sexism in the mental health field, depending on the point of view of the interpreter' (1978: 93). However, the evidence of bias from these studies is certainly sufficient to cast doubt on the value of patient statistics as the sole basis for comparative claims about mental disorder in men and women although, of course, gender differences in service use are of interest in themselves.[6]

Moreover, the procedures usually employed for assessing diagnostic bias almost certainly underestimate its importance. The standard procedure involves the use of analogues – that is, the construction of ana-

scriptions of cases for diagnosis where only the gender of the
⌐ is changed. Though designed to control all variables but
the task involved is very different from the assessment of cases
in   cal contexts, where the sheer presence of the individual almost
inevitably makes gender more immediately apparent and more significant than in written texts, since gender is such a basic component of
social identity.[7] Gender is, consequently, likely to be more salient in
face-to-face clinical encounters than in research situations where only
written case histories are assessed.[8] Studies of decision making in practice provide some support for this view. An important study by Hilary
Allen (1987) of mental health assessments in the criminal justice system
found very clear and systematic biases in the assessments of men and
women who had committed a criminal offence. The study showed far
more frequent reference to details of the individual's mental life in
women's case notes rather than men's, and this even applied to psychiatric reports on men 'where one might have expected the most
explicit consideration of the defendant's mind' (ibid: 35). The accounts
of women's conduct also differed:

> Any material narrative in these reports tends to focus, not on what these
> women *do*, but on what *happens* to them. Indeed, the documents tend to
> undermine the sense of these women doing anything at all, by presenting
> them as perpetually moved by others' agency, rather than their own. They
> are dominated and dependent; they are victims of circumstance (ibid: 40).

For a number of reasons, therefore, patient statistics, even when they
include the full range of treated cases, do not provide a very secure
foundation for claims about gender differences in mental disorder even
within a single country at a single moment of time.

Community Surveys

Do community surveys offer a better prospect for providing adequate
measures of the distribution of mental disorder as many have suggested? Since they include untreated cases, they must surely provide a
rather better means of determining gender differences. Certainly, as
was apparent in Chapter 2, their findings sometimes cast doubt on the
inferences that might be drawn of the basis of patient statistics alone, as
in the case of the relation between marital status and mental disorder.
However, the measures of disorder generated by community surveys

are themselves by no means unproblematic, the problems primarily centreing on the instruments used to screen for cases of disorder. What is the nature of the instruments and the problems they generate?

The objective of community surveys is to derive measures of medically defined mental disorder across a population, including untreated as well as treated cases. The ideal solution might, consequently, appear to be to send clinicians to screen people for mental disorder in the community, in order to determine its social distribution. Clinicians could be specially trained to try and ensure they employ a standard classificatory schema in an uniform way. However, on grounds of resources and cost this is rarely practicable and few studies of this kind have been attempted. One survey of 2,550 individuals was carried out in Sweden in the 1950s using psychiatrists with a similar training to make the assessments (Essen-Moller 1956). But it employed what has been described as 'a somewhat idiosyncratic diagnostic classification of mental illness and abnormality', these commentators adding that 'it is perhaps because of this that it has not had a greater impact' (Brown and Craig 1986: 174). Pragmatic considerations necessitate the development of alternatives.

Screening instruments devised to detect 'cases' of mental disorder in the community without a full clinical examination vary enormously. They fall broadly into three types: (a) single-scale symptom inventories of general psychological ill-health which aim to capture the overall level of the individual's symptomatology on a single dimension; (b) multiple scale inventories designed to detect the presence or absence of a range of disorders; and (c) syndrome-specific inventories designed to measure the presence or absence of one particular disorder, whether broadly or narrowly defined, such as depression, anxiety or anorexia nervosa. I shall consider each in turn.

Unidimensional scales embody single, linear constructions of mental health and disorder and employ more or less arbitrary cut-off points to determine either the overall number of cases of disorder in the group surveyed, or else to allocate individuals to different levels of impairment – mild, moderate, severe and so forth. The shorter scales of psychiatric symptoms derived from the widely used General Health Questionnaire (GHQ) developed in the UK in the 1960s and early 1970s (Goldberg 1972), with questions on losing sleep over worry, feeling constantly under strain, and so on, fall into this category. So, too, does the Langner Mental Health Scale developed a decade earlier for the Midtown Manhattan survey (Langner 1962), but subsequently much criticised. These scales are usually scored on a simple additive basis, with high scores treated as indicative of worse psychiatric health. Such general scales do not measure mental disorder in a way that accords with the medical conceptualisation of disorder as a set of discrete clinical entities. Instead they treat it as a single continuum, which raises immediate difficulties as to where to draw the cut-off point in identifying cases of disorder, and of how the measure relates to categorically defined disorder. Put another way, the measures do not generate diagnoses, but only a general assessment of the degree of mental disorder. For critics of the categorical model this is a virtue, but it is a limitation if we are trying to find good measures of medically defined disorder.

Another problem is that these instruments do not involve clinical assessments – a practical virtue, since they can be administered quickly with little training – but a further limitation as measures of clinical disorder. Clinical assessments are typically based on the observation of behaviour (and at times physical and psychological tests) – on the signs of illness – as well as on symptom reports. Symptom inventories, though standardised and circumventing some of the unreliability of clinical assessments, rely only on symptoms reported by respondents to measure disorder – that is, on the subjective assessments made by the individual in question. These self-assessments may not match those of clinicians. One study (Conover and Climent 1976) on a group of new patients in Columbia making contact with the local mental hospital – a homogeneous group in which cultural differences should have been minimised – found the match between the patients' self-assessments and clinicians' diagnoses following a mental-state evaluation was rather poor. Both patients and clinicians used a list of the same sixteen symptoms, a procedure designed to increase agreement; they agreed on their presence or absence in only 54 per cent of cases, although there was a moderately strong relationship between the ranking of the two sets of scores. The lack of agreement ranged across all types of symptoms and there was evidence that clinicians under-reported some symptoms because they failed to get sufficient information from patients, whereas patients, who generally tended to over-report rather than under-report, if and when they did under-report, did so because they were reluctant to admit to shameful symptoms (unfortunately the study did not examine the correspondence of patients' and clinicians' assessments by gender).

In theory, discrepancies like this over *individual* symptoms should not matter if clinical cases can be differentiated in terms of responses across the set of questions (that is, if the instrument is validated against clinically assessed cases). However, validation is often defective. In the case of early instruments, validation 'was either ignored (the rule), or focused on small, diagnostically homogeneous groups of patients' (Dohrenwend et al. 1970: 162). Validation of more recent instruments, including the GHQ, has been more thorough (see Bowling 1991: 111–3), but is still not entirely satisfactory. Instruments and items are typically validated by their capacity to distinguish clinical and community samples, not by the selection of individual cases, and different instruments often select out different cases (ibid: 187). Moreover, although validation against clinical samples appears to be a reasonable strategy, it means that the criteria for defining a case 'ultimately depends on the nature of the primary care and hospital services in which each set of researchers develop their notion of a significant psychiatric illness' (Goldberg and Huxley 1980: 18). Consequently, the samples of clinical (that is, treated) cases used to validate the instruments are already contaminated by the very biases the instruments are designed to eradicate.

A further related problem concerns the range of psychiatric symptoms encompassed by the single-scale instruments. For purposes of speed and efficiency the scales are frequently short and include only a highly selected set of symptoms, particularly those common across a range of disorders, such as problems with sleeping, anxiety, feeling under strain and finding it difficult to concentrate. Symptoms specific to, say, psychoses or behaviour disorders are not usually included. Consequently, although those with severe mental health problems (including psychotic symptomatology) may well score highly, the selectivity introduces biases. On the one hand, since the symptoms included are frequently typical of neurotic conditions, those with anxiety states and depression are likely to have scores indicative of poorer mental health. On the other hand, since symptoms of certain 'less severe' conditions, such as alcoholism, drug addition, sexual deviations and eating disorders are excluded, the instruments are less likely to identify people with these problems as cases. It is significant that the symptoms generally included are precisely those particularly typical of female rather than male mental disorders, indicating an in-built gender bias in the screening instruments.

A further source of gender bias relates to the instruments' reliance on self-assessments. This is problematic since, as we have seen, evidence indicates there are gender differences in the willingness to report psychological symptoms, as well as in the willingness to seek medical help for psychiatric problems. The former finding has not, however, gone uncontested. Clancy and Goye (1974) argued, for example, that it is not a significant source of bias. Their claim was based on a study in which they obtained social disapproval scores using a standard instrument. They found little difference in the desire for social approval between men and women, or in their assessments of the undesirability of having psychiatric symptoms, and concluded that gender differences in symptom reporting could not account for the gender differences in psychiatric scores. However, in a further study Gove found that if mental health scores were adjusted to allow for the desire for social approval and assessments of the undesirability of having psychiatric symptoms, along with a third factor, the tendency to 'yeasay', the differences between male and female symptom scores were reduced (though still significant). This suggested that in this sample at least, the women's higher scores had been inflated by 'response bias' factors (Gove et al. 1976). Moreover, it is important to note that the type of measures of response bias used in these studies almost certainly do not measure the possible biases at issue very adequately – one of which is a gender difference in the tendency to forget symptoms over time (men are more likely to do so over the longer term, see Angst and Dobler-Mikola 1984).[9] As a result, studies like Clancy and Gove's, which show some gender differences in response bias, reinforce rather than undermine studies like Phillips and Segal's (1969) which showed a greater willingness to report psychological symptoms in women than in men.

Of course, it might be argued that in the case of mental disorder the distinction between the 'subjective' and 'objective' components of disorder is mistaken and that subjective reports are the *sine qua non* of mental disorder: that if an individual does not report a particular symptom in response to questioning, it would be improper to attribute it to them.[10] There can be no distinction between *feeling* disturbed and *being* disturbed. However, if the aim is to identify medically defined mental disorder, exclusive reliance on self-assessments is problematic, since medical thinking with its positivist foundation assumes that someone can be ill without knowing it and this extends to mental disorder. Clinicians assume that someone can be depressed without consciously recognising it or being willing to report it, let alone assuming that someone can be grossly psychotic yet claim to have no psychological problems. Indeed, one does not have to be an uncritical devotee of psychoanalytic thinking to accept that denial may play an important role in contaminating self-assessed symptoms. Such contrasts between subjective (self) awareness and objective (external) evidence, which apply to assessing specific symptoms as well as to categories of disorder, are important to lay as well as medical thinking (lay distinctions argu- ably underlie medical thinking). They are consistent with a realist phi- losophy of science and need to be retained, even if we reject the categorical model of mental disorder.

Unidimensional symptom inventories are, therefore, arguably better described as measures of 'distress' or 'malaise' than medically defined mental disorder. These terms do at least suggest the subjective compo- nent of what is measured and fit the manifest content of the questions with their focus on symptoms of anxiety, distress, sleeplessness, and so on. But we still need to remember the limitation of their reliance on self-assessment. They are best referred to as measures of 'self-reported distress' since this indicates both their content and their source. Some researchers do refer to them as measures of distress or malaise; too many, in a careless elision, then proceed to treat them as adequate indices of categorically defined mental disorder in aggregate, which they are not. As measures of *subjective* distress they have some value for comparative purposes as long as we remember their dependence on self-assessments and their potential gender-bias.[11]

Some community surveys employ more sophisticated instruments, which attempt to measure a set of symptom syndromes rather than operating with a single scale. In so doing they get closer to measuring categorically defined mental disorder. However, multiple disorder instruments have several limitations when used to identify gender dif- ferences. In the first place, even though they have the handicap of being lengthier, they tend to be selective as to which disorders they incorporate. For example, the Present State Examination (PSE) devel- oped in the early 1970s (Wing, Cooper and Sartorius 1974), is widely used in Britain. Yet, while usually treated as a good instrument for measuring overall psychiatric morbidity, it does not attempt to measure alcoholism, organic states, or personality or eating disorders as clinical syndromes, even though one or two questions relate to isolated symp- toms from these syndromes (see Goldberg and Huxley 1980: 27). Con- sequently, it tends to generate quite a high ratio of female to male cases. Selectivity is also a feature of the Schizophrenia and Affective Disorders Schedule (SADS), a semi-structured clinical interview devel- oped in the United States later the same decade (Endicott and Spitzer 1978) and arguably, as its title suggests, even narrower in scope than the PSE.

Far broader than either the PSE or SADS is the Diagnostic Interview Schedule used in the Epidemiologic Catchment Area programme (ECA). It was developed specifically for the ECA study, drawing on both SADS and the Renard Diagnostic Interview, and covers DSM-III diagnoses such as drug and alcohol abuse and anti-social personality (Myers et al. 1984). Significantly, unlike many other studies, the ECA study yielded almost equal sex ratios in the prevalence of disorders (Regier et al. 1988). However, although probably the most comprehensive instrument so far, it is still selective (certain less common DSM-III diagnoses such as post-traumatic stress disorder are not covered). It is also tied to a particular diagnostic framework (the DSM-III now replaced by the DSM-IV), and so has an historical and social specificity that makes comparisons with other studies using different instruments difficult. Put another way, it still operationalises the notion of mental disorder in a distinctive way and sets its boundaries more narrowly than the classification to which it relates.

We have to accept, therefore, that the findings of studies using different instruments are dependent on the particular operational definitions and measurements of mental disorder the instruments embody, which may not correspond very exactly with the conceptualisation of mental disorder that is the starting point of the research question or with psychiatric classifications used in clinical contexts.[12] Other measures embodying different definitions of mental disorder may generate different results (Brown and Craig 1986; Van den Brink et al. 1989), including varying gender differentials. This means that broad-ranging generalisations about gender differences cannot be justified unless similar findings are visible across a range of studies with different samples and different instruments.

Another problem is that more complex symptom inventories, like the unidimensional screening instruments, still rely on self-assessments of the presence or absence of symptoms to determine whether an individual constitutes a case, with all the problems this raises about denial, the reliability of memory and the desire for social approval. Yet, even more than the single-scale inventories, they are likely to be viewed as offering satisfactory, gender-neutral measures of aggregate mental disorder.

A further problem with community surveys is that regardless of the instrument used, samples, even when drawn on a random basis, are not usually drawn from the whole population. Certain groups, especially children, are often excluded. So, too, are those living in institutions such as prisons (or indeed mental hospitals). This latter exclusion is significant for the study of gender differences, since institutional populations often have a gender imbalance (men are far more likely than women to end up in prison and the mental health of prison inmates is often poor). Significantly, the ECA study which sampled institutional populations is one of the few studies to confront the problem directly.

Some of the same limitations also apply to the syndrome-specific screening instruments, such as the scales for measuring depression. In this case, since there is no claim to provide an aggregate measure of mental disorder, there is no longer the problem of the exclusion of certain syndromes such as alcoholism. But other problems remain. First, the measures still rely on self-assessments. Second, though validated against clinical samples and sometimes identifying similar *levels* of disorder in populations, they tend to pick out different individuals as cases (Brown and Craig 1986; Zimmerman and Coryell 1990). Indeed, these instruments raise very obviously the whole problem of the boundaries of particular disorders. I have already noted that in clinical contexts diagnostic reliability is typically greater for broader diagnostic categories than for more specific ones. Yet, determining the precise boundaries of one condition and differentiating it from another is just what is called for if the task is to measure the occurrence of specific syndromes rather than mental disorder in general. To some extent this problem is circumvented by the use of screening instruments which operationalise categories of disorder in particular ways and then apply them in a mechanical fashion. Score highly on a scale designed to measure depression and you count as a case of depression whether or not your overall constellation of symptoms, if examined clinically, might lead to an alternative diagnosis. However, any validation – and validation is often poor – is dependent on diagnostic decisions made in clinical contexts which are themselves far from perfect, and we still have the problem that different instruments yield different results.

Consequently, like the multi-disorder inventories, single-disorder instruments have limitations. Moreover, since they do not attempt to cover the spectrum of psychiatric conditions, they obviously cannot offer the prospect of generating a good aggregate measure of mental disorder in the community.

For these reasons community surveys, like patient statistics, do not provide very good measures of gender differences in medically defined mental disorder. The limitations of the two sources of data differ, but neither offers a very firm basis for general claims. Before considering the implications of these observations further, I want to consider one disorder in more detail in order to illuminate some of the issues under consideration. I have chosen depression because of its importance to aggregate gender differences.

The Case of Depression

Depression is arguably the psychiatric disorder *par excellence* of the second half of the twentieth century. Although it only emerged into prominence as a common mental disorder and object of research attention in the period following the Second World War, as I have noted (see p. 22), it is now one of the most frequently diagnosed disorders, especially at the primary care level, and it plays a key part in generating gender differences in aggregate levels of mental disorder. In the 1980–81 GP Survey in England and Wales, affective psychoses and depressive neurosis accounted for almost half of the female 'excess' of consultations (see Royal College of General Practitioners 1986: Table 8).

The emergence of depression as a prominent mental disorder is undoubtedly tied in part to changes in mental health services in the postwar period. In particular it is linked both to the expansion of services dealing with less severe disorders and to the development of a range of treatments – first Electro Convulsive Therapy (ECT) and then psychotropic drugs – which have been considered especially effective in cases of depression (see Clare 1976: Chapter 6; Stafford-Clark and Bridges 1990: 249–54). These two changes have contributed to a cultural climate in which depression is considered a very suitable candidate for medical intervention, both by doctors and the lay public, although claims as to the efficacy of the varying drugs treatments and ECT are hotly debated.[13]

The emergence of depression as a significant mental disorder is also tied to developments in psychiatric nosology. The term initially entered psychiatric classifications as a symptom of melancholia, the condition usually juxtaposed to mania – 'real' madness (see Foucault 1967: Chapter 5; Jackson 1986). By the nineteenth century a range of texts held depression to be the hallmark of melancholia. For example, Samuel Tuke in his famous *Description of the Retreat* (1813), commented on his statement of cases: 'the cases are arranged under three classes, viz., dementia, melancholia and mania... Under the class melancholia, all cases are included in which the disorder is chiefly marked by depression of mind, whether it is, or is not, attended by general false notions' (quoted in Lewis 1967: 82–3). A prominent psychiatrist in 1890 began his characterisation of melancholia: 'The most marked and conscious feeling of the malady – the leading symptom – is the depression of spirits which always characterises it' (Mercier 1890: 338).

The use of the term depression as a disease label rather than as a symptom of disease began to take hold with Kraepelin's introduction in 1889 of the polarity of dementia praecox (renamed schizophrenia by Eugen Bleuler in 1911) and manic-depressive psychosis. This new opposition not only helped to undermine the old polarity of mania and melancholia, thereby contributing to the diminishing importance of the term melancholia, it also helped to secure currency for the use of depression as a disease label – albeit primarily as one component in a binary term.[14] However, manic-depressive psychosis was a relatively broad category which could include a range of mixed states of mania and depression, as well as states where either mania or depression predominated.

With the transformation in meaning of the category of neurosis from a disorder of the nerves, via the Freudian concept of psycho-neurosis, to a disorder of psychogenic origin, the psychosis–neurosis polarity began to structure psychiatric nosology. This new polarity generated in turn a contrast between two types of depression – psychotic or 'endogenous' depression, and neurotic or 'reactive' depression. This contrast, which featured in psychiatric texts and classifications throughout the immediate postwar decades, was called into question in the 1980s, especially in the United States. The DSM-III (American Psychiatric Association 1980) demarcated a broad group of Affective Disorders differentiated in two major ways: first, in terms of whether they are unipolar or bipolar – that is, whether they involve swings from elation to depression (bipolar: the old manic-depression), or not (unipolar); and second in terms of severity. The more severe are termed 'Major Affective Disorders', and include 'Major Depressive Episodes'; the less severe belong to the category 'Other Affective Disorders'. This framework is largely retained in the DSM-IV, although the group as a whole is now labelled 'Mood Disorders' (American Psychiatric Association 1994).

What is clear from this brief nosological history of the concept of depression is the way its meaning has changed very markedly over time. Moreover, even when clinicians are operating with an agreed classificatory framework, the boundaries between the different types of depression and other mental disorders are usually far from clear cut. I noted earlier the difficulty of distinguishing anxiety and depression, and it is also clear that the boundaries between different types of depression are not precise (see Brown and Craig 1986). This immediately raises problems for any epidemiological endeavour, since the way in which the boundaries of the category are set can differ between the groups being compared across time or place. We need, therefore, to attend to the different ways in which depression is measured and to the differing conceptualisations of depression any data embody.

I indicated in Chapter 2 that both patient statistics and community surveys do typically show higher levels of depression in women than men, although this does not apply to bipolar disorder (Weissman and Klerman 1985). When Weissman and Klerman surveyed the available data in 1977 they pointed out that, though patient statistics showed some exception to the general pattern, the community surveys did not – a feature that they suggested added weight to the conclusion that (unipolar) depression is more common in women than men.[15] Quite what contribution gender differences in the willingness to report symptoms make to this observed gender difference in levels of depression, is difficult to determine. However, it is important to note that, as I have already suggested, some of the gender difference visible in community surveys may arise from woman's willingness to report relatively mild symptoms of distress (Newman 1984), and that few screening instruments control for this tendency.

Moreover, Weissman and Klerman's (1977) claims about the supposed universality of the gender difference is questionable. Certainly the number of community surveys screening for depression in developing countries is not large (the authors listed two: one carried out in India, the other in Iran); altogether they listed only seven studies from outside the United States, suggesting the possibility of a fair degree of cultural specificity in the supposedly general finding. Studies carried out since Weissman and Klerman's initial survey support this conclusion. They indicate that the female predominance in depression identified via screening instruments is not universal, a number of studies finding no significant differences between men and women from certain social groups in the symptoms of depression reported. For example, one US community survey found the female predominance, as measured by self-reported symptoms, was specific to whites, and the difference between male and female rates for blacks was not significant (Comstock and Helsing 1976). Another, of the Amish in Pennsylvania, using DSM-II diagnoses on the basis either of clinical records or the SADS scale, found no significant difference between men and women (Egeland and Hostetter 1983). The same is true of several US studies of college students (Hammen and Padesky 1977). Outside the US, with the exception of a study of college students in Australia, the community surveys do show a female predominance, but the number of studies is limited (Mitchell and Abbott 1987).

An important issue raised by Weissman and Klerman (1977) and Egeland and Hostetter (1983) is the extent to which men's higher levels of alcohol use and alcoholism may mask depression. One possibility is that:

> depression and alcoholism are different but equivalent disorders. Women get depressed. Men are reluctant to admit being depressed or to seek treatment and mitigate this by drinking. Thus, men self-prescribe alcohol as a psycho-pharmacological treatment for depression (Weissman and Klerman 1977: 103).

As support for this possibility they cite studies showing that many treated alcoholics have symptoms of depression (Tyndel 1974; Winokur 1972).[16] However, whilst alcoholism may mask symptoms of depression, it may also curtail them. Egeland and Hostetter's study of the Amish is of particular interest here, with its finding of no difference in levels of depression in men and women. Since alcohol (as well as drug use and delinquency) are culturally prohibited amongst the Amish, it does not offer a possible mechanism for dealing with psychological difficulties.

The view that alcoholism and alcohol abuse constitute some sort of alternative to depression for men, has been applied to other disorders. Sylvia Canetto (1991) argues, for instance, that substance abuse in men and suicide attempts in women are psychological equivalents. Such ideas can be incorporated into a rather broader claim, that in Western culture men and women respond to psychological difficulties rather differently: women typically internalise their feelings and difficulties, becoming anxious and depressed; men turn them outwards either into excessive drinking or into aggression and violence (see Cloward and Piven 1979) or, if they do internalise them, express them through physical symptoms.

Certainly a range of studies provide evidence that even when men and women are assigned the same diagnosis, their symptomatology differs (see, for instance, Goldstein 1992; Padesky and Hammen 1981). Other studies show clear differences in emotional expression between men and women in Western cultures, and in the capacity and willingness to articulate emotions (Duncombe and Marsden 1993). In particular, the public expression of certain emotions in men (anxiety, fear, misery) is discouraged in many circumstances as indicative of vulnerability and dependence, and as incompatible with ideas of masculinity and the importance attached to control and achievement. In contrast, expressions of rage and anger, which may enhance power and the capacity to control others, are not curtailed in the same way (Thompson and Walker 1989). On the other hand, the expression of anxiety, fear and sadness as well as of feelings of love and affection are more permissible in women, who are typically expected to do the 'emotion work' within the family (Hochschild 1983; James 1989; Duncombe and Marsden 1993). There are, of course, also class factors in this. For instance, the expectation of a 'stiff upper lip' is especially strong in relation to British upper-class men. Moreover, expectations governing the expression of emotion are highly context dependent (crying in public is very different from crying at home).

In subsequent chapters I explore some of these issues further. The salient point here is that the wide range of evidence of gender differences in emotional expression in Western culture is likely to contaminate the measurement of depression, affecting self-assessed symptoms and clinical evaluations, since both involve the awareness, articulation and identification of feelings. Individuals using excessive drinking as a 'solution' to psychological difficulties are less likely to report the standard symptoms of depression, as these experiences are less likely to be part of their consciousness of their situation. Any depression may be more visible in systematic clinical examinations, but may still be more likely to go unnoticed or deemed only secondary in men because of these cultural factors, especially if alcohol problems become the focus of attention early in the clinical encounter.[17]

This examination of the case of depression shows very forcibly the difficulties of measuring gender differences in the distribution of depression. The lack of precision over what constitutes depression, reflected most obviously in the changing construction of different, often rather poorly demarcated, categories of depression, raises considerable problems for establishing the extent of gender differences, which are probably exaggerated by existing practices and procedures. Findings are both construct and method-dependent. Nonetheless, what is notable is that, despite the very important exceptions, many studies have shown that 'unipolar' depression, even though conceptualised and measured in a range of ways, has tended in Western societies to be more of a female than a male disorder. This consistency suggests the gender difference is not simply an artefact of measurement. Whilst many would attribute the difference to biology (see Chapter 8), the cultural variation we have already noted in the gender difference suggests such explanations have limited value, and we need to look to social factors in order to understand it, including gender differences in modes of expression.

Conclusion

This examination of the two types of epidemiological data which provide the basis of comparative claims about the distribution of mental disorder in women and men, and of the specific case of depression, reveals major limitations in both sources of data. Above all it highlights the way in which comparative claims are often problematic because of the variability in the definitions and measures of disorder incorporated into the data. Patient statistics on their own provide an insecure basis for comparisons because of the way in which the institutional activities and practices from which they are derived set the *de facto* boundaries of mental disorder very differently across time and place and exclude untreated cases. It is these organisational activities and practices, as well as lay judgements, rather than formal medical definitions, that largely determine the distribution of cases of mental disorder – though both organisational practices and lay assessments are influenced by medical definitions.

Similarly the screening instruments used in community surveys embody varying definitions of mental disorder and are frequently gender-biased. Even when they avoid unidimensional measures of mental health and disorder, they usually include only a restricted set of disorders (they are particularly prone to exclude disorders more common amongst men), and embody particular constructions of the selected disorders derived from a particular classificatory schema at a particular moment in time. Such selectivity inevitably shapes the gender differences they generate. Moreover, once we move away from patient statistics to community surveys in order to include untreated as well as treated cases, we are invariably forced to rely on self-reports of symptoms. And these self-reports may be subject to further biases beyond those that arise from the selective definitions of disorder the instruments embody. These biases include those associated with the cultural acceptability of particular symptoms, an acceptability which can vary between women and men, as well as by age, social class and ethnic group.

What conclusions can, therefore, be drawn from this analysis of epidemiological data? I want to mention five. First, and most importantly, critical examination of the data affirms the suggestion made in Chapter 2 that there can be no universal generalisation that mental disorder is more common in women than in men. Epidemiological findings must be treated as *construct specific* – that is they are specific to the particular construction of mental disorder they embody. For example, the female predominance in levels of disorder found at present in quite a wide range of aggregate data derived both from patient statistics and community surveys, holds at best for a definition of mental disorder that usually excludes the realm of violent and criminal activity (including child abuse) as well as much alcohol and drug abuse. The marginal status of these conditions in service provision is repeated in screening instruments where they have, until recently, hardly featured. Change the boundaries of mental disorder as it is measured in whatever context to include more of these cases and you are likely to change the gender balance.

Second, and related to this, the whole idea of establishing the 'true' prevalence or incidence of mental disorder in general or even of particular mental disorders is a chimera.[18] The notion of true prevalence or incidence not only assumes agreed and accepted diagnostic categories, it also assumes reliable and valid measures that cover untreated as well as treated cases. Yet, even if we accept for pragmatic purposes the value of a particular definition of mental disorder as a general category, or of one specific disorder, there is no prospect of measuring the presence or absence of either the general or the particular condition sufficiently accurately that would make it appropriate to talk of a true prevalence. Measures derived from patient statistics are clearly inadequate, and the screening instruments used in community surveys depend on self-reported symptoms that are liable to cultural contamination.

Third, though the idea of a true prevalence is a chimera, if and when a particular epidemiological finding is supported across a wide range of studies, including both patient statistics and community surveys, then that observation obviously has a more secure foundation in relation to the specific times and places studied. This is the case with the observation that in advanced capitalist societies in the second half of the twentieth century there has tended to be an inverse association between social class and mental disorder. It equally applies to several of the linkages between gender and particular types of disorder in Western societies considered in Chapter 2, such as that between women and both anorexia nervosa and depression, and that between men and alcoholism and psychopathic or anti-social personality disorder, although the gender differences may well be exaggerated by measurement biases and can change over time.

Fourth, data on the reliability and validity of the different measures of mental disorder do raise serious questions about the value of the categorical models of mental disorder fashionable in medical circles. Exploration of this issue in any detail is beyond the scope of this book (see Bentall 1990), yet it needs to be noted that the lack of consistency in measures of various disorders is salient not only to the issue of gender differences, but also to the study of the aetiology of psychiatric disturbance.

Fifth and finally, we have to conclude that both patient statistics and data from community surveys often tell us more about the mental health services in a particular society, and the particular way the category of mental disorder is being constructed and measured, than they do about the distribution of mental disorder in particular populations. Epidemiological data are themselves social products. At one and the same time they both reflect and describe the activities of psychiatrists and other mental health professionals, and are products of those activities, helping in turn to shape both lay and professional ideas and practice – a set of interrelated ideas and practices that are themselves also shaped by external forces.

Let us turn, therefore, to ways of understanding the observed gender differences, focusing not on the character of the epidemiological data but on category construction.

Chapter 6

Gender and Constructs of Mental Disorder

What we consider 'madness', whether it appears in women or in men, is either the acting out of the devalued female role or the total or partial rejection of one's sex-role stereotype (Chesler 1972: 56).

Much psychiatric theory regarding women is revealed as more ideological than scientific. It contains images and symbols of women which, when examined, prove to be archetypes and stereotypes. These have changed and developed but have always been presented in a mythical manner as representing the actual nature of women for all times. Such images and symbols are part of the network of ideas which have been used to enforce women's roles and to control the activities of women through the centuries. In appropriating them as scientific theory, psychiatry functions as a form of social control through, over and above its actual practices of treatment and incarceration (Penfold and Walker 1984: viii).

A range of feminist writers of different theoretical persuasions have followed Phyllis Chesler's influential study *Women and Madness* (1972) in suggesting that gender is embedded in the very construction of concepts of madness and mental disorder. In order to explore these claims further, I want to begin by outlining Chesler's analysis of the way the concept of mental disorder is constituted in relation to gender. I then use her argument as the foundation for a detailed consideration of whether, and the mechanisms through which, gender is embedded in constructs of mental disorder. Employing a framework in which I distinguish official constructions of mental disorder, the delineation of normal cases and the process of case identification, I contend that gender is embedded in constructs of mental disorder. I argue that at the level of official constructions the relation between gender and categories of mental disorder is indirect rather than direct, and stems from the differential relation of constructs of disorder to gendered behaviour. I further argue that this differential relation stems from the linkage between gender and attributions of agency and rationality which are tied to issues of power. In contrast, at the levels of normal cases and case identification, the central mechanism linking gender to constructs and attributions of disorder is the particularism that is an inherent feature of clinical practice. This ensures that gender is incorporated into both the construction of normal cases and case identification.

Chesler's Analysis

Chesler's analysis of gender and constructs of mental disorder merits attention because, although some of her concepts and language may seem outmoded, her analysis still offers the clearest and fullest formulation of the intersection of gender and categories of mental disorder. Indeed, as Hilary Allen (1986) contends, the body of feminist work following on from Chesler has adopted 'without question the same unspoken assumptions about the kind of issue upon which a feminist analysis of psychiatry must be grounded' (ibid: 86).[1]

Theoretically, Chesler's analysis is built from two major foundations: the writings of anti-psychiatrists, such as Thomas Szasz, R.D. Laing and T.J. Scheff (see Chapter 4), and the theorisation of social roles, including gender relations, derived from structural functionalism (see Chapters 3 and 4). From the former, she derives her emphasis on madness and mental disorder as labels and the theme of social control; from structural functionalism the analysis of sex roles, and of sickness and disorder as failures of role performance. What she provides is a powerful feminist reading that interweaves these two sets of ideas and gives them a distinctively feminist gloss. In her analysis, gender, or to use her term sex roles, are placed centre stage.

Chesler's starting point is that the way behaviour is defined and interpreted is crucial to understanding differences between women and men in patterns and levels of disorder. Men, she contends, are generally less likely to be labelled mentally disordered than women, even if they are disturbed:

Many men *are* severely 'disturbed' – but the form their 'disturbance' takes is either not seen as 'neurotic' or is not treated by psychiatric incarceration. Theoretically, all men, but especially white, wealthy, and older men, can act out many 'disturbed' (and non-'disturbed') drives more easily than women can (1972: 38–9).[2]

The reaction to disturbed behaviour in women is much harsher, notwithstanding the fact that more neurotic behaviour is expected:

> The greater social tolerance for female 'help-seeking' behavior, or displays of emotional distress, does not mean that such conditioned behavior is either valued or treated with kindness. On the contrary. Both husbands and clinicians experience and judge such female behaviour as annoying, inconvenient, stubborn, childish and tyrannical. Beyond a certain point, such behaviour is 'managed', rather than rewarded: it is treated with disbelief and pity, emotional distance, physical brutality, economic and sexual deprivation, drugs, shock therapy, and long-term psychiatric confinements (ibid: 39).

In Chesler's analysis, gender is intimately linked to madness since it is departures from sex role expectations (or from the expectations of class and ethnicity) that are defined as disordered.[3] This means that men do not escape judgements of mental disorder, for if they reject masculine identities and act in more female ways they are liable to be viewed as disturbed:

> Men who act out the female role and who, for example, are 'dependent,' 'passive,' sexually and physically 'fearful' or 'inactive,' or who, like women, choose men as sexual partners, are seen as 'neurotic' or 'psychotic'. If they are hospitalized they are usually labelled as 'schizophrenic' or 'homosexual' (ibid: 56–7).

However, since madness embraces not only 'the total or partial rejection of one's sex role stereotype', but also 'the acting out of the devalued female role' (ibid: 56), women are doubly disadvantaged. They are liable to be identified as disturbed if they *either* deviate from the female role by being more masculine *or* if they fully act it out, as this frequently quoted passage indicates:

> Women who fully act out the conditioned female role are clinically viewed as 'neurotic' or 'psychotic'. When and if they are hospitalized, it is for predominantly female behaviours such as 'depression', 'suicide attempts', 'anxiety neuroses', 'paranoia', or 'promiscuity'. Women who reject or are ambivalent about the female role frighten both themselves and society so

much that their ostracism and self-destructiveness probably begin very early. Such women are assured of a psychiatric label and, if they are hospitalized, it is for less 'female' behaviours, such as 'schizophrenia', 'lesbianism', or 'promiscuity' (ibid: 56).

This is the 'Catch 22' of female mental health: that for women both close conformity to, and departure from, female roles are liable to generate definitions of psychiatric disorder. Chesler suggests, therefore, a marked asymmetry in the situation of men and women, that arises from a devaluation of women, which Chesler sees as a fundamental feature of patriarchal societies. Women are liable to be viewed as disturbed if they 'act out' either masculine or feminine roles; men only if they act out feminine roles. Moreover it is easier, Chesler contends, for men to escape from psychiatric labels if they do not conform to their sex role: 'men in general are still able to reject more of their sex-role stereotype without viewing themselves as "sick", and without being psychiatrically hospitalized' (ibid: 57).

This asymmetry, resulting from the ready pathologising of women as mentally disturbed which parallels other gender asymmetries, is evidenced by the well-known Broverman study (Broverman et al. 1970) on judgements of mental health that Chesler cites. The study examined clinicians' conceptions of mental health using gender stereotypic items about behaviour. It showed not only that the conception of women's adult mental health differed from that of men's, but also that the conception of men's mental health was far closer than women's to that of adult mental health, gender unspecified – a finding confirmed in other studies (Jones and Cochrane 1981). It appears, therefore, that as long as men conform to the conception of male mental health they can escape being defined as disturbed. Women, however, by conforming to the female conception are simultaneously in danger of departing from the general conception of adult mental health. What is appropriate for women is close to mental disorder. Consequently, they are in danger of not meeting the required standards whether they act in masculine or feminine ways.

Chesler's argument is, therefore, a dual one. On the one hand, she gives a feminist gloss to anti-psychiatrists' ideas of social control, arguing that the use of labels of mental disorder helps to regulate male and female behaviour and ensure it conforms to normative expectations, so that psychiatry is intimately involved in what Allen calls 'gender role maintenance' (1986: 95), and what I call gender regulation. On the other hand, since the female role is itself devalued and is linked to definitions of the pathological, there is a double jeopardy for women, for even if they conform to their gender roles they are likely to be deemed disturbed. Significantly, Chesler sees gender as permeating definitions of mental disorder across the full psychiatric spectrum, a point which Allen contests, arguing that this only occurs on the periphery with a limited set of disorders such as hysteria, sexual deviation and disorders associated with the female reproductive life cycle (ibid: 98).[4]

It is easy enough to criticise Chesler's theorisation in terms of sex roles (see Chapter 2). But the language of sex roles is not decisive to her analysis. The key issue is the way in which gender impinges on the construction of categories of mental disorder. In order to explore this issue more fully I want to distinguish three levels of category construction: the official constructions of mental disorders, the elaboration of normal cases, and individual case identification. I consider each in turn.

Official Constructions

Official psychiatric classifications of mental disorders, which are developed both for diagnostic and statistical purposes, nowadays maintain a clear and conscious universalism in relation to gender in their formal descriptions of the symptoms of each disorder. Nosological descriptions of disorders are designed to allow them to be applied to either men or women – to be neutral as to gender as well as to class, ethnicity, time and place. This universalism is integral to the scientific ideas and values on which official constructions are grounded, and at the level of formal description is sustained reasonably effectively. For example, psychoses associated with childbirth do not constitute a separate disorder in present-day classifications, which are based on symptomatology not aetiology, and childbirth is viewed simply as a precipitating factor. Occasionally some reference to gender-specific symptoms, such as amenorrhoea in anorexia nervosa, creeps into formal descriptions of disorders, as do occasional statements about the likely gender balance of patients. The glossary for the WHO's *ICD-10 Classification of Mental and Behavioural Disorders* when delineating anorexia nervosa says almost immediately: 'The disorder occurs most commonly in adolescent girls and young women, but adolescent boys and young men may be affected more rarely' (1992: 176), although reference to gender is excluded from the official diagnostic guidelines.

However, the formal, surface, gender-neutrality of the diagnostic criteria does not mean that the categories are themselves constructed entirely independently of gender, since the official categories refer to many aspects of mental life and behaviour which are themselves gendered. Indeed, the very ubiquity of gender (see Chapter 3 above) makes gender neutrality in the formal constructions an impossibility other than at the surface level.[5] But what part exactly does gender play in official constructions if we move beyond the surface descriptions?

I want to suggest that once we look beyond the surface descriptions we find an indirect relation (cf. the distinction between indirect and direct discrimination in sex discrimination legislation) between gender and the official constructions of mental disorder. This is because, although formally described in universal terms, the characterisation of specific disorders refers to mental life and behaviour that is to a greater or less extent gendered (and also specific to class and ethnicity). Consequently, gender is indirectly embedded in the formal constructions of mental disorder. For example, to the extent that fear, anxiety and sadness are deemed more appropriate, reasonable feelings in women than in men, then the categories of disorder constructed around pathologies of these feelings will end up identifying more female than male disturbance. This is not an argument about double standards in diagnostic assessments of male and female pathology (an issue I consider below). It is an argument about the *construction* of categories of disorder around gendered feelings, thoughts and behaviours. We would expect, given the way in which masculinities and femininities are currently constructed, to find more cases of pathological depression, anxiety and phobia in women than men, since feelings of misery, anxiety and fear are deemed more appropriate in women, just as we would expect more alcoholism and drug abuse among men, given the existing, though changing, ways in which patterns of drinking and drug taking are linked to gender. Similarly, eating disorders are likely to be more common in women to the extent that appearing slim is more of a normative requirement for women than men.[6]

This analysis, although formulated rather differently, lends some support to Chesler's thesis about the importance of sex roles (gender expectations) to definitions of at least some mental disorders. However, it differs from Chesler's argument in one major respect. It does not, as it stands, assert an especial devaluation of the female role or an especial affinity between women and madness. The argument here suggests a symmetry in the situation of men and women in that either can be viewed as pathological if they 'overstep the mark' in relation to feelings and behaviours which are at least in part gendered: if they give what psychiatrists call an 'exaggerated' response to reality. Being somewhat anxious, concerned and fearful is part of being a middle-class woman in Western societies; but if you are too anxious, over-concerned or fearful you may be deemed over-emotional, irrational and disturbed. Similarly, higher levels of social drinking, aggression and even violence may be part of being manly, but a man may sometimes, nonetheless, be viewed as having a mental disorder if his drinking is excessive or he becomes inappropriately or unreasonably violent or aggressive (not it should be noted, *contra* Chesler, if he acts in a more feminine manner).

However, this argument needs to be qualified. We do not have to accept Chesler's claim that male 'excesses' are not liable to judgements of psychiatric disturbance, to contend that exaggerations of masculinity have often tended to be defined not as mental disorder but as delinquency: that is, they may be viewed as unacceptable but not as raising questions of possible psychological disorder. Consequently, as Chesler herself contends, there has been something of an asymmetry in the response to male and female exaggerations: problematic female behaviours have tended to be viewed as mental disorder; problematic male behaviours as evidence of wrongdoing.[7]

Put another way, we can say that the boundaries of mental disorder have, at least in twentieth-century Western societies, come to be set in ways that incorporate more 'problematic' female than male thought and behaviour. Or even more simply, we can say that men's mental life and behaviour, if and when they are deemed problematic, are more likely to be regulated through attributions of wrongdoing, women's through attributions of mental disorder. It does not follow, however, that women are more tightly regulated than men. There is considerable evidence in many contexts of tight and often harsh regulation of male behaviour, for instance in the military, as well as in work contexts, particularly in less advanced industrial economies. But the mechanisms of regulation often differ, with, in general terms, a greater focus on controlling male behaviour and a greater regulation on female mental life.

This contrast should not, however, be overstated or overgeneralised. The 'acting out' of masculinity, most obviously through certain forms of sexual and physical violence, can be deemed evidence of mental disturbance as the categories of criminal insanity and psychopathy attest, and there are male images of mental disorder no less than female. Moreover, some of these behaviours are at present increasingly liable to be problematised as mental disturbance, as is evidenced by the changing perceptions of sexual violence and child abuse. Indeed, this could be one factor in the decline in gender differences in mental disorder visible in patient statistics in the past decade or more. To recognise this, however, does not detract from the importance of the point that the boundaries of mental disorder have historically come to be constituted in ways that are indirectly far from gender-neutral. The gender bias in the construction of categories of mental disorder is far more clear cut in the case of the neuroses and behaviour disorders than of the psychoses and the organic mental disorders – an observation which seems to fit Allen's claim that there is a solid, middle ground where issues of gender play little part. However, before examining whether, and the mechanisms through which, gender influences the construction of normal cases and the identification of mental disorder – an analysis which shows this conclusion needs to be qualified – we need to consider the factors that underpin the gender bias in official constructions of mental disorder.

Gender, Agency and Rationality

How can we understand the gender bias in the construction of official categories of mental disorder? Why have sexual and child abuse usually not been seen as problems of mental health, whereas depression has? Central to any understanding of this question are the issues of agency and rationality, their importance in modern societies and their relation to cultural constructions of masculinity and femininity. We have already noted in Chapter 4 how the boundaries between mental disorder and wrongdoing, and between normality and mental disorder, relate to issues of agency. The realm of wrongdoing or deviance, as of normality, is a world in which we assume individuals to be agents: persons who are responsible for their thoughts and actions which are judged by social standards. In contrast, the realm of mental disorder is a world in which individuals are assumed to be subject to forces which they themselves cannot immediately control – they are passive rather than active. These contrasts are not formulated with any reference to gender. However, since assumptions or denials of agency are in practice gender-related, it follows that gender underpins the allocation of categories of problematic thought and action to the realms of mental disorder or deviance. What is typically problematic amongst men is more likely to be assigned to the category of wrongdoing; amongst women to the category of mental disorder.

The tendency in modern societies to assume human agency in men but to deny it in women and to see them as more passive has been widely noted. John Berger in a frequently cited passage in *Ways of Seeing*, provides the classic statement of this view: '*Men act* and *women appear*. Men look at women. Women watch themselves being looked at' (1972: 47). In a similar vein, Allen's analysis of case notes of men and women defendants in the criminal justice system indicates, as I earlier observed (see Chapter 5), that the notes on women focus 'not on what these women *do*, but on what happens to them' (1987: 40). And, like others, she links this to the tendency to see 'woman as the hapless victim of her own biology' (ibid: 28) – a link with biology explored more fully in the next chapter.

For many writers the passive–active opposition is at the core of the cultural contrast between masculinity and femininity. Freud, typifies the position in his essay 'Femininity' where he comments 'when you say "masculine", you usually mean "active", and when you say "feminine", you usually mean "passive"' (1973: 147–8). The pervasiveness of such cultural linkages in Western societies means that thoughts and behaviours more typical of women, if considered problematic, are more likely to be appropriated to the category of mental disorder; those more typical of men to be defined as deviant. This is one factor helping to ensure that exaggerated fears come to be constituted as mental pathology (viz. the various phobias); and exaggerated anger as wrongdoing if it generates 'unacceptable' violence. This point further qualifies Chesler's analysis of gender asymmetry. Chesler's view of a *difference* in response is confirmed; however the source is less the devaluation of the female role *per se*, than the tendency to deny women agency – a tendency that affects both the way mental disorder is constructed through the allocation of types of problem to the terrains of mental disorder or deviance, and through the assessment of individual cases.

A similar argument applies to the related issue of rationality. I argued in Chapter 4 that rationality, which is highly valued in modern societies, is central to the concept of mental disorder – indeed, it is through its opposition with rationality that the concept takes on its meaning. But, like agency, assumptions of rationality are not independent of gender. A further crucial opposition between reason and emotion helps to situate women on the side of irrationality and men on the side of reason. As I noted in the previous chapter, culturally women have tended, especially in certain social and historical contexts, to be viewed as more emotional than men. Images of women frequently emphasise their softness, dependence and responsiveness to the feelings of others, as well as their tendency to feelings of anxiety, sadness and fear. In this way women are constituted as emotional, sensitive and irrational. Men in contrast are constituted as more independent, tough-minded and rational, and when they display the emotions of rage and hate, this is less likely to be constituted as being 'emotional'. Men tend to be viewed as controlled and rational beings even in their displays of emotion.[8] Indeed, in this respect standards of rationality are male standards.[9] And it is these oppositions, in which women are linked with the emotional and irrational and men with the rational, that underpin the tendency to constitute the boundaries of mental disorder in ways that incorporate more of the terrain of women's than men's problems (the readiness to include eating disorders versus the contest over the inclusion of alcoholism is salutary). It also helps us to account in particular for the way in which mental disorders have come to be constituted around forms of emotional expression especially associated with women.

The gendered nature of rationality and its contrast with the irrational and emotional has been explored most fully in relation to science (see, for instance, Harding and O'Barr 1987). Eighteenth-century Enlightenment thought, with its attachment to rationality and progress – qualities that we now take to be characteristic of modernity – increasingly viewed science as the epitome of objectivity and rationality and as linked with masculinity. By the twentieth century the familiar polarisation of male, scientific and rational with female, intuitive and emotional, was well-established:

> Our science-based culture depends on abstract studies, mostly in the physical sciences, and on techniques relating to engineering skills. Both science and engineering are identified with male accomplishments, with the capacity for mathematical and logical reasoning, with mechanical skills; they are literally and metaphorically masculine activities. Women by contrast, are stereotypically identified with so-called caring jobs, nursing, teaching and social work. They are deemed to be uniquely gifted in the realm of human relationships by virtue of their greater emotional sensitivity. The model for female accomplishments is motherhood. The corresponding popular imagery is of soft, tender sympathy overriding reason and intellect (Brown and Jordanova 1981: 224).

However, notwithstanding the value attached to science in Enlightenment thought, until the twentieth century science had a more marginal position within the academic realm; the classics were the most prestigious subjects and women were not entirely excluded from scientific activity (Phillips 1990). During this century, science's growing significance has helped to strengthen its linkages with masculinity and rationality. And, whilst male irrationality can still prove threatening, rationality is more likely to be presumed in the case of men simply because it is part of the definition of being a man – of being manly. Significantly, it is the predominantly female territory of emotional disorders centred on emotional sensitivities that has seen the greatest expansion within the formal domain of psychiatry in the twentieth century, and where the linkages with gender are the strongest.[10]

The linking of assumptions about agency and rationality with masculinity, and of irrationality and the denial of agency with femininity are tied, I would suggest, to issues of social power. They are, consequently, underpinned by structural differences in power between men and women. Agency and rationality tend, other things being equal, to be attributed to the more powerful and denied to the more powerless. Indeed, such attributions are the cultural representation and realisation of differences in power. Of course, the relationships here are complex and not easy to unravel. Nonetheless, attributions of irrationality, passivity and dependence also constitute one of the mechanisms through which power can be maintained and even enhanced. Significantly, these linkages between gender and assumptions of rationality and agency are also salient at the level of both normal cases and case-identification.

Normal Cases

Gender is salient not only to the way in which the boundaries of mental disorder are historically constructed, but also, as we shall see in the following section, to the identification of cases in clinical practice. Here the relation with gender is less a matter of 'indirect' discrimination than of a direct fracturing of the universality that official classifications and scientific discourses require. As Allen (1987) argues very convincingly in relation to the criminal justice system, a system formally delineated in universal terms may, nonetheless, *require* diversity to be taken into consideration.[11] After describing a number of cases in which the personal characteristics of the accused are taken into account, she comments:

At a deeper level than this, however, one can trace in this series of cases the intrication of assumptions about gender difference into the very *logic* of legal discourse. These rulings rehearse certain old and unresolved questions about justice itself: faced by human diversity, does justice inhere in judging similar behaviours alike, or in taking account of human differences between the perpetrators... Sexual division is here taken as a fundamental apriori of legal reasoning; it structures the legal argument, not simply at the level of the description of particular legal subjects, but at the abstract level of the legal logic itself (ibid: 30).

The point, she contends, is that 'ultimately legal discourse simply cannot *conceive* of a subject in whom gender is not a determining attribute: it cannot *think* such a subject' (ibid). The same I would argue applies to psychiatric reasoning. The very objectives of clinical medicine require attention to individual cases, and in so doing require an attention to the individual's particular personal characteristics, including their gender. This is the sphere of the individual case history, rather than the generalised official delineation – the ideographic rather than the nomothetic. Put another way, we may say that whereas universalism is a requirement of the scientific medicine in which official classifications are grounded, particularism is a *sine qua non* of clinical medicine.

These two countervailing requirements intersect in the construction of typifications (Schutz 1964) of specific disorders – that is, in the elaboration of what I call, following Sudnow (1965), 'normal cases' which describe the typical personal and social characteristics of patients with a view to facilitating diagnosis. These typifications are grounded in studies of the epidemiology and aetiology of each disorder which are informed by scientific discourse; they are, nonetheless, directed to individual characteristics and so move away from the universalism of the formal descriptions of the disorders.

The formal descriptions of symptomatology are fleshed out by a range of information about the disorder: about its onset, causes and prognosis, as well as by illustrations of symptomatology and, in this elaboration, material about the likely personal and social characteristics of patients is incorporated. Some of the elaboration may be provided in diagnostic manuals, as it is in the DSM-IV Manual (American Psychiatric Association 1994). Much more of it is detailed in psychiatric texts and case books (see, for instance, the *DSM-IV Casebook* (Spitzer et al. 1994) and in the training given to psychiatrists, which has traditionally included the presentation and discussion of selected case histories in the form of vignettes.[12] In this way normal cases of particular disorders are constructed, constructions which may change markedly as ideas about the particular disorder change. They also vary according to theoretical proclivities of those who produce the particular text.

Gender plays a far more explicit role in the construction and elaboration of normal cases than in official symptom specifications. First, and most obviously given the salience of gender, there is no way of constructing a supposedly typical case without some reference to gender, usually as part of the attribution of a social location and identity for the individual in question. This can be seen very clearly in textbooks like Stafford Clark and Bridges's *Psychiatry for Students*, which illustrates different disorders by describing typical cases. Inevitably the social identity, including the gender of the individual, is mentioned. A case of anxiety begins 'Mrs J.H., a housewife of 26 with a son of four and a baby daughter of 18 months, had begun to suspect that her husband might be becoming interested in one of the girls at his work...' (1990: 64). We are presented here with information not only about gender, but also about the woman's age, marital status, occupation and family structure. The powerful image of a 'trapped housewife' tied to the home readily comes to mind. Another case, also of anxiety, begins 'A 20-year-old medical student was certain that he had developed pulmonary tuberculosis... Discussion revealed a number of anxieties related to his parents, girlfriend, his digs and his forthcoming examinations' (ibid: 64). Here the social information is a little more restricted, but in addition to gender we are told about the individual's age, occupation and marital status.

Construction of these normal cases is clearly designed to facilitate diagnosis, just as descriptions of middle-aged, male, heavy-smokers are intended to aid the diagnosis of lung cancer: a diagnosis which should be based on the presence or absence of symptoms not on the social characteristics *per se*. At a minimum, however, the danger is that personal characteristics contaminate diagnosis as when doctors fail to diagnose 'childhood infections' like mumps in adults or lung cancer in a man who does not smoke – a contamination more likely with mental than physical disorders, since there is usually less independent corroborating evidence on which to base a diagnosis (Busfield 1989a: 65). Even more importantly, these typifications help to generate cultural images of particular disorders in the wider society, which in turn contribute to the constructions of masculinity and femininity. In the process, the categories of disorder and of masculinity or femininity become interwoven as, for instance, in the increasingly pervasive images of anorexic women.

The second way in which gender features in the construction of normal cases is in the information provided about the usual gender balance of each disorder. Psychiatric texts often describe both male and female cases; but they also make it clear that there is a definite imbalance in some conditions. Indeed, as we saw in Chapter 2, few conditions are said to be distributed uniformly by gender. A disorder's link with either men or women is strengthened not only by statements about the likely gender balance, but also by examples of gender-specific causes and circumstances. Some descriptions, for instance, refer to the female reproductive cycle, others to contextual details which may have aetiological relevance, as with the 26 year-old housewife with two young children at home. Consequently, in the glosses that fill out the vignettes of normal cases, a disorder is quite frequently associated rather more with one gender than the other. Disorders attributed a gender imbalance extend beyond the neuroses and behaviour disorders, to those where the link with gender is less marked, such as senile dementia and psychotic depression (but not manic-depressive psychosis) – disorders which form part of the middle ground of psychiatry.

Normal cases are also linked with gender in one further way: through their relation to the performance of duties and responsibilities commonly assigned, at least in part, on the basis of gender: a man's paid employment outside the home, women's work as housewives or their caring roles within the broader family. The description of a case of mania in Stafford Clark and Bridges's text begins:

> A young surgeon (aged 34) in a university town in the Midlands began to arrange his operating list earlier and earlier in the mornings, and to instruct the Sister in charge of the out-patient clinic to book more and more cases for him at his out-patient clinic. By the time he was arriving at the operating theatre and expecting to start operating at 5.30 am, and had informed the out-patient department that no less than 25 cases were to be booked for his afternoon clinics, it became evident that his general judgement was no longer to be trusted (1990: 104–5).

Another case, this time of psychotic depression, starts: 'This was a patient who came complaining of inability to think clearly, or perform his normal work, which was that of a designer and producer of cartoon films' (ibid: 98). And a women with an obsessive-compulsive disorder is described as follow:

A highly intelligent woman who had obsessive fears about pregnancy, eventually contrived to undergo a hysterectomy at the age of 45. But in fact, after the operation she found that her rituals of glove-wearing, hand-washing, and total inability to deal normally with household chores, were quite unaffected by the fact that she no longer had a uterus, and therefore could not under any circumstances become pregnant. She had to perform the same rituals in order to reduce the anguish which arose in exactly the same way (ibid: 84–5).

In all these cases performance of tasks assigned at least in part on the basis of gender, enters the description and is one factor that occasions the assumption of some underlying mental pathology: the surgeon and the cartoon designer not managing their work properly, and the woman's inability to do her 'household chores'.

But again, what precise part does gender play? The psychiatric position is that gender is basically irrelevant: it may determine the assignment of particular duties and responsibilities, but judgements of pathology are matters of the mental processes that underlie task performance. From this perspective gender differences, like those of age, class nd ethnicity, only condition the manifestation of disorder and are to be treated as no more than background noise 'as much distorting as revealing the pure – and sexually undifferentiated – form of the medical pathology' (Allen 1986: 98). However, on closer examination this position is difficult to sustain.

First, it is far from clear that symptoms of mental disorder can be differentiated from their socially conditioned manifestation in the way psychiatric discourse tends to assume (see Busfield 1989a: 94–9). Clearly, as I argued earlier (Chapter 4), there are analytic distinctions between a judgement of social behaviour (including task and role performance) and a judgement of the reasoning that underlies behaviour. However, I have also argued that in practice judgements of rationality and irrationality often take task performance (including what people say) as their starting point – as Parsons's analysis (1951) with its definition of health as the effective performance of social roles (see Chapter 4) makes clear (see also Wootton 1959: Chapter 7). Consequently, even though the judgement of rationality is a judgement of mind not of behaviour *per se*, it is far from clear that this separation between the social characteristics of individuals and the tasks they are required to perform can in practice be differentiated from some pure, gender-neutral mental pathology.

Second, the gender-based assignment of tasks and duties is itself maintained by the way in which judgements of mental pathology are derived, in the first instance, from task performance. Although for analytic purposes task may be independent of the gender (or class or ethnicity) of the person carrying it out, structurally and culturally it often is not, given the high degree of gender segregation (and class and ethnic stratification) of the labour market and in the allocation of tasks more generally. Consequently, even when an analytic distinction can be made, gender and task do become inextricably linked, and judgements related to task or role performance inevitably reaffirm the gender-based assignment of tasks and responsibilities. We are back, therefore, to the gender regulation that is at the heart of Chesler's analysis. However, again the argument is not identical to Chesler's. In Chesler's theorisation, mental disorder is *defined* in terms of deviation from (or in the case of women exaggerations of) a person's sex role, with acting in feminine ways especially devalued. My claim here is that while mental disorder is not defined in terms of gendered tasks and roles, these are, nonetheless, sustained by attributions of irrationality that are not independent of task performance.

The claim that psychiatry helps to maintain gender relations in society is a version of a standard criticism or psychiatry: that by working with definitions of mental disorder which in practice emphasise adjustments to the social milieu, psychiatry contributes to social conformity (Davis 1938; Scheff 1975). It is countered, especially by psychoanalysts, by the argument that the psychiatrist's task is to facilitate the capacity to deal with one's social milieu, not to conform to it. Undoubtedly some psychiatrists and therapists do perform that facilitating role which may, for instance, enable a woman to call existing gender relations into question. Regrettably, however, as a range of studies have shown (Warren 1987: Chapter 5; Miles 1988: Chapter 6), many others merely encourage conformity and repress resistance and change, not least because of their reliance on physical methods of treatment and their reluctance to analyse the values embedded in their own practice.

In the construction of normal cases we see, therefore, a departure from the principles of universalism that inform official symptom descriptions, towards a particularism in which gender plays a significant part. Not only do the delineations of normal cases of particular disorders usually refer to gendered subjects, but in many instances disorders are said to be more common in one gender than the other, so that gender comes to form part of the constructions of that disorder, as with the images of depressed, anxious or anorexic women. In addition, and most importantly, the detail of normal cases shows the way in which judgements of disorder are bound up with the performance of tasks assigned in part on the basis of gender, so that task and gender are inextricably linked. It is here that the regulation of gender is most obviously manifest and where Allen's claim of a solid, middle ground where gender is not important finds little support.

Case Identification

At the third and final level, that of the identification of particular cases, the key issue is that the person who is assessed for possible mental pathology is always a gendered subject. As I noted in the previous chapter, attributions of disorder often involve the judgements of a range of people, lay and professional, including the individual them- selves and do not depend exclusively on psychiatrists' assessments (though they are officially the final arbiter). Consequently, at least in the initial stages of case identification, we are in a domain even further removed from the formal gender-neutrality of official constructions. This is the sphere where it is the sense that something is wrong, that a person is not coping properly, that they are being irrational, that their feelings are 'unreasonable' and excessive, that they are acting strangely, which may occasion contact with a GP, who then determines whether a visit to a specialist is necessary.[13] And it is here that the aspects of gender-embedded task performance, visible in the typifications of mental disorders, and the attributions of irrationality, are especially salient. And it is here that cultural images of disease often play an important part.

We do not, of course, necessarily expect the same skill in judgements of mental disorder by lay persons as by professionals, and tend to assume that specialists' judgements are superior to those of lay persons and escape from the impact of stereotypic images. Yet, as I noted in the last chapter, a range of evidence calls the accuracy of psychiatric judgements into question; the evidence indicating, for instance, a lack of agreement between psychiatrists in diagnostic assessments under clin- ical conditions. However, even where agreement is high, as it can be in a research context, systematic biases may exist. The Broverman study

(Broverman et al. 1970), for instance, showed that clinicians had different conceptions of female and male mental health, men's being closer to the gender unspecified conception, suggesting the possibility of double standards in clinical evaluations of men and women. Regrettably, however, the study did not show how the differing conceptions were applied in assessing actual cases. Gove and his colleagues (Tudor, Tudor and Gove 1977) have argued, *contra* Chesler, that the study suggests the standards applied to men are more stringent than those for women, since the male stereotype is closer to the overall (gender unspecified) ideal. But it can equally be argued that if the overall standard is applied to both men's and women's behaviour, then women are more likely to be judged to be disturbed in as far as they conform to the female stereotype, since this is further away from the overall ideal. This latter interpretation is in line with the cultural tendency to deny agency and rationality to women. Moreover, claims as to gender bias do not rest on the Broverman study alone. What is clear is that, despite endeavours to standardise classifications and diagnostic instruments, and despite methodological techniques which are likely to underestimate the level of bias in research studies, the studies do continue to show some bias. Given the salience of gender in our daily lives and in our apprehension of individuals, it would be surprising if they did not. Can we really expect psychiatrists to exclude gender altogether in their assessments, given the clinical requirement to attend to individual diversity?

Moreover, the identification of cases of mental disorder is not solely a matter of specialist psychiatric evaluation. As I have already noted, in practice the judgements of lay people and other professionals with varying lengths of training in the mental health field – GPs, social workers, psychologists, mental health nurses and care assistants – influence decisions about the presence of mental disorder. Consider, for example, the identification of Alzheimer's disease in an individual – part of the mainstream of psychiatric practice. Alzheimer's is included under the group of dementias in the ICD-10 Classification (World Health Organisation 1992), where it is described as 'a primary degenerative cerebral disorder' (ibid: 47). Like other dementias it is characterised by 'a disturbance of multiple higher cortical functions, including memory, thinking, orientation, comprehension, calculation, learning capacity, language and judgement' (ibid: 45). As we would expect, the detailed description of the diagnostic criteria retains a formal gender-neutrality, although the rather fuller DSM-IV in its gloss on the condition notes that dementia is slightly more common amongst women (American Psychiatric Association, 1994: 141). However, the distinction between normal and pathological ageing is far from clear cut (Armstrong 1983: Chapter 9), and once we consider how impairment of higher cortical functions is judged in practice the issue of gender begins to enter the picture.[14] The problem is that, although there are some standardised psychological instruments designed to measure intellectual performance and to highlight intellectual deterioration which may be more or less gender-neutral, and there are also some physiological measures of brain functioning which may be used, the diagnosis of a case of Alzheimer's depends on such instruments and measures only in the last instance.[15] Much of the pathway to becoming a clinical case depends on more informal judgements and a range of other information about intellectual performance. A judgement of pathology depends on the judgements of an individual's family, friends, relatives, GP and other professionals, as to whether he or she is managing their lives as well as might be expected. Such judgements not only affect referral, but also constitute some of the evidence on which the psychiatrist's assessment is based.

The significance, of everyday activities is recognised in the WHO glossary. The preliminary discussion of dementia notes:

> Dementia produces an appreciable decline in intellectual functioning, and usually some interference with personal activities of daily living, such as washing, dressing, eating, personal hygiene, excretory and toilet activities. How such a decline manifests itself will depend largely on the social and cultural setting in which the patient lives (1992: 45).

But the glossary's note of caution is hardly adequate. Although the list of activities is constructed in gender-neutral terms, the significance attached to interference with normal activities ensures that gender is embedded in case identification as it is in the construction of normal cases, because even in old age tasks are frequently assigned on the basis of gender.[16] Dementia may be suspected if a woman has difficulty boiling a kettle properly, managing money when shopping, keeping the house clean and so forth; it may be suspected if a man has difficulty filling in his football coupon or forgets the way to his house when driving. Moreover, whilst task performance is central for both men and women, there are grounds for believing that any deterioration in performance is more visible in women. On the one hand, amongst older couples, when men have retired from paid employment women usually

still have to continue with their household responsibilities where incapacities will be manifest. On the other hand, since women tend to live
longer than men and are more likely to end up living on their own,
intellectual deterioration is likely to be more noticeable to friends and
outsiders who have any responsibility for them (that is, the external surveillance of those who live on their own is arguably greater than that of
surviving couples).[17]

One of the consequences of the move to community care is that the
role of lay people and professionals with more limited mental health
training is increasing. In this context, official medical definitions of disorder often have less significance and broader notions of coping and
task performance become if anything more important.[18] As a result,
gender is likely to be even more salient in case identification. This is
partly because the ideological commitment to the universal standards of
science is likely to be lower and the use of standard instruments of psychiatric assessment less common in most community settings, but also
because of the way in which coping and managing are so often judged
in terms of the performance of gender-assigned tasks and duties. This
means that the boundaries of mental disorder will themselves shift over
time, since official constructions, the elaboration of normal cases and
case identification are interrelated.

Conclusion

It is hard to avoid the conclusion that gender plays a pervasive part in
official constructions of mental disorder, in the elaboration of normal
cases and in case identification. The relation between mental disorder
and the regulation of gender is not simply contingent (Allen 1986: 95);
rather, since gender is such a key feature of social relations and a
major dimension of social difference, gender inevitably features in constructions of mental disorder.[19] On the one hand, official constructions,
though delineated almost entirely in gender-neutral terms are indirectly
related to gender since they construct as problems of mind (that is, as
irrationality), feelings, mental processes and behaviour which are themselves gendered. Here, the gendered nature of notions of rationality
and agency, with the strong linkage between what it is to be a rational,
autonomous individual and being a man and the corollary – a tendency to see women as passive, emotional and irrational – underpins
these processes of categorisation. On the other hand, the elaboration of

normal cases and case identification are founded on a particularism that *requires* attention to individual characteristics, including gender. Constructs of mental disorder are, therefore, inherently gendered, and are linked with the regulation of gender. And the relationship between gender and mental disorder is reciprocal. For whilst gender is embedded in constructs of mental disorder, the constructs of disorder which are developed and elaborated by a range of mental health professionals, incorporating ideas about causation and treatment as well as about symptoms, in turn contribute to the way in which gender is itself constructed.

In the next chapter I want to develop the analysis further by looking at the interconnections between mental health services, the boundaries of mental disorder and the balance of patient populations in historical context.

Chapter 7

The Historical Context

If doctors found themselves diagnosing nervous exhaustion more frequently at the end of the nineteenth century, they may have been prompted to do so by the ease with which they could flourish the new, all-inclusive designation for a very mixed bag of symptoms... On the other hand, they may well have been under strong pressure from patients to dispense the neurasthenic diagnosis. Once propagated, disease entities assume dimensions that the medical profession cannot always predict or control. Those that take root and thrive most luxuriantly are the ones that best further the confluence of patient's and physician's needs (Oppenheim 1991:99).

In this chapter I want to build on the analysis of gender and mental disorder I have developed so far, by setting it in a broader context of changes in mental health services. I have argued that theoretically mental disorder is best understood as a shifting, changing category which classifies certain social problems as problems of mind, a process that involves attributions of irrationality and unreason. I have also argued that, given the generally greater reluctance to attribute rationality and agency to women than men and particularly to see them as more 'emotional', women may be particularly prone to be categorised by clinicians as having certain mental disorders (both in terms of the development of general categories and of individual cases). It is necessary, however, to examine how these processes operate in socially and historically specific situations, and how the development of particular institutional arrangements, which are themselves shaped by a range of social forces, affect the processes of category construction and the gender balance of patient populations.

The aim of this chapter is to outline the broad contours of such an analysis by examining the development of the category of mental dis-

119

order and the gender balance of patient populations in the context of the historical development of mental health services in Britain. I have already noted in Chapter 5 how mental health services structure epidemiological data, including the gender balance of patient populations. This argument needs now to be taken one stage further by exploring the complex interaction over time between categories of mental disorder, mental health service provision, and the gender balance of patient populations. While attention to the activities and interests of the medical profession and other professionals is essential to this endeavour since they are key actors in the development of mental health services, it is also important to examine the problems and difficulties (the social needs) to which professionals are responding, and their social distribution – problems themselves a product of social institutions and social arrangements – as well as the activities of government, policy makers and social reformers that help to shape the professional response.[1] In turn we need to be aware how service developments and the activities of professionals themselves contribute to the way problems are defined, interpreted and dealt with in specific social contexts. The lines of impact are by no means one way.

Within the confines of a single chapter I can only begin to provide a general indication of the way in which a complex set of forces interact to generate a particular landscape of identified mental disorder. My analysis is designed to be suggestive: more detailed, specific studies are needed. In the interests of brevity my main focus will be on nineteenth and twentieth-century developments. However, it is necessary to begin by saying something about preceding centuries.

Societal Categories of Madness and Mental Disorder

Madness and lunacy first gained currency as societal not medical terms which were widely used in common parlance. Within both lay and medical thinking they were relatively narrow categories used to group certain behaviours (and the individuals who manifested them) considered in some way severely disruptive or threatening to social values and, because of this and the irrationality that appeared to be involved, as indicative of madness. Michael MacDonald (1981: 121–32) persuasively argues that in the seventeenth century, madness was indicated in popular eyes by frantic behaviour, excess talk, odd language and the threat or actual carrying out of some criminal action that was common in type (such as murder, theft or assault) *but often distinctive in object.* Attacks on kith and kin, self-violence and the destruction of personal property (highly valued because of its cost and scarcity) were especially likely to be interpreted as irrational and consequently as evidence of insanity. The behaviour in question might involve some delinquent or criminal action, but it also had the added dimension of irrationality.

MacDonald further notes how in addition to madness, which was likely to be given the medical diagnosis of mania (the terms mania and madness were often used interchangeably), a range of less severe mental problems were recognised in everyday thought. These were described using terms such as 'light-headed', 'troubled in mind', 'melancholic', 'mopish', 'anxious' and 'fearful', terms that categorised experiences and behaviours that were troubling either to the individuals themselves or to those around them – perhaps because they were adversely affected task performance but also because they were seen as also involving some disturbance of mental functioning – some form of irrationality. These less severe, but nonetheless frequently distressing, mental problems, along with madness proper were embraced, as MacDonald shows, within a framework of magic, religious and scientific ideas. Individuals with such problems, if they escaped penalty for some offence within the criminal justice system, were liable, depending on the degree, severity and chronicity of their problem, and their social standing, either to be viewed as relatively harmless and left alone or to be encouraged to seek help from some cleric or healer, whether on a charitable or commercial basis, the remedies offered often combining the same mixture of magic, science and religion.

Gender permeated lay and medical categories of mental disorder then as now even though the construction of gender appropriate emotions and behaviours was not precisely the same. Interestingly, MacDonald's (1981) analysis of the persons seen by the astrological physician, Richard Napier, does not show any clear gender imbalance in the relatively limited number of lunatics whom he saw. Yet madness and mania were if anything more linked to men than women. If, for instance, we consider lunatics confined under the jurisdiction of the courts, there was a clear preponderance of men (MacDonald 1986). And in London, Bedlam, the only separate institution for inmates in England until the eighteenth century (its use for inmates dates back to the thirteenth century – Allderidge 1979), had more male than female inmates in the sixteenth and seventeenth centuries (MacDonald 1986). Moreover, about 80 per cent of lunatics supervised by the Court of

Wards between 1542 and 1646 (when it was abolished) were men; male pauper lunatics were also more likely than female in this period to end up in houses of correction (ibid).

This bias towards a male presence in the institutional arrangements for the mad was paralleled by the representations of madness up until the nineteenth century. Mad people, especially those deemed to be suffering from mania, were often portrayed in this period, as I earlier indicated, as wild, raging animals insensitive to normal feelings and experiences such as cold and hunger and this wild figure of the mad person often had a masculine face (see Showalter 1987: 8). Even melancholia (see p 90–1 above) was frequently portrayed at this time through masculine images: 'The emblems of melancholy were a love-sick youth, a celibate scholar, an idle gentleman' (MacDonald 1986: 263). Melancholia, like mania, was a medical category widely used in lay contexts and, as these images suggest, had clear connotations of social rank and standing – connotations derived no doubt from the class background of those seeking medical help (mopishness was its plebeian, non-medical counterpart: see, for example, MacDonald 1981: 162–3). Hypochondriasis was another medical category (see Chapter 2) also initially associated with men of higher social standing, and significantly, characterised by enfeeblement of the will (Oppenheim 1992: 142–37).[2]

It is clear, however, from MacDonald's analysis of Richard Napier's case notes that overall women were more likely than men to be found amongst those with milder mental disorders like these, or with other loosely categorised as 'light-headed', 'troubled in mind', 'anxious' or 'fearful', which did not attract formal medical labels. I noted in Chapter 2 that this gender imbalance is of some interest, since it parallels the present-day imbalance in affective disorders and anxiety states. MacDonald (1981: Chapter 3) links these mental problems to a range of social stresses including troubled courtships, marital problems, bereavements and economic difficulties – the latter a factor of significance to a much higher proportion of men than women, and the psychological impact of these experiences, especially the significance of interpersonal and family problems for women, may well have contributed to the gender differences in the more minor mental problems brought to Napier's attention (see Chapter 10 for a fuller discussion of stress and mental disorder).[3] Yet it may also be the case that in this period there were not only differences between men and women in the way in which psychological difficulties were expressed (see Chapter 5), with men being more likely to turn them outwards and women inwards, but also that there were gender differences in assumptions of agency and rationality, so that women were more likely to be seen as having emotional problems that needed attention.

Institutions for Lunatics

Separate institutions primarily catering for lunatics rather than the more extensive category of persons 'troubled in mind' were established from the seventeenth century onwards, with Bedlam serving as a frequent standard for comparison – usually unfavourably. The institutions became the linchpin of nineteenth-century mental health provision and the places where psychiatry clearly emerged as a separate speciality within medicine and where madness was transformed into mental illness. By the mid-nineteenth century there were three major types of institution: private madhouses, voluntary (charitable) asylums and public asylums, stratified in terms of the inmates' social standing and differing considerably in their scale and character.

The first to emerge were the private madhouses which date back to the seventeenth century and perhaps even earlier (Parry-Jones 1972). They were commercial enterprises catering for two groups: persons of relatively high social standing whose families could afford the costs of care, and paupers who were sent there under a system of contracting out within the framework of the poor-law system. Their development had a number of origins. First, there were the financial gains to be made from looking after some awkward and disruptive individual in a world where market capitalism was spreading, and the practice often began with an individual who had a reputation as a healer agreeing to take in one or more mad persons within their own household. As the private madhouses started to take in more mad people the financial gains could be considerable and, like other commercial enterprises, they were often passed down from one generation to the next (see Parry-Jones 1972; MacKenzie 1992). And, as with other businesses, advertisements were used to emphasise the merits of the institution and the care provided in order to attract a suitable clientele. Second, and equally important to the growth of private madhouses, was the advantage to families of divesting themselves of the day-to-day care of a difficult and disruptive individual, albeit at a relatively high financial cost – a prospect that could seem doubly attractive if there was some chance of cure (which was frequently stressed in the advertisements). Third, there was the need within the poor-law system to make provision for inmates who could not be dealt with easily within the workhouses which were being increasingly established to deal with the economically dependent – hence the willingness of the poor-law authorities to make contracts with private madhouses (usually at much cheaper rates and with lower standards than for private inmates).

Initially at least, there was not much of a gender imbalance in the inmate populations of private madhouses.[4] The evidence indicates that by the early decades of the nineteenth century, marginally more men than women were being admitted (most inmates were assigned a diagnosis of mania (Parry-Jones 1972: 13) though some were diagnosed as suffering from dementia or melancholia). But women's death rates tended to be lower than men's (and death rates in institutions were typically higher than in non-institutional populations).[5] In consequence, there were sometimes more women than men in the resident population. The higher male admission rates were probably due both to the greater attraction of getting rid of the more difficult and disruptive lunatics (often men), and to the greater willingness of families to pay for the care of male family members (perhaps because it seemed a more advantageous economic investment).

Voluntary asylums (Busfield 1989a: Chapter 6) were the second type of institution to emerge. Most were established in the second half of the eighteenth century following the wave of new charitable general hospitals mainly founded in the first half of the eighteenth century (see Woodward 1974). The motivations and factors underpinning the establishment of voluntary asylums differed from those that led to the private madhouses. The voluntary asylums, like the voluntary hospitals, were set up by reformers and philanthropists concerned to ensure a healthy population and a healthy workforce, with a view to giving access to qualified medical care in a cost-effective manner to those who could not afford to pay for the services of a physician or surgeon at home.[6] They tended to be more medical in character than the private madhouses, often with more active therapeutic regimes, and catered for a different social group: those in middling circumstances or the respectable poor. Relatively few in number, they provided both a general institutional model for the public asylums, the final type of specialist institution, and the location in which new practices such as moral treatment, with its focus on constructing a well-ordered social environment, were developed.

Like the private madhouses, voluntary asylums catered largely for disruptive, difficult individuals, frequently diagnosed as suffering from mania. Again the number of male admissions and residents tended to be marginally higher than female. This was not only because economic arguments were likely to encourage families to have male family members admitted when they depended on their wages if there was a prospect of their return to health, but also because the voluntary asylums were increasingly reluctant to deal with chronic, long-term patients (defined as persons whose disorder had lasted more than a year). Consequently, gender differences in mortality rates had rather less impact on these institutions than on the private madhouse populations.

Public asylums, which were established from the first half of the nineteenth century onwards, were the third major type of specialist institution to emerge (see Scull 1993: Chapter 6; Busfield 1989a: Chapter 7). Like the voluntary asylums they were founded on a wave of reformist enthusiasm by those who argued there needed to be an input of public money if all parts of the country were to have their own asylum (it was often difficult for reformers to secure sufficient funds from voluntary donations to establish a voluntary asylum). Initially they were designed to cater for three groups of inmates – private lunatics whose families could afford to pay for their care, criminal lunatics (existing institutional provisions for this group were considered totally inadequate), and pauper lunatics who disrupted workhouse routines (who might otherwise have been sent to a private madhouse). Of particular importance to the success of the campaign to establish public asylums was the claim that the new asylums not only treated inmates more humanely than the voluntary asylums and private madhouses (there had been a series of scandals surrounding care in these institutions), but also that they would cure inmates. Consequently, although the public asylums were expensive to establish (they were usually purpose-built) and to run (more expensive than the workhouses), they offered the chance of reducing the long-term burden of dependency by restoring inmates to health – an issue crucial to the poor-law authorities who were given permissive powers via an Act of 1808 to collect rates to fund them.

Equally important to the success of the campaign to establish public asylums were three other factors. First, the coincidence of two very different but both strongly pro-institutional ideologies: the pro-institutional philosophy of moral treatment with its belief that the well-ordered institution was itself therapeutic; and the pro-institutional philosophy of the poor-law system with its belief that economic support should be provided in institutions as a means of deterring individuals from seeking support unless absolutely necessary. Second, the increasing political power of the reformers who were largely drawn from the class of new entrepreneurs whose new power found expression in the 1832 Reform Act. And third, and linked to this, the declining power of local authorities who were opposed to central regulation and consequently to central legislation requiring that asylums be provided. The result was that in 1845 the provision of public asylums became mandatory.

Despite the initial optimism on which they were founded, by the second half of the nineteenth century the public asylums were, like the workhouses, increasingly functioning as places of last resort providing custody rather than care and treatment, almost entirely for pauper patients (Busfield 1989a: Chapter 8; Scull 1993: Chapter 6). But this did not prevent expansion in inmate numbers which increased rapidly throughout the century, reaching over 80,000 by its end, or in the size of the institutions, the average size being close to a thousand inmates by the end of the century. In part, this was because of the institutional bias of the poor-law system which meant that families in need of help and support for difficult and disturbed individuals could only obtain poor-law relief in institutions. In part it was the result of the custodial, last resort character of the institutions themselves (those admitted were held on a compulsory basis). Admitting those whose problems were well-advanced with little prospect of cure and providing little in the way of active therapeutic intervention, ensured the asylums were silted up with chronic cases who constituted the bulk of asylum residents. Much of the expansion in numbers resulted from this accumulation of chronic cases – often people who were not 'mad' in the sense that their behaviour was by then especially uncontrolled or threatening, but whose mental capacities had been in some way or another undermined.[7]

The expansion of the asylum system had major implications, primarily for the development of the new profession of psychiatry. On the one hand, the asylums provided an empire which could be colonised by an emergent breed of medical specialists – psychiatrists – whose power and influence was grounded in the asylums which they tended to dominate.[8] Within medicine as a whole the standing of the new specialists was not, after the early years, especially high, not least because new requirements that doctors should be resident deterred any who wished to retain a private practice. In addition, the poor-law authorities who funded the public asylums constrained their practice in crucial ways. Yet within their own domain the doctors' power over asylum attendants and patients was still considerable. On the other hand, asylums yielded a set of captive patients who provided the basis on which new concepts, theories and treatments could be developed. Of particular importance were psychiatrists' classificatory endeavours which reached their height towards the end of the nineteenth century. Equally important were new concepts such as moral insanity and monomania which did not so much change the boundaries of mental disorder in its broadest sense, as change the boundaries of which problems were best dealt with within an institutional environment.

Those admitted to public asylums were, however, still a highly selected group of the economically dependent – the awkward, difficult and incapacitated who would disrupt the life of the workhouse or who required a level of day-to-day care neither the workhouse nor the family could readily provide. In this context it is not surprising that often as many men as women were admitted to public asylums. As with the voluntary asylums the focus on difficult, threatening behaviour helped to ensure a strong male presence amongst admissions, and criminal lunatics constituted a significant group proportion of asylum inmates where male numbers outstripped female (Broadmoor did not open as a separate asylum for criminal lunatics until 1863). Equally, general paresis of the insane (GPI) brought a steady flow of male patients to the asylum. Yet, as the data given in Chapter 2 show (see Table 7), female admissions were almost on a par with men's in the final decades of the nineteenth century, and other data show this was also the case in the decades prior to this. Women's economic dependence was one reason. Women were less likely than men to have alternative means of support and so were more likely to become paupers (Thane 1978) – a situation in which behaviour considered unacceptable and inappropriate (and consequently 'unreasonable'), such as having an illegitimate child, could well bring them to the attention of the authorities and make a stay in the workhouse or asylum seem like a suitable remedy. Women were, as a result, liable to end up in pauper institutions, whether the workhouse or the public asylum.

Women's greater economic dependence may also have been one reason why, if we look not at admissions but at residence data, there were, as Showalter (1987: 17) notes, overall more women than men in public asylums. Another important factor, however, in public asylums as in the voluntary and private madhouses, was differential mortality. Mortality was higher in the public asylums than outside, and men's mortality in the asylums was higher than women's, just as it was outside (GPI was but one condition contributing directly to the higher male mortality in the public asylums).[9]

The gender imbalance in the asylum populations can be seen in Table 7.1 which gives the location of all known lunatics on January 1880.

TABLE 7.1   *Distribution of Lunatics at January 1880 by Type of Institution, Status of Patient, and Gender*

Institution	Private		Pauper		Total	
	Male	*Female*	*Male*	*Female*	*Male*	*Female*
Public asylums	211	273	17,903	21,701	18,114	21,914
Voluntary asylums	1,409	1,293	81	48	1,490	1,341
Private madhouses:						
(a) metropolitan	1,026	828	180	428	1,206	1,256
(b) provincial	745	809	247	286	992	1,095
Naval and						
military hospital	309	19	–	–	309	19
Broadmoor	180	50	188	65	368	115
Workhouses	–	–	5,126	6,865	5,126	6,865
Metropolitan						
District asylum	–	–	2,080	2,393	2,080	2,393
Private single						
patients	186	282	–	–	186	282
Outdoor paupers	–	–	2,293	3,687	2,293	3,687
Total	4,066	3,554	28,098	35,473	32,164	39,027

SOURCE   *34th Report of the Royal Commissioners in Lunacy*, 1880: 1.

The Table also shows that by 1880 public asylums confined more than half all known lunatics. We can see, too, the gender differences by type of institution that I have already noted, as well as the fact that Broadmoor, the only criminal lunatic asylum, had more men than women inmates. So too, not surprisingly, did the Naval and Military Hospital for lunatics.

Significantly, as in the twentieth century, the unmarried had a disproportionately high chance of admission to an institution compared with the married, not least because they were more likely to lack alternative means of support, and admission rates of unmarried men were typically higher than of unmarried women. Amongst the married, where admission rates were generally lower than amongst the single, women's admission rates were higher than men's (the current picture) for those under 35, but not at older ages. The data are presented in Table 7.2.

TABLE 7.2   *Admissions of Lunatics by Gender and Marital Status**

| Age | Marital status | | | | | | | | |
| | Single | | Married | | Widowed | | Total | |
	M	F	M	F	M	F	M	F
Under 15	0.3	0.2	0.3	0.2				
15–19	2.9	3.0	1.8	3.1			2.9	3.0
20–24	7.9	7.2	1.3	4.4			6.7	6.3
25–34	17.9	14.9	4.6	6.8	10.0	10.8	9.3	9.6
35–44	29.8	23.8	9.4	9.1	17.3	14.0	12.8	11.9
45–55	28.0	27.0	10.2	9.9	17.7	14.4	12.7	12.2

* rates per 10,000 population

SOURCE   *53rd Report of the Commissioners in Lunacy*, 1899, Appendix A, Table XX

Outside the Asylum

The second half of the nineteenth century was a decisive period in the history of psychiatry. Inside the asylum the new breed of asylum doctors were emerging as a relatively strong professional grouping with their own claims to special expertise. There was an increasing focus on what went on within the brain (autopsy was becoming routine), on the importance of heredity, on the value of classifications and an extension of the boundaries of the groups considered suitable for asylum care. Moreover, outside the asylum there were also major developments in professional practice with the construction of new disease categories and new forms of treatment – developments influenced by the changing position of middle-class women who were increasingly expected to concentrate their lives on their families. These changes were crucial to the character of the twentieth-century mental health services, particularly to the emergence of the psycho-neuroses and the provision of a broader range of services for less severe disorders where women are over-represented.

In the second half of the nineteenth century outside the asylum the troubled in mind faced a fragmented, diverse, stratified array of provision from different healers, few of whom specialised in the treatment of mental problems, just as they had in the seventeenth century. The more affluent might seek help from private doctors specialising in mental disorder, who often held honorary posts in the voluntary asylums and were sometimes also proprietors of private madhouses.[10] Far more might take their mental problems to some general doctor or healer, just as they had to Richard Napier in the seventeenth century. The evidence suggests there were still more women than men consulting with a range of more minor mental and nervous complaints in this period, although nervous disorders were not exclusive to women and were quite commonly identified in men (Oppenheim 1991: Chapter 5).

The flow of individuals with mental problems which either they or others around them found disturbing provided, for some, a relatively lucrative basis for private practice, and alienists, neurologists and other doctors competed for patients who could afford to pay for their services. It was in this competitive market that some doctors specialising in mental and nervous problems developed new theorisations and concepts of mental disorder, and new treatments which specifically related to the less severe problems. For instance, the term neurasthenia was introduced by G.M. Beard in the United States in 1869 to cover a very ill-defined set of symptoms – a form of nervous exhaustion – and the term anorexia nervosa was first used in Europe in the 1870s. Whilst anorexia nervosa was from the first particularly associated with women, neurasthenia, which was viewed as a disease of civilisation – the results of technological developments and rapid change – was initially associated with upper-class men, only gradually taking on a more female image (presumably because it was a convenient label for the diffuse mental complaints women brought to medical attention). Hysteria, too, was a common diagnosis in this period, already well-established as a disease of psychogenic origin. It was especially associated with women (although there was some discussion of male hysteria), and it was still commonly counterpoised to male hypochondriasis.

The treatments offered by the diverse groups of healers were themselves varied. Hypnosis (a term coined in 1843 as an alternative to 'mesmerism') had first been introduced towards the end of the eighteenth century. The practice was rejected by many doctors, but was widely used within and outside official medicine. Various forms of electrical treatment directed to parts of the body other than the brain were also commonly used and some new treatments were developed. One fashionable treatment was the so-called rest-cure developed in the United States by S. Weir Mitchell for soldiers suffering from battle fatigue after the Civil War. However, it was soon used more widely and Weir Mitchell thought it an admirable antidote to the more heroic interventions (which included clitoridectomy on women), and preferable to the excessive use of drugs. There is no doubt that some treatments were harsh and others, while apparently more humane, could be used in quite a punitive fashion (feminist writers have documented the repressive use of the rest-cure on some women patients (see, for instance, Wood 1974)).[11] Moreover, whether used punitively or not, the danger of the use of the rest-cure was that it encouraged passivity and invalidity and so reinforced and helped to sustain women's exclusion from public life.

It was the terrain of less severe mental disorders, many associated with women, on which Freudian ideas had such an impact. Freud's decision to enter private practice in Vienna (see Freud 1935) in order to make a living (he was keen to get married), brought him into contact with these milder mental problems and a disproportionate number of women patients. Whilst the type of problems with which he dealt with were hardly new, he, like other medical men, introduced new concepts that helped to transform the formal psychiatric lexicon. Crucial in this transformation was the introduction of a contrast between psychoses ('madness' proper, dealt with in the asylum) and what he termed the psycho-neuroses. Psycho-neuroses were, he claimed, disorders of psychological origin and it was these to which he gave almost all his attention (in line with the demands of his practice). The resultant set of ideas and practices he developed, psychoanalysis, provided not only a new framework for thinking about less severe mental problems, but also a new form of treatment (the so-called 'talking' cure). And since psychoanalytic theory emphasised the continuity between normal and abnormal psychological processes, it helped to broaden the terrain of problems considered suitable for professional intervention, whether grounded in psychoanalytic ideas or not. Indeed, psychoanalytic ideas also helped to contribute to a new proliferation of mental health professionals, which has become especially marked with the development of community care – professionals whose expertise is often partly grounded in a range of psychodynamic ideas and therapies – psychoanalysts, psychiatric social workers, psychologists and psychiatric nurses.

The female predominance in patients with more minor mental problems dealt with outside the framework of institutional care, which was visible in the closing decades of the nineteenth and the early decades of the twentieth century, is of considerable interest. It echoes, of course, the gender imbalance at the beginning of the seventeenth century noted by MacDonald, and so cannot simply be attributed to the impact of the activities of healers seeking a basis for building a successful (both socially and materially) private practice or to changes in the position of middle-class women. What the professionals did in this period was to transform into a medical language and medical images, problems long recognised in lay thinking and give them a new life and new identity. In this respect they broadened the formal territory of diseases of the mind and helped to make them appropriate objects of medical attention for a broader group of persons.

The gender imbalance in these 'milder' mental health problems which, even in the seventeenth century, might be brought to the attention of some healer or cleric if their services could be obtained, has to be tied as in the seventeenth century to three factors: first, to gender differences in the expression of problems which may have been enhanced by nineteenth-century ideas about ladyhood and women's nature (see Chapter 8); second, to the differential tendencies to view men's and women's problems as casting doubt on their mental functioning and to deny agency, especially in relation to feeling and emotion – tendencies which exist independently of medical activities and practices but which again were almost certainly strengthened by nineteenth century ideas about women; and third, to gender differences in the types of problems and difficulties experienced. Here again the fact that the end of the nineteenth-century was a period in which gender divisions were particularly heightened may have helped to reinforce the association between women and the less severe mental problems, especially amongst women of the middle and upper social classes.

Community Care

The twentieth century has witnessed a number of key developments in ideas and practice of especial relevance to the gender balance of patient populations. In the first place, the range of services has expanded, with a greater emphasis on services for those with less severe problems, including some publicly funded services. Second and related to this, there has been a major shift away from the large-scale nineteenth-century asylum, even for those with more severe psychiatric problems, and the introduction of policies of community care. Third, with the decline of the asylum the professional dominance of psychiatrists has diminished somewhat, a decline heightened by the proliferation of other mental health professionals. All these changes have brought female mental disorders like depression and anxiety to the forefront, although recent cut-backs in public services may begin to reverse this trend. These changes need to be examined in some detail.

During the first decades of the twentieth century, the character of public asylums changed little. Proposals to transform them into more medical, therapeutic institutions using various strategies designed to encourage early, and it was assumed more effective, treatment did not get the necessary legislative support (one proposal was for the introduction of voluntary admission) and the numbers confined continued to increase. In Britain it was only in the 1930s, following the breakdown of the poor law system and the acceptance of a more expansionary role for state welfare, that the legislative changes to permit voluntary admission and state-funded out-patient clinics were secured (changes which arguably in turn encouraged more active therapeutic regimes within the newly renamed mental hospitals: see, for example, Unsworth 1987; Busfield 1989a: 333).

Another factor encouraging acceptance of policies of voluntary admission and the development of out-patient clinics was the high level of psychological breakdowns amongst soldiers in the First World War. Shell-shock and war neuroses (see Chapter 11 below) amongst officers as well as privates during the war and after, did not seem to merit the opprobrium of compulsory detention or the pauperisation usually necessary for admission to a public asylum. And since the evidence suggested that conditions like shell-shock had a psychogenic rather than a physical origin, they facilitated the spread of Freudian ideas with their emphasis on the psycho-neuroses. In consequence, publicly funded services that would cater for the neuroses as well as the psychoses came to seem increasingly necessary. In Britain the number of psychiatric out-patient clinics increased rapidly during the first half of the century and, following the 1930 Mental Treatment Act, so did the number of voluntary admissions.

In the event, however, it was women more than men who were increasingly brought into the psychiatric fold. For, with the transformation of service provision, came a transformation in the social character of the patient population including its gender balance. Above all, the changes introduced a range of common nervous complaints, not just shell-shock but also anxieties, phobias and depression, into everyday specialist practice for people from a broader range of backgrounds. And increasing attention to these conditions, now given official psychiatric labels, brought a greater gender imbalance. For, like hysteria which they largely replaced, although not exclusively female, they were usually predominantly female diagnoses. In the mental hospitals themselves new patient populations began to be visible amongst those admitted on a voluntary basis. It was not so much that persons with psychoses and dementia were admitted earlier in the development of their disorder as had been envisaged, but that persons with diagnoses falling in the psycho-neurotic range were increasingly admitted. And this was even more true of the new out-patient clinics than of the asylums.

Yet, despite these major changes in the first half of this century, in many respects the custodial character of the old asylums changed very little. Naming them mental hospitals and admitting new groups of patients to acute units did not deal with the problem of the long-stay wards. The new therapeutic developments of the 1930s − ECT, psycho-surgery, insulin therapy − might in theory help to prevent chronicity, but only habit training was designed specifically to rehabilitate the long-stay patients.

It was in this context that the policy of community care was developed and introduced − a policy which was in effect formally accepted in Britain with the Report of the Royal Commission on Mental Illness and Mental Deficiency, published in 1957. Community care, as initially envisaged, aimed to develop services such as halfway houses and training centres outside the mental hospital, primarily for those with long-term problems usually with diagnoses of psychoses who either no longer needed active *medical* care or whose symptoms could be controlled by the drugs developed in the 1950s and subsequently. These services were still to be publicly funded and it was the cost of alternative provisions that hampered the implementation of community care in the 1960s and 1970s.

However, although the policy of community care when introduced had a relatively narrow meaning (rehabilitative, after-care service for those with chronic problems who should be encouraged to leave the hospital), the concept itself was highly imprecise. The term was commonly defined merely negatively, as any care that did not involve residence in a large institution. Consequently, any services for those with mental health problems provided outside the mental hospital could potentially fall within its orbit – including special psychiatric units attached to general hospitals, residential care in smaller institutions, primary care provided by GPs, as well as community mental health centres (CMHCs) – whatever the severity and chronicity of the problem and whether publicly or privately funded. Indeed, the term does not require that there be any professional service at all, and informal care by family and friends, let alone homelessness and neglect, can all fall within the framework of community care. This ambiguity about what exactly is meant by community care has allowed a major shift in its meaning to occur since the beginning of the 1980s. Cost-cutting and ideologies of privatisation have ensured that instead of new public services it is private care – whether commercial or that provided by family and friends – that is continually emphasised.

The impact of policies of community care for those with mental health problems on patient populations has largely confirmed the patterns that were already developing in the 1930s and 1940s. Since 1954 the in-patient population of mental hospitals in Britain has declined markedly (as it also has in the US: see Scull 1984). In practice the long-stay inmate population have been subject less to a process of deinstitutionalisation than to one of transinstitutionalisation (see Brown 1985:91), often ending up in boarding-houses, nursing homes, homes for the elderly, or even prisons, as well as a few purpose-built facilities. In the US the process of 'decarceration' (Scull 1984) was especially rapid, and many of the elderly (often women) were discharged from mental hospitals. The result was that groups with diagnoses of alcoholism and drug addiction (mainly men) became proportionately more important in the state mental hospitals with obvious implications for the gender balance of patient population. In consequence, the gender balance of psychiatric residents in the US mental hospitals also changed in the postwar period. Whereas in the mid-1950s there were somewhat more female than male admissions to state and county mental hospitals, by the 1970s there were more male admissions, a situation that has continued since then (President's Commission on Mental Health, 1978: 100; National Institute of Mental Health 1987: 77).

In Britain the reduction in overall numbers in psychiatric beds as part of the policy of community care was initially rather less marked and less rapid than in the US, and even in the 1980s, when the numbers declined more rapidly, the elderly still constituted a very major in-patient group. Nonetheless, patients with diagnoses such as alcoholism and drug addiction played a proportionately larger part in the spectrum of disorders dealt with by the mental health services in the 1980s than the 1950s, and the psycho-neuroses (excluding neurotic depression), were quantitatively less important (such patients were less likely to be admitted to a psychiatric bed). Table 7.3 provides data on some of the diagnoses assigned to persons admitted to psychiatric beds in England in 1970, 1976 and 1986 and shows significant changes even in this relatively short period of time.

Many of the services that fall under the umbrella term of community care, deal in practice not with those with chronic difficulties requiring

TABLE 7.3   *Admissions by Selective Diagnostic Group, percentages, England*

Diagnostic group	1970 %	1976 %	1986* %
Affective psychoses	14.2	13.0	12.5
Senile dementia	6.0	5.7	10.6
Neurotic disorders	13.7	12.5	7.7
Alcohol dependence	3.5	5.8	7.8
Personality and behaviour disorders	9.3	10.4	7.2
All diagnoses	100	100	100

* Data for 1970 and 1976 are based on the 8th Revision of the International Classification of Diseases, data for 1986 are based on the 9th Revision, so comparisons must be treated with caution.

SOURCE   *In-patient Statistics from the Mental Health Enquiry for England 1976*, Table A2.1; 1986, Booklet 12, Table A1.1

residential care but with the less severe mental health problems that now play such an important part in the psychiatric spectrum. Community mental health centres have provided an important model for service provision for these groups. First developed with federal support in the US in the 1960s, they offered limited in-patient care for acute cases, as well as emergency, drop-in and out-patient services, employing a range of mental health professionals; but some began to founder in the 1970s when federal funding was cut back (see Brown 1985: Chapter 3). Translated to the British context in the 1980s, they provided only out-patient, drop-in and emergency facilities, and in both countries have tended to provide for new patient populations with the less severe problems (ibid: 64; Sayce et al. 1991) – persons now too often dismissively described as the 'worried well'.[13] Such clients, often with problems of anxiety and depression, are more likely than the residents of mental hospitals to be middle class and to be women. However, the increasing commercialisation of state health services in Britain and the increasing resource constraints which are directing attention to the more severely disturbed, especially the most disruptive and dangerous, are already putting them under threat.[14]

Another important development now also affecting the gender balance of mental health patient populations, is the shifting division of labour between health and social services in Britain. The Griffiths Report's (Department of Social Security 1988) recommendation that social service departments should be the lead agencies in developing community care packages for individuals, which was eventually accepted by the Government, is contributing to a process in which the boundaries between health and social problems, and between health and social care, are being realigned. What was once seen as a health matter is now seen as a matter for social services. Such a shift may be desirable; however, a key problem is the lack of co-ordination between different welfare agencies.[15] Given the way in which local authority services are structured, and the difficulty of securing state benefits, the move to social services does not, for instance, ensure that adequate housing will be provided.

We can see, therefore, that twentieth-century developments in service provision, especially the expansion of non-residential forms of psychiatric service and the greater access to primary care, have been linked with, and have helped to shape, changes in the way in which the boundaries of mental disorder are set and the gender balance of patients with diagnosed mental disorders. That a female predominance should also be manifest in community surveys, which were almost entirely developed after the Second World War is not, therefore, surprising, since as I argued in Chapter 5, many of the screening instruments employed in community surveys primarily measure symptoms of the more 'minor' psychiatric disorders that are now very common diagnoses in primary and out-patient care.

Conclusion

This history of mental health services in Britain and the examination of its implications for psychiatric patient populations has necessarily been brief. Nevertheless, I hope it is sufficient to demonstrate the complex processes underpinning the gender balance of patient populations. The shifting terrain of mental disorder is shaped by a range of forces. On the one hand, there are lay judgements of what is problematic mental functioning, which involve attributions of irrationality often occasioned by disruptive difficult, dangerous or disturbing behaviour, attributions which are themselves affected by factors such as gender, class and ethnicity, by the distribution of power, and by the social and cultural preoccupations of society at a particular moment in time. On the other hand, there are the range of institutions, most particularly the mental health services, which have been developed to cater for mental health problems. These, by means of the activities of professionals, provide the intellectual categories through which we now apprehend mental disorder; they also structure the flow of patients including their gender balance. Such institutions are not, however, merely the product of the activities of professionals, although professionals may benefit from them and may try to ensure they support their own interests. The institutions have also emerged as mechanisms, shaped by policy makers, the interests and ideas of government, and other powerful groups, to deal with the problems presented to individuals or to groups by forms of 'unreason', in societies that have always been stratified in diverse ways and where power is not distributed evenly. The way in which such forces operated in the case of one disorder, shell-shock, are explored in Chapter 11.

It is necessary, however, to shift the focus of the argument. Up until now I have focused primarily on categories of mental disorder and on mental health services. We need now to examine the intersection of gender with the processes of *becoming* mentally disturbed as it is defined at specific times and places. To what extent does gender impinge on these processes. Are women biologically more vulnerable to the psychological processes we term mental disorder as has frequently been argued? Does women's oppression drive them mad? In the chapters that follow I examine these questions further.

Part II

Gender and the Origins of Mental Disorder

Chapter 8

Biological Origins

> The monthly activity of the ovaries which marks the advent of puberty in women has a notable effect upon the mind and body; wherefore it may become an important cause of mental and physical derangement. Most women at that time are susceptible, irritable and capricious, any cause of vexation affecting them more seriously than usual; and some who have the insane neurosis exhibit a disturbance of mind which amounts almost to disease. A sudden suppression of the menses has produced a direct explosion of insanity, or occurring some time before an outbreak it may be an important link in its causation (Henry Maudsley, *Body and Mind*, 1873).

The theories and ideas of psychiatrists and other mental health professionals about the origins of mental disorder exert a profound influence. Most obviously, they directly influence and legitimate patterns of treatment. There is, of course, no necessary symmetry between professionals' ideas about causation and their decisions about treatment. A GP may believe, for example, that a woman is depressed because of her husband's intolerable behaviour, yet still prescribe some psychotropic medicine as a remedy. There can be various reasons for discrepancies like this, including the therapeutic knowledge and skills of the practitioner, the costs of different treatments, assumptions about their relative efficacy, and so forth. Nonetheless, a symmetry between ideas about causation and treatment practices is quite common, not least because the two often develop in reciprocal relation (the development of psychoanalytic theory and psychoanalysis as treatment is a clear example). Certainly psychiatrists' frequent emphasis on the physical causes of mental disorder parallels their widespread prescription of psychotropic medication.

However, from a sociological perspective, this way of thinking about the importance of professionals' ideas concerning the origins of mental disorder is too restricted. On the one hand, professionals' theories help to shape the whole way in which society interprets and responds to mental disorder; indeed they structure the very meaning of the concept itself. For instance, as we saw in Chapter 4, an emphasis on the physical origins of mental disorders tends to lead to an assimilation of mental disorders to models of physical illness, whereas an emphasis on their psychological origins locates the problem more at the level of mind than body and is less conducive to such assimilation. In either case, mental disorder tends to be seen as a problem of individual pathology. In contrast, if an emphasis is given to the social origins of mental disorder there is a greater willingness to identify the problem, whether it is seen as of mind or behaviour, not as one to be analysed in terms of the individual but of the wider society. Moreover, professionals' theories also shape ideas about the social groups with whom mental disorders are associated. Claims, for example, that women are biologically predisposed to higher levels of mental disorder help to construct images of women as weak and vulnerable and have been used to legitimate their exclusion from paid employment and public life. Indeed, one of the contributions of feminism has been to document the way in which any differences between men and women's behaviour are frequently attributed to biology.

On the other hand, professionals' ideas about the origins of mental disorder need to be viewed through the prism of ideology and social interest, and should not be treated merely as a matter of detached, value-neutral science. We need to be aware of the professional interests and professional struggles that shape the direction of scientific attention. Consequently, just as the boundaries of mental disorder are contested and cannot be established objectively, and depend on historical struggles, often between different groups of professionals as well as policy makers, so ideas about the origins of medically defined mental disorders are contested, and competing claims cannot be settled entirely by resort to the facts. This is because what we count as a satisfactory explanation, what we count as *the* cause of a disorder depends on our objectives and our interests (see Hart and Honoré 1959; Busfield 1989a: 108–10). It is undoubtedly the case that there are some biochemical correlates of states of depression which are necessary conditions for those states. Whether we regard these correlates as *the* causes of the disorder, depends not only on the adequacy of empirical studies in establishing the correlations, but also on whether we deem the existence of these correlates a satisfactory stopping point in the explanatory quest. For those, like doctors, whose skills and expertise are largely grounded in the natural sciences and whose focus is on the body, they may well be. For many, however, they are not and tell only a very partial (if not inaccurate) story.

My argument here that science is not value-neutral, and that contests between different disciplinary experts cannot be settled simply by resort to the facts, although facts will often be very germane, is founded on the observations of philosophers and sociologists of science that scientific knowledge is socially situated (see Harding 1991: 80–1; 96–7) and far from value-free, whatever its claims to the contrary. It is the product of socially located actors with their own values and interests which shape the selection of problems to study, the approaches adopted, the methods employed and the criteria of what constitutes science (as well as its claims to value-neutrality, objectivity and impartiality). What is needed is an approach, or a set of approaches, in which the social conditions of knowledge production are made explicit, a process essential to Harding's 'strong objectivity' (ibid: 149–52). The result of adopting such a stance will not be the abandonment of all claims to good science, but the generation of better science.

In this chapter, I want to begin my examination of ideas about the impact of gender on the origins of mental disorder as it is constituted according to time and place, by considering both general claims as to the biological origins of mental disorders and more specific claims as to the biological origins of gender differences in the landscape of reported disorder. Many of the claims that have been made about the biological basis of gender difference, especially nineteenth-century ideas, have been subject to detailed and systematic criticism by feminists as 'bad science' (ibid: 54–8) and as permeated by sexism. We need, therefore, to consider to what extent sexism is still pervasive in professional thinking about the causes of mental disorder.

The weight attached to biology in understanding the origins of mental disorder, as well as the precise character of biological theorising, has varied over time, between societies, and in relation to different types of disorder. Moreover, commentators do not always agree in their assessments of its importance in professional thought at a particular historical moment and may also disagree as to the weight particular writers themselves attach to biology, as the debate about Freudian theorising attests. Analysts of twentieth-century medical thought have, perhaps rather too readily, tended to see medicine as giving exclusive attention to the biological origins of mental disorder and as operating with a single model, frequently referred to in the literature as *the* medical model, in which mental disorder is assumed to have physical causes and to be amenable to physical treatments.[1] This ignores other major influences on psychiatric thinking such as psychoanalysis, and we need to be wary of any simple assumption that medical or psychiatric thought about mental disorder is exclusively biological – a point recognised by some writers who talk of bio-social or bio-psycho-social models of disorder (see Engel 1977, 1980; Roth and Kroll 1986: Chapter 5).[2] Yet the key, though fluctuating role, played by biological thinking in psychiatry cannot be doubted.

The emphasis on biological factors has arguably been even greater in thinking about gender differences in mental disorder than in theorising about mental disorder more generally. It is here that we find the striking tendency to see the female as biologically inferior. What we observe is a set of assumptions not just about biological difference, but about the biological weakness and vulnerability of the female, with a typical gender asymmetry: the supposedly general account of human biological functioning is assumed to apply to the male but not to the female who is held to require special consideration. In this way, the male is positioned as normal, the female as some deviation. One consequence is that the specific attention given to female biology by some authors is not matched by any analysis of what might be distinctive to male biology. This asymmetrical shaping, with the assumption of a biologically based female inferiority, can be seen very clearly if we look at nineteenth-century ideas about the origins of mental disorder. It would be hard for any present-day writer to claim there was much in the way of scientific objectivity in these ideas and that sexism had no place. Consideration of such ideas might seem only of scholarly interest were it not for the striking parallels with current formulations.

Nineteenth-Century Ideas

Teasing out the influence of biological thinking on ideas about insanity in the nineteenth century is not easy. Andrew Scull for one, contends that in the first half of the nineteenth century there was a growing acceptance of somatic interpretations of insanity, grounded in assumptions about the link between the brain and mental functioning. Mental pathology, it was increasingly argued, necessarily involved brain pathology as these claims illustrate: 'Madness has always been connected with disease of the brain and its membranes'; 'Insanity may be defined as "Disordered" function of the brain generally'; 'Insanity has been considered in all cases, to be a disease of the brain' (quoted in Scull 1974: 251–2) Yet this equation between madness and brain disease, which at one level asserted a physical causation for madness and its character as a physical illness, was not considered the end of the aetiological search. Factors in the individual's environment were also held to contribute to the development or madness in conjunction with an individual's constitution (heredity). Consequently, two divisions cross-cut discussions of the causes of insanity. On the one hand, there was the heredity-environment contrast. On the other, lists of the causes of insanity were frequently divided into moral and physical, a rather different division since physical causes, such as accident or injury, might be environmental rather than the result of heredity.[3] Moral causes embraced environmental factors, such as business anxieties and family and domestic troubles, but these were juxtaposed to all types of physical causes whether arising from the environment or heredity.

The environmentalism in ideas about causation, which was especially influential in the first half of the nineteenth century, underpinned the strong environmentalism of the principles of moral treatment fashionable during the period (Rothman 1971: 128–9; Busfield 1989a: Chapter 6). Yet, despite this environmentalism, some viewed moral causes as only 'exciting' causes – that is, occurrences that occasioned madness at a particular moment in time, with the suggestion that individuals were constitutionally predisposed to madness and the environmental cause was only a precipitant. This bias towards heredity, especially visible in some writings in the second half of the nineteenth century, seems at times to have been linked to a desire to absolve the individuals or community from blame for the problems in question. Samuel Tuke, discussing the causes of lunacy in his influential account of the care provided at the Quaker asylum in York, 'The Retreat', which became the standard bearer of moral treatment, commented:

> It will, I trust, be readily admitted, that the habits and principles of the Society of Friends, are at least not more unfriendly to mental sanity, than those of other societies; and this opinion will derive some confirmation, from observing the large number of cases, in which the disease has been ascertained to be constitutional or hereditary (1813: 211–2).

There seems little doubt, however, that as the nineteenth century progressed the emphasis on biology in medical thinking increased (Clark 1981). On the one hand, the search for pathological lesions of the brain associated with mental disorders intensified – a search encouraged by new work in anatomy and pathology (Foucault 1973) and by the differentiation of general paresis of the insane, which in the 1820s was shown to be related to brain lesions. On the other hand, there was growing emphasis on the importance of heredity. In France this was particularly associated from the late 1850s onwards with the work of Auguste Morel and his ideas about degeneration. Using a Lamarckian framework that assumed acquired characteristics could be transmitted between generations by heredity, Morel argued that the undesirable habits and customs of one generation would be passed on to the next: mental disorders were the mere manifestation of the underlying pathological substratum of degeneration (Harris 1989: 55). Consequently, whilst the environment was important, pathology had a somatic base and was biologically transmitted between generations.

In Britain, Henry Maudsley, a key figure in psychiatry in the second half of the nineteenth century, who was influenced by Morel's ideas about degeneration, viewed heredity as a major cause of mental disease:

> It would be scarcely an exaggeration to say that few persons go mad, save from physical causes, who do not show more or less plainly by their gait, manner, gestures, habits of thought, feeling and action, that they have some sort of predestination to madness. The inherited liability may be strong or weak; it may be so weak as hardly to peril sanity amidst the most adverse circumstances of life, or so strong as to issue in an outbreak of madness amidst the most favourable external circumstances (Maudsley quoted in Skultans 1975:213).

'Circumstances of life' were of some importance if there was only a weak morbid predisposition. So too was human will – a concept very closely related to what I have called agency. A weak will made madness more likely: 'Suicide or madness is the natural end of a morbidly sensitive nature, with a feeble will, unable to contend with the hard experiences of life' (ibid: 211) – an assumption highly pertinent, as I have already indicated, to issues of gender.

In the nineteenth century gender differences in mental disorder were attributed almost entirely to biology, notwithstanding the environmentalism of the first half of the century, and the continuing belief in the second that difficult experiences and will-power had a part to play in the aetiology of insanity. This was but one facet of a general assumption that differences between men and women were a product of nature not culture. Part of being a woman was a tendency to problems of the nerves.

The constellation of nineteenth-century ideas about women's distinctive biological vulnerability and inferiority has been well documented by feminists since the 1970s, especially in relation to the US. The constellation portrays women as in the sway of their reproductive organs. A woman was 'driven by the tidal currents of her cyclical reproductive system, a cycle bounded by the pivotal crises of puberty and menopause and reinforced each month by her recurrent menstrual flow' (Smith-Rosenberg 1974: 24). Carol Smith-Rosenberg terms this the 'ovarian' model of female behaviour since the activities of the ovaries were held to account for the characteristics considered typical of women. An American physician in the 1850s asserted, for example, that the reproductive organs:

> exercise a controlling influence upon her entire system, and entail upon her many painful and dangerous diseases. They are the source of her peculiarities, the centre of her sympathies, and the seat of her diseases. Everything that is peculiar to her, springs from her sexual organisation (ibid: 24).

Ideas like this were not new, but the increasing knowledge of the physiology of the reproductive system facilitated more elaborate and convincing explanations of the impact of the reproductive organs on women. Women rather than being in control of themselves (having agency) were under the control of their biology.

In Britain and Europe, as in America, there was a similar emphasis on biology as the source of gender differences in character and behaviour in medical and scientific thinking. George Man Burrows, an English physician, noted in his *Commentaries on Insanity* (1828) that 'Every body of the least experience must be sensible of the influence of menstruation on the operations of the mind' (Skultans 1975: 224). He viewed the menopause as an especially problematic period, emphasising that it sapped energy:

> The critical period, as it is called, when menstruation ceases, is certainly a period favourable to the development of mental aberration. The whole economy of the constitution at that epoch again undergoes a revolution. The moral character, at the age when the menses naturally cease, is much

changed to what it was on their first access; and every care or anxiety produces a more depressing and permanent impression on the mind. There is neither so much vital nor mental energy to resist the effects of the various adverse circumstances which it is the lot of most to meet with in the interval between puberty and the critical period (ibid: 225).

Henry Maudsley, one of the most forthright proponents of such views, accepted George Man Burrows's belief that reproductive changes in women used up energy, both physical and mental. Consequently, he argued that women should avoid using too much energy on other activities in order to negotiate these changes successfully. This was the basis of his well-known attack on higher education for women which, he asserted, threatened their biological function of reproduction because it consumed mental energy:

> It will have to be considered whether women can scorn the delights, and live laborious days of intellectual exercise and production, without injury to their functions as the conceivers, mothers, and nurses of children (quoted in Sayers 1982: 8).

The underlying assumption was that women's mental energy was limited and was needed for reproductive tasks. Once puberty was reached a woman had to ensure the health of her reproductive organs and forego the demands of an intellectual life. Such ideas could, therefore, be readily used to confine women to their domestic roles and attack 'any behaviour considered unfeminine' (Smith-Rosenberg 1974: 27).

But were such arguments specific to women? Smith-Rosenberg contends they were. She argues that, whilst it was assumed that men had to experience developmental changes, these were thought to be less frequent in men and less difficult to negotiate. Indeed:

> The extent to which the reproductive organs held sway over woman's body had no parallel in the male. Male sexual impulses, nineteenth century physicians and laymen alike maintained, were subject to a man's will; they were impulses that particular men could at particular times choose to indulge or repress (ibid: 24).

Men had the power (the will) to control their bodies ¬ agency was assumed; women did not. Sally Shuttleworth in a recent survey of medical discourse in the mid-Victorian era makes a similar claim: 'While male health was believed to be based on self-control, woman's health depended on her very *inability* to control her body' (1990: 57). In women, unlike men, agency was not to be assumed.

Shuttleworth's argument makes a contrast between the assumed undesirability of retaining bodily fluids in the female and the desirability of so doing in the male. She contends that it was the suppression or cessation of menses (cf. Burrows above) that was especially problematic: 'The intensity of emotion associated with womanhood is directly aligned with the flow of bodily fluids; only if such "superabundance" is drained from the body can emotional tranquillity be preserved' (ibid: 57). In contrast, the parallel concern about the loss of semen in men reveals a very different model in which the need is to *retain* bodily fluids. Indeed, the uncontrolled loss of semen was given a medical label – spermatorrhoea. Anxieties about the loss of semen were also manifest in the prohibitions surrounding male masturbation. Excess masturbation, it was believed, could lead to insanity, and a special form of masturbatory insanity was identified. Vieda Skultans quotes a Scots physician's description of the effects of masturbation:

> that vice produces a group of symptoms which are quite characteristic, and easily recognized, and give to the cases a special natural history. The peculiar imbecility and shy habits of the very youthful victim, the suspicion and fear, and dread, and suicidal impulses, the palpitations and scared look, and feeble body of the older offenders, passing gradually into dementia or fatuity, with other characteristic features familiar to all of you, which I do not stop to enlarge on, all combine to stamp this as a natural order or family (1979: 73).

She suggests the chronic masturbator represented the antithesis of all the valued characteristics of the period. 'He is the polar opposite of nature's gentleman: the person who can get by on the strength of inner resourcefulness and outer accomplishments. He provides the prototype of uncontrolled and undisciplined behaviour' (ibid: 76).

However, we need to analyse the contrast in ideas about men's and women's relation to their bodies with some care and, in particular, to be aware of the complexities arising from the intermingling of ideas about gender, reproduction, bodily fluids, bodily and mental energy and will-power. The concern about male masturbation and the loss of semen assumed there was a limited quantity of semen, which as a form of bodily energy was not to be wasted or dissipated. An important objective was to ensure this bodily energy was used appropriately for reproductive purposes. However, although men's mental energy could be influenced by the unnecessary loss of semen, it was assumed that normally men had plenty of psychic energy (will-power) to avoid this. In contrast, whilst a woman's bodily fluids were assumed to be relatively unlimited, at least till the menopause, these fluids were not indicative of unlimited energy either bodily or mental. Rather than being the source of energy, women's reproductive changes – puberty, menstruation, childbirth and the menopause – were the consumers of energy, both physical and mental, that was assumed to be very limited and had to be conserved at all cost.

Women's biological inferiority lay, therefore, in their more limited energy (mental as well as bodily), and in the way in which reproduction consumed mental as well as physical energy. Above all it lay in the weakness of the female will (Oppenheim 1991: 181). As a result, women's reproductive functions held more sway over their lives than men's. Ironically, of course, though the decisive contrast was that men's will-power was assumed to be greater than women's, and their health more dependent on self-control than on the influence of their bodies, in practice self-control and will-power were routinely required of women – both in the curtailment of their activities to the domestic sphere, and to take another example, in relation to sexuality. Women were expected to show a high degree of control of their sexuality, whereas it was considered harder for men to control their own sexuality because of the strength of their sexual drives. Nonetheless, for all the requirements for self-control, women's will-power (agency) was, as noted in Chapter 6, less likely to be recognised and was assumed to be inferior. The ideology and the reality were markedly discrepant.

Twentieth-Century Ideas

What then of twentieth-century ideas? Are the same assumptions of women's biological inferiority and vulnerability present in twentieth-century theorising?

Biological thinking has been a dominant though not the sole strand in psychiatric thought and practice in the twentieth century. Its importance is linked to the power of the natural sciences in the intellectual foundations of medicine, which were strengthened in the nineteenth century, and is evidenced in the way in which biological explanations have had primacy within psychiatry. For example, the search for the causes of various forms of senile dementia, a condition agreed to have an organic base, rarely moves beyond trying to establish the physical causes that may be involved.

The importance attached to biology in the field of mental disorder is also visible in twentieth-century treatments: electro-convulsive therapy (ECT) and other shock therapies, psychosurgery, and most important of all, drugs. The use of a panoply of psychiatric medication is now routine, even in contexts where psychiatrists pride themselves on their therapeutic eclecticism and also use other forms of treatment and intervention (Samson 1995). The impact of such physical treatments on mental states, albeit that they usually control symptoms rather than providing a cure, has done much to legitimate and reinforce the search for biological causes – a process in which the drugs industry has played an active part.

However, biological ideas have undergone major transformations in the twentieth century. On the one hand, the development of genetics has provided an understanding of the mechanisms of hereditary transmission which has, amongst other things, led to the rejection of Lamarckian ideas about the transmission of acquired characteristics which were so central to Morel's and Maudsley's ideas about degeneration. On the other hand, there has been a shift from a search for structural lesions of the brain associated with mental disorder to the search for biochemical correlates. In both cases the search for explanations has been polarised, with the construction of mutually exclusive oppositions either between heredity and environment or between biogenesis and psychogenesis, or less frequently, between biogenesis and sociogenesis. Consequently, the debate about the role of heredity has often focused on attempts to quantify the precise contribution of heredity and environment to the aetiology of particular mental disorders. The value of these attempts has been questioned, not least because of the way in which human mental functioning and behaviour is dependent on the interaction of heredity and environment (Lewontin et al. 1984). It seems likely, however, that in the case of the more severe mental disorders such as schizophrenia, a hereditary predisposition does play some part in aetiology (Gottesman and Shields 1982; Gottesman 1990). There is also evidence of the role of genetic factors in some of the rarer forms of Alzheimer's disorder. With the less severe disorders some genetic loading seems possible, but its contribution is less significant.

The contrast between biogenesis and psycho- or socio-genesis is equally problematic. The opposition is usually a reflection of disciplinary and professional rivalries and interests, and all too frequently

ignores the extent to which biological, psychological and social explanations may complement one another rather than necessarily being
mutually exclusive alternatives. A mental state such as depression certainly has a physical base, but it also results from psychological and/or
social processes, just as lung cancer in someone who smokes heavily
may also have been made more likely by psychological and social
factors that not only encouraged heavy smoking, but also may have
had a direct interactive effect with the smoking. Work on the biochemistry of mental disorder has, however, not been especially successful to
date, part of the problem being the lack of consistency in the identification of cases. Early studies were also adversely affected by the fact that
the clinical samples were usually of persons living in institutional environments whose circumstances, such as diet, generated some of the biochemical differences between patient and control samples (Clare 1976:
192) However, these failures are not necessarily indicative of the potential success of future research, although the imprecision of diagnostic
boundaries should make us cautious about what we can expect. Nonetheless, there seems little doubt that we are likely to see considerable
advances in the field of the biochemistry of mental disorder, as of the
biochemistry of human mental life more generally.

Given the importance attached to biology within psychiatric thought
in particular, and the importance it is frequently given in accounts of
overall gender differences, it is not surprising to find that biology is frequently invoked to explain identified gender differences in the distribution of mental disorder, notwithstanding the high degree of variation in
these differences across time and place. As in the nineteenth century,
much of the emphasis in explaining the gendered landscape is on
reproductive differences between men and women, especially on geneti-
cally based hormonal differences. Instead of the impact of the womb or
ovaries through some imprecisely specified mechanism, it is women's
hormonal activity associated with puberty, menstruation, childbirth and
the menopause that are seen as central both to higher aggregate levels
of identified disorder and to the particular type of mental disorders in
women, especially the tendency to depression. The precise understanding of the impact of women's reproductive biology has, of course,
changed since the nineteenth century and the gross sexism reflected in
ideas of the period is less apparent, notably with regard to explicit
assumptions of biological inferiority. Nonetheless, on close inspection,
we find many ill-founded claims about the impact of women's reproductive biology on their states of mind, with relatively few comparable

arguments being made about men. It is, therefore, hard to escape the conclusion that women are still assumed, by virtue of a distinctive biology, to be more psychologically vulnerable than men.

In order to substantiate this argument I want to examine present-day ideas linking menstruation, childbirth and the menopause to mental disorder, since these are the biological processes still frequently claimed to have an adverse effect on women's mental health. I shall then examine contexts where men's biology is invoked to help account for mental disorder. I begin the discussion about the role of biology in explaining mental disorder in women with menstruation, potentially the most important of the three aspects of women's reproductive biology because of its frequency.

Pre-Menstrual Tension

In a fascinating analysis of the language used in scientific texts, Emily Martin (1987) has shown very effectively the way in which even in the twentieth century in Western societies negative cultural assumptions about menstruation permeate supposedly neutral and objective descriptions of menstruation. Menstruation, she suggests, is viewed teleologically in terms of a purpose (childbearing) that has failed – and is construed as a failure of production. The language is of degeneration, dissolution and loss, a language that contrasts markedly with the positive images of male reproductive physiology as well as with the descriptions of equivalent processes elsewhere in the body, which are viewed as processes of renewal not degeneration. Martin also analyses the general cultural view of menstruation as dirty and embarrassing and something that must be dealt with outside the public view (ibid: Chapter 6).

These negative, pathologising tendencies in the constructions of menstruation, which have an impact on the way women deal with and experience the process, have been further enhanced with the introduction and increasing use of the concepts of pre-menstrual tension (PMT) and pre-menstrual syndrome (PMS). These concepts not only extend the length of the problematic period of the menstrual cycle (the days before menstruation as well as of menstruation itself), but also extend the pathologising tendencies from body to mind. They bring the menstrual cycle squarely into the realms of psychiatry and mental health.

The term pre-menstrual tension was first introduced in the 1930s (Frank 1931; Israel 1938) to characterise tension occurring in the days prior to menstruation. According to Frank, while 'normal' women may suffer some discomfort during this period, including 'increased fatigability, irritability, lack of concentration and attacks of pain' (1931: 1053), others experience much more severe pain, and some suffer 'grave systemic disorders' including epileptic attacks, severe asthmatic attacks and hystero-epileptic attacks. Frank's own discussion of 'cases' concentrates on the latter group, and at this stage PMT is arguably presented as more of a physical than psychological disorder. Frank does talk of this group of patients suffering 'indescribable tension from ten to seven days preceding menstruation', a suffering that 'manifests itself in many reckless and sometimes reprehensible actions' (ibid: 1054), but his focus is more on physical than psychological manifestations and he puts the condition down to an excess accumulation of the female sex hormone.[4] He also recommends physical treatment.

It was Katherina Dalton, a British doctor, whose book *The Pre-menstrual Syndrome* was published in 1964, who did much to popularise the condition and constitute it as more of a mental than a physical disorder. Dalton had already written a number of articles linking menstruation with crime, accidents and psychiatric disorder and whilst, like Frank, she asserted the hormonal causes (progesterone) of PMS and the need for hormonal treatments, her focus was far more on psychological than physical symptoms.

The status of PMT and PMS as psychiatric rather than physical disorders (neither Frank nor Dalton were psychiatrists) has been officially established only quite recently. It was included in the DSM-III-R under the label 'late luteal phase dysphoric disorder' (American Psychiatric Association 1987) and in the DSM-IV has the marginally less cumbersome title of 'premenstrual dysphoric disorder' (American Psychiatric Association 1994). Because of controversies over the disorder, including strong criticism from feminists, it is to be found only in the Appendices of the DSM-III-R and DSM-IV as a diagnostic category needing further study, although significantly it does have a DSM code number.[5] The DSM-III-R manual noted that, whilst advisory committees felt that there was sufficient research and clinical evidence regarding the validity of this and one or two other categories 'to justify their inclusion', critics 'believed that not only was adequate evidence of the validity lacking but these categories had such a high potential for misuse, particularly against women, that they should not be included' (American Psychiatric Association 1987: xxv–xxvi). The condition does not, however, yet feature in the ICD classification of mental disorders, even though the latest revision (1992) postdates the DSM-III-R. The inclusion in the DSM of pre-menstrual disorder resulted from a successful battle by the American psychiatric establishment on a number of fronts, including a battle with gynaecologists over whether it should be viewed as a physical or mental disorder (Figert 1992). Equally important were debates about the scientific status of the concept itself. Here its lack of precision and the contradictory nature of the empirical data present considerable problems.

The imprecision of the category of 'premenstrual dysphoric disorder' can be seen if we look at its symptoms. The DSM-IV lists eleven:

> (1) feeling sad, hopeless, or self-deprecating; (2) feeling tense, anxious or 'on edge'; (3) marked lability of mood interspersed with frequent tearfulness; (4) persistent irritability, anger and increased interpersonal conflicts; (5) decreased interest in usual activities, which may be associated with withdrawal from social relationships; (6) difficulty concentrating; (7) feeling fatigued, lethargic, or lacking in energy; (8) marked changes in appetite, which may be associated with binge eating or craving certain foods; (9) hypersomina or insomnia; (10) a subjective feeling of being overwhelmed or out of control; and (11) physical symptoms such as breast tenderness or swelling, headaches or sensations of 'bloating' or weight gain, with tightness of fit of clothing, shoes, or rings. There may also be joint or muscle pain. The symptoms may be accompanied by suicidal thoughts (American Psychiatric Association, 1994: 715).

The vagueness and lack of specificity of these symptoms, which echo the catch-all nineteenth-century construct of neurasthenia, are all too apparent. What we have is simply a list of the different ways in which a person may feel got down, miserable or, one might say, oppressed. The DSM-IV attempts to introduce more precision by adding that for a diagnosis to be made at least five of the list of symptoms must have been present for most of the time during the last week of the luteal phase, including at least one of the first four symptoms; that they must have occurred during most menstrual cycles in the previous year; and that they must be absent during the week following menses. But these qualifications do not add much specificity to this diverse, eclectic set of symptoms. Arguably specificity comes from the linkage between the symptoms and the pre-menstrual period. However, the linkage between the supposed symptoms and this phase of the menstrual cycle is not well-established empirically. Although quite a high proportion of women do claim changes in mood and behaviour in relation to the menstrual cycle, more direct measures of mood and behaviour do not provide clear support for their patterning in relation to phases of the cycle (Weissman and Klerman 1977; Laws et al. 1985:40–3). The problem is that *any* changes in women's mood and behaviour may easily be 'read' both by the woman herself and by others as due to the bodily changes associated with the menstrual cycle. And regrettably the empirical studies which sustain such interpretations are often inadequate including, for instance, only negative feelings, relying on retrospective reports and failing to study comparable samples of men (Tavris 1992: Chapter 4).[6]

This is not to deny that some women do experience changes in mood as a result of hormonal changes associated with menstruation: 'But the *content* of these moods and wishes often depends on a woman's attitudes, expectations, situation, personal history and immediate problems and concerns' (ibid). Nor is it to deny that pain, tension and discomfort occur during the pre-menstrual period for some women (though many more women experience pain during menstruation itself). Such experiences help to account for the welcome some women have given the concepts of PMT and PMS. Their use in one or two well-publicised court cases in the 1980s indicate some of the possible attractions to some women as *ex post facto* constructions of disturbed and difficult behaviour which can be blamed on the 'time of the month' (now not the period of menstruation, but the period prior to it). However, as an explanation of criminal activity in women they are over-powerful and do not fit well with the fact that crime is far more common in men than women. The potential gains in pleading mental disorder for a relatively small number of women are far outweighed by the potentially wide-ranging pathologising of women's mental life that is involved on the basis of insubstantial evidence.

It is hard to avoid the conclusion that the construction of pre-menstrual syndrome as a psychiatric disorder is evidence of the willingness to see women as moody and irrational, as governed by their bodies, and to deny their agency. What is striking, moreover, is that the inclusion of pre-menstrual disorder in the DSM, fractures the usual principles (see Chapter 6) of universality and symptomatological classification of official constructions of psychiatric categories.[7]

Pregnancy and Childbirth

The idea of a link between pregnancy or childbirth and changes in mood and emotion is also an old one, both in lay and medical thinking. William Battie writing in his *A Treatise on Madness* (1758), commented: 'And it is moreover a repeated observation that Madness frequently succeeds or accompanies Fever, Epilepsy, Child-birth, and the like muscular disorders' (1962: 52–3). The concept of puerperal mania or puerperal insanity which gave formal expression to that linkage did not, however, emerge until early in the nineteenth century when the fevers associated with the puerperium were shown to be of an infectious nature and so could be distinguished from puerperal insanity, a condition where mental disturbance did not result from the fever of infection. The category was, however, imprecise and referred to any mental disorder occurring in the period from pregnancy to several years after confinement (Smith 1981: 151).

In view of the relative frequency of pregnancy in women of childbearing age, and of puerperal fever in the nineteenth century, it is perhaps not unexpected that puerperal insanity was quite a common diagnosis for female in-patients. A study by J. Batty Tuke (1865) of admissions to Edinburgh Royal Asylum over the period 1846 to 1864 found that puerperal insanity accounted for 7.1 per cent of all female admissions. Tuke followed other writers of the middle of the century in distinguishing three types of puerperal insanity: insanity of pregnancy; true puerperal insanity arising during the period of confinement; and insanity of lactation (often occurring after more than six months of nursing and indicative in Tuke's view of the dangers of prolonged lactation). Interestingly, he also noted that melancholia was a more typical symptom in the insanities of pregnancy and lactation than in true puerperal insanity (accounting for over half the cases in the former, but only about one in five of the latter (ibid: Tables I, II and III)).

In the nineteenth century the importance of puerperal insanity as a diagnostic category was tied to the way in which it was quite frequently invoked in cases of infanticide, which were far more common in countries like Britain and the US in the nineteenth than the twentieth century. Identifying a woman who had killed her child as mad helped to ensure she was not held responsible for her actions. Roger Smith, in his analysis of cases of infanticide, comments: 'Female criminal lunatics came nearest to enabling medical discourse to describe legally exculpatory conditions' (Smith 1981: 160). Like others he points to the way in which women were linked to nature adding: 'This reflected a shared assumption that woman was closer to nature than man; medical discourse was therefore more appropriate to women's lives' (ibid: 160).

During this century the construction of the relation between childbirth and mental disorder has changed considerably. In the first place,

the increasing focus on symptomatological classification (PMS notwithstanding) means that terms like puerperal insanity and its twentieth
century counterpart, puerperal or postpartum psychosis, are no longer
prominent in psychiatric nosologies. The mental states at issue have to
be classified syptomatologically as cases of depression, schizophrenia or
whatever, and childbirth noted as an aspect of aetiology rather than a
defining characteristic. Second, the focus has increasingly shifted
towards depression as one of the sequelae of childbirth and to a debate
as to whether the psychological effects associated with childbirth have
physiological or psychological origins, although 'puerperal psychosis'
remains as the twentieth-century equivalent of puerperal insanity.
However, it is relatively uncommon and of rather limited interest in
discussions of overall gender differences in mental disorder.

Some fearfulness and sudden mood changes following childbirth are
quite frequent in Western societies, though estimates as to just how
common vary considerably (Yalom et al. 1968). However, these 'baby
blues' (Oakley 1981: 125), which occur in the first few days after childbirth, are usually considered normal and are distinguished from postpartum depression which is more severe, though in many cases still
relatively short-lived. In some it is not. Oakley found that nearly a
quarter of her sample of 66 women having their first babies in the mid-
1970s experienced 'more enduring depressed feelings' (Oakley 1981:
143). Weissman and Klerman in their review of the evidence assert that
'there is overwhelming evidence that the longer postpartum period (up
to six months) carries an excess risk for more serious psychiatric disorders' (1977: 105), with an excess of manic-depressive psychosis quite
commonly reported. However, childbirth is an event associated with
major social and psychological changes, as well as changes in women's
hormones, and there is no decisive evidence to indicate that it is the
latter not the former that generate any depressed mood. Probably some
complex interaction between the social, psychological and biological is
involved in which hormonal changes generate an emotional sensitivity
whose exact content is shaped by a woman's social situation. However,
even if hormonal changes associated with childbirth do make depression (as well as happiness) more likely, this cannot account for the
major part of the higher levels of psychological distress reported by
women overall, not least because much of the depression diagnosed in
women or reported by them is not associated with childbearing. On the
one hand, changing rates of depression over time bear no relation to
changing levels of fertility. On the other hand, as the various postwar

surveys show, much of women's reported depression occurs outside the childbearing years and there is still a marked gender differential outside as well as during women's reproductive span. Clearly any depression associated with childbirth, even if it is in part caused by hormonal changes, cannot get us very far in accounting for the overall gender differences in reported depression.

The Menopause

Finally, what part if any is the menopause now held to play in contributing to mental disorder in women? Martin argues that, like menstruation itself, the menopause is viewed negatively within Western culture and that, even more than menstruation, medical texts associate it with degeneration and decay: 'ovaries cease to respond and fail to produce. Everywhere else there is regression, decline, atrophy, shrinkage, and disturbance' (1987: 43). The hormone oestrogen is viewed as central to this process and the menopause, a natural process occurring in all women, is constituted as an oestrogen-deficiency disease. The point according to Martin is not that the ovaries cease to produce oestrogen (which they do), but that this is viewed entirely negatively, rather than as a protective physiological function. It might be argued, *contra* Martin, that ageing processes are generally viewed in this negative way in medical texts, so that there is no particular gender bias here. However, while reproductive capacities in men do not cease, the production of sperm declines. Yet this is given little emphasis or negative construction in medical texts and is not regarded as equivalent to the menopause.

In view of the tendency to pathologise the menopause in Western societies, it is not perhaps surprising to find that in the twentieth century no less than in the nineteenth it has been commonly assumed by doctors that the menopause can have a pathological impact on women's mental health. Until recent decades, the concept of involutional melancholia served as an important mechanism linking the menopause with psychiatric symptoms.[8] Involutional melancholia, usually regarded as a psychotic disorder, was said to occur in both men and women during the 'involutional period', that is, the period when the organs of the body were said to atrophy (held to be 40 to 55 or 60 in women, and 50 to 65 in men). This physiological process was believed to precipitate symptoms of melancholia in some individuals for the first time in their lives (the diagnosis was only to be given to those who had not previously had any mental disorder). Although formally gender-neutral in construction, because of the way in which the menopause has been considered a problematic, pathological process without a male equivalent, the diagnosis was, not surprisingly, more frequently assigned to women than men. Men, it was felt, might suffer from an awareness of unfulfilled ambitions and missed opportunities (note the later timing of the involutional period in men), but the emphasis on biological processes associated with the menopause ensured a gender imbalance in diagnosed cases.

Although involutional melancholia continued to feature in psychiatric texts in the 1960s, the distinctiveness of the syndrome was increasingly called into question (Batchelor 1969: 232–4), writers arguing that the symptoms were not specific to the syndrome and that no clear boundary could be drawn between involutional melancholia and other affective psychoses, such as manic-depression or endogenous (major) depression. Recent psychiatric classifications do not list it as a separate condition; the DSM-III-R indicated that what was formerly classified as involutional melancholia should be categorised as a major depressive episode (American Psychiatric Association 1987: 562), but it is not mentioned in the DSM-IV.

The abandonment of a mental disorder which could be specifically defined in relation to the menopause cannot, however, be taken as evidence that the menopause is no longer thought to have any impact on women's mental health, even though the linkage is less visible in psychiatric classifications. Certainly the growing use of hormone replacement therapy (HRT) attests to medicine's belief that the menopause very often heralds changes that merit therapeutic intervention, and HRT is sometimes prescribed more for its supposed therapeutic potential in relation to insomnia, irritability, nervousness and depression and for its energising qualities as for its supposed benefits for hot flushes, vaginal dryness and other menopausal symptoms of a more physical nature.

Significantly, the data on reported depression in relation to the menopause do not suggest that the menopause increases women's risks of depression. This was the finding of Weissman and Klerman's survey of the literature (1977) and the Epidemiologic Catchment Area survey showed women's levels of depression marginally lower amongst those aged 45–64 than women aged 25–44 (Myers et al. 1984). Moreover, a number of writers have argued that where the menopause is linked temporally to depression, the origins of depression lie in the social changes occurring around the time of the menopause, in particular the departure of children from the parental home and the loss of the maternal role (Bart 1970: 72).

Men's Reproductive Biology

Whilst women's reproductive hormones have been held responsible for much of the 'excess' mental disorder detected in women, men's reproductive biology is given far less attention in psychiatric ideas. As we have seen, medical texts portray men's reproductive biology far more positively than women's, and there is no male equivalent of the tight medical regulation of women's reproduction, either in terms of the range of pathological conditions associated with menstruation and the menopause, or the biochemical regulation of women's reproductive capacities, through contraceptive pills, HRT, and so forth.

Yet men's reproductive biology does not entirely escape attention within psychiatry. It features in two main areas: first, in relation to the various forms or sexual pathology that are part of the psychiatric lexicon. At present, sexual disorders constitute only a relatively small part of the psychiatric terrain in quantitative terms, but they are primarily diagnosed in men (see Chapter 2) and male hormones are attributed much of the responsibility. In the DSM-IV, under the general heading of sexual and gender identity disorders, three types are listed: the paraphilias (literally deviation in love, i.e., that to which the person is attracted), which include fetishisms, paedophilia, sexual sadism, sexual masochism and voyeurism; sexual dysfunctions characterised by inhibition in sexual response; and gender identity disorders. In the discussion of paraphilias, whilst there is no specific reference to male hormones, there is frequent reference to sexual 'urges'. Moreover, psychiatric texts do discuss the importance of sex hormones in relation to these disorders (see for instance, Stafford-Clark and Bridges 1990: Chapter 12), focusing primarily on the androgens. What is striking is that in these discussions of sexual disorders, hormones are defined as relating to sexuality not reproduction. This, it might be argued, is because the disorders are sexual not reproductive disorders. Yet, in the contrast with the disorders linked to women's distinctive biology, it situates women on the side of reproduction; men on the side of sexuality.

Here, too, psychiatric discussions reflect and reinforce widespread cultural assumptions. For, whereas in the nineteenth century men were expected to subject their sexual desires and urges to strong self-control, in the twentieth century the strength of biological urges has been increasingly emphasised and is used to excuse and justify any lack of control (Plummer 1975). The contrasting constructions of male and female sexuality have been well documented and cannot be detailed here. What is important, however, is that women's reproductive biology is subject to more pathologising tendencies than men's reproductive (sexual) biology; moreover, whereas in this pathologising process the focus is on women's emotions and reasoning, if and when it occurs in relation to men it is more on behaviour than mind.

Male hormones also enter discussions of what the DSM-IV terms the 'attention-deficit and disruptive behaviour disorders', which are said to commonly develop in childhood or adolescence, and the 'anti-social personality disorder'. The disruptive behaviour disorders include hyperactivity, conduct disorder and oppositional defiant disorder. Aggressive behaviour is emphasised in all of these, and all are said to be more common in men than women. The same applies to 'anti-social personality disorder'. All fall under the heading of what is often now more broadly and loosely termed 'challenging behaviour', and in psychiatric texts the question of an excess of male hormones is frequently raised. And where the aggression or violence in question is severe, treatments frequently involve drugs that control male hormones.

As this analysis suggests there are, however, still important differences in the biological focus in relation to men and women. Not only is there a greater tendency in the twentieth century as there was in the nineteenth, to invoke biology in any discussion of women, but there is also a greater tendency to focus on women's minds than on their behaviour.

Conclusion

It would be a mistake to claim that biology has no role to play in the feelings, behaviour and experiences, currently deemed irrational and constituted as different types of mental disorder. There is too much evidence of the impact of biological processes on mental states and behaviour to make such a claim credible, though we lack imaginative models to study the interaction of the biological and the social (Benton 1991). Yet the primacy given to biological explanations of mental disorder within psychiatry does not stem from the fact that they can be shown to be more important than other aetiological factors across the spectrum of mental disorders. Rather it stems from the emphasis psychiatrists, as members of the medical profession, have typically given to physical processes (and physical treatments) – an emphasis that links to the professionalisation of medicine and the development of its own fields of expertise and competence. Psychiatrists have frequently chosen to treat any physical factor as *the* cause of a particular mental disorder, ignoring or giving little weight to any psychological or social factors that may be involved. It is true, of course, that the importance of particular biological factors is likely to vary between different disorders, especially if we focus on the contribution of genetic factors, but recognition of this point does not undermine the general argument that where we place our focus is determined more by professional and political interests than it is by scientific facts.

The concentration on biology in examining gender differences in the origins on mental disorder is over-determined. On the one hand, the biological bias of psychiatry supports and sustains such an explanatory orientation. On the other hand, the tendency to 'naturalise' all gender differences, to see them as rooted in nature not culture, strengthens and confirms this biological orientation and, in contexts where women are typically subordinated, is frequently associated with assumptions of female biological inferiority. Not surprisingly, therefore, twentieth no less than nineteenth-century ideas about mental disorder in women stress women's vulnerability to their reproductive biology. By virtue of the hormonal changes associated with menstruation, childbirth and the menopause, women are assumed to be prone to disorders of mind as well as of body. Yet, with the possible exception of childbirth, the evidence of any direct links between reproductive biology and specific mental states is poor.

Men are not, as we have seen, entirely exempt in psychiatric theorising from any assumptions about the impact of their hormones on their psychological states, but the constructions about the impact of their hormones are very different. Men are believed to be subject to powerful sexual and aggressive urges, which far from being a mark of their inferiority, affirm their power and domination. Such urges do need to be controlled, but they are believed to disturb behaviour more than mind.

Theories of the biological origins of gender differences in mental disorder are grounded, therefore, more in ideologically-based cultural assumptions about men and women than in properly substantiated scientific knowledge. Let us turn, therefore, to the accounts developed by feminists which emphasise the significance of female psychology in understanding gender differences in the origins of mental disorder.

Chapter 9

Feminist Psychologies and Gendered Individuals

'It is essential to understand clearly that the concepts of 'masculine' and 'feminine', whose meaning seem unambiguous to ordinary people, are among the most confused that occur in science. It is possible to distinguish at least three uses. 'Masculine' and 'feminine' are used sometimes in the sense of activity and passivity, sometimes in a biological, and sometimes again in a sociological sense. The first of these three meanings is the essential one and the most serviceable in psycho-analysis. *When, for instance, libido was described ... as being 'masculine', the word was being used in this sense, for an instinct is always active even when it has a passive aim in view.* The second, or biological, meaning of 'masculine' and 'feminine' is the one whose applicability can be determined most easily. Here 'masculine' and 'feminine' are characterised by the presence of spermatozoa or ova respectively and by the functions proceeding from them. Activity and its concomitant phenomena (more powerful muscular development, aggressiveness, greater intensity of libido) are as a rule linked with biological masculinity; *but they are not necessarily so, for there are animal species in which these qualities are on the contrary assigned to the female.* The third, or sociological, meaning receives its connotation from the observation of actively existing masculine and feminine individuals. Such observation shows that in human beings pure masculinity or femininity is not to be found either in a psychological or a biological sense. *Every individual, on the contrary, displays a mixture of the character-traits belonging to his own and to the opposite sex; and he shows a combination of activity and passivity whether or not these last character-traits tally with his biological ones*' (Freud, *Three Essays on the Theory of Sexuality*, quoted in Mitchell 1975: 46–7 [her italics]).

Feminists have largely rejected a focus on biology in seeking to understand the origins of mental disturbance in general and of women's mental disturbance in particular. Instead, many have turned to psychological theories, especially psychodynamic theories grounded in Freudian ideas, to provide the formulation for their analysis of mental disorder, drawing, like Freud, primarily on clinical data. In so doing they have paid particular attention to the way the psychological make-up of women is structured and shaped mainly in early childhood, making implicit or explicit comparisons with men's psychological development. In this chapter I want to explore these feminist psychologies to see whether they provide fruitful ways of helping us to understand the gendered landscape of patient populations by casting light on how women's and men's psychological development may take rather different paths.

One of the striking features of feminist psychologies is their composite character: their reliance not only on psychodynamic underpinnings, but also on ideas about gender drawn from sociology and anthropology. Their strength lies in the detailed attention they pay to the complex dynamics of human mental life which are typically involved when someone becomes disturbed, to the gendered character of these dynamics and, consequently, to the gendered nature of psychological and emotional expression. Their limitations lie in their over-readiness to generalise about male and female psychological development and to downplay the importance of cultural and situational factors in contrast to personality dynamics. This latter criticism has found its strongest and most effective expression in the argument that Freud's focus on sexual phantasies and unconscious processes directed attention away from the reality of the sexual abuse of women (see Chapter 11). In this chapter I first examine the general features of feminist psychologies. I then consider feminist accounts of anorexia nervosa, some of which move well beyond feminist psychologies and give greater attention to social and cultural issues.

Feminists and the Freudian Heritage

Despite feminists' trenchant criticisms of the sexist character of Freud's ideas about women, in the late 1960s and early 1970s feminist theorising about male and female psychology has, with one or two significant exceptions (for instance, Gilligan 1982), been primarily influenced by various readings of the work of Freud and his followers.

The early feminist critiques of Freud are well-known and centre on the picture Freud conveys of women as both biologically and psychologically inferior to men. Men are presented as the norm: women as biologically inferior because they lack a penis – Freud refers to their 'genital deficiency' (1973: 166) – and as psychologically inferior because of their envy of men's penis.[1] The female personality is in Freud's account (1973) characterised by masochism, narcissism, deceitfulness, shame, envy and jealousy. Such ideas have, according to a number of feminists, had a profound and deleterious impact on the way in which we think about and treat women. Kate Millett, in her influential text *Sexual Politics*, put the case like this: 'the effect of Freud's work, that of his followers, and still more that of his popularizers, was to rationalize the invidious relationship between the sexes, to ratify traditional roles, and to validate temperamental differences' (1972: 178).

However, the feminist defence of Freud emerged quite rapidly. Juliet Mitchell's analysis in *Psychoanalysis and Feminism* which, drawing both on psychodynamic and feminist ideas, attempted to rescue Freud from his critics, was especially influential. Feminist critics she contended were right in arguing that popularisers of Freud have provided a justification of a bourgeois and patriarchal status quo. The mistake, however, is to see Freud as offering a *prescription* for gender difference rather than a *description* of it: 'However it may have been used, psychoanalysis is not a recommendation *for* a patriarchal society, but an analysis *of* one' (1975: xv).[2] Freud's writings should be read as presenting an invaluable account of how, in a society characterised by patriarchy – defined by her as the law of the father – anatomically different males and females come to take on the characteristics of men and women, their masculinity or femininity. Feminists, she contends, cannot afford to neglect Freud's writings because of the need to understand the complex psychology of that process. Indeed, at present, psychoanalytic ideas offer almost the only framework for thinking about the development of female psychology (the focus of her study) which attributes a depth and complexity to the human mind, most obviously through the concept of the unconscious, sufficient to match the complexity of empirical reality.[3] With his assertion of the power of unconscious desires, ideas and phantasies, of the conflicts and tensions within the individual and of the importance of early childhood experiences, Freud has provided a framework that can cope with issues such as an individual's resistance to change, the mismatch between stated beliefs and actions, the deep-seated, embedded quality of feeling and ideas, and so forth. Consequently, feminists interested in the way in which gendered individuals develop have had little choice but to try and build on his foundations, his sexism notwithstanding, rather than to reject his ideas wholesale.

Mitchell's own composite account is grounded on an analysis of patriarchal society indebted to the French anthropologist Lévi-Strauss, a Marxist analysis of capitalism, and a reading of Freud derived from the French psychoanalyst Jacques Lacan. According to Lacan's psychoanalysis the *id* rather than being the repository of biological drives is the repository of unconscious culturally transmitted ideas: 'thus in "penis-envy" we are talking not about an anatomical organ, but about the ideas of it that people hold and live by within the general culture' (Mitchell 1975: xvi). It is the symbolic 'phallus' not the biological penis that is important: consequently psychoanalysis can offer us an understanding of ideology. Gender relations, sexual relations and male and female psychology are not, therefore, to be viewed as biologically given, but as socially generated; bisexuality not masculinity or femininity is the starting point. As Freud himself says in his essay, 'Femininity':

> In conformity with its peculiar nature, psychoanalysis does not try to describe what a woman is – that would be a task it could scarcely perform – but sets about inquiring how she comes into being, how a woman develops out of a child with a bisexual disposition (1973: 149)

That feminists, whether pro-Freud or anti-Freud, have read him so very differently is to be expected, given the ambiguities and contradictions in his writings. Mannoni (1971) persuasively argues that two rather different conceptions of the mind compete in Freud's writings. On the one hand, there is the biological, mechanistic, scientific model of the mind – the psychology of instincts or drives as in his *Three Essays on The Theory of Sexuality* (1977); on the other hand, there is the focus on symbols and meaning, the interpretative and anti-positivistic – the psychology of desires and phantasies as in *The Interpretation of Dreams* (1976). Feminist critics have stressed Freud's biological determinism (cf. Friedan 1963: 107); feminist defenders, like Mitchell, his emphasis on social meaning.

Mitchell's account of the shaping of male and female psychology has its limitations, not the least of which is her analysis of the patriarchal nature of society drawing on the work of Lévi-Strauss – an analysis in which the possibility of change seems limited.[4] She has, therefore, also been attacked for her pessimistic view of the future of women (Segal 1987: 127–8). Whether she succeeds in rescuing Freud from accusations that he assumes women's biological and psychological inferiority is debatable. Certainly she does not seek to challenge Freud's characterisation of women in present-day society, nor to challenge Freud's emphasis on the importance of unconscious sexual phantasies.[5] Her approach is, however, essentially political: to extract from Freud, ideas that can be used to understand women's psychological development. What her work offers is a way of understanding socially generated differences in psychological states and emotional expression between men and women, that focuses, as did Freud, on early childhood.

Mitchell's work draws upon Lacanian interpretations of psychoanalytic ideas. Other feminists have turned to the interpretations of the object relations school. This approach develops the work of Melanie Klein, a follower of Freud, who settled in England in 1926 and became a major figure in British psychoanalysis. Klein emphasised the role of internal 'objects' and internal 'object-relations' in the individual's psychic structure. An internal object is a phantasy of a real object – an object being some person or thing in the person's external environment – and does not correspond directly with the external object. The two worlds, the outer world of material objects and the inner world of phantasy, continually interact and cannot be kept entirely separate. In the words of Klein:

> The young child's perception of external reality and external objects is perpetually influenced and coloured by his phantasies, and this in some measure continues throughout life. External experiences which arouse anxiety at once activate even in normal persons anxiety derived from intrapsychic sources. The interaction between objective anxiety and neurotic anxiety – or, to express it in other words, the interaction between anxiety arising from external and from internal sources – corresponds to the interaction between external and psychic reality (quoted in Guntrip 1961: 226).

Hence, it may be less external events and experiences than the objects of inner phantasy that are disturbing.[6] Klein attached especial importance to the earliest phases of development, analysing the child's early object relationships, particularly the child's relation to the mother (see Segal 1964, 1979). In her view the first two years of life are crucial, whereas in Freud's account of early development the decisive period surrounds the Oedipus complex around the age of three or four. Klein also attached considerable importance, following Freud's later work, to the idea of innate, destructive impulses or a death instinct, arguing that destructive impulses, which are present from birth and commonly projected onto others, play a key role in the child's inner phantasy world.

Klein's ideas were further developed into a distinctive object relations school of psychoanalysis by a group of psychotherapists working in Britain, including W.R.D. Fairbairn, D.W. Winnicott, Michael Balint and Harry Guntrip. Guntrip describes the object relations approach as providing a synthesis of the psychobiology of Freud and the psychosociology of the 'culture' school of American psychoanalysts, such as Karen Horney, Eric Fromm and H.S. Sullivan, to form a psychodynamic theory of the person. A key difference between the object relations school and Klein's own approach is the emphasis given to innate drives and to biology. Object relations theorists reject the notion of innate, destructive impulses, which Klein had adopted and developed (Guntrip 1961: Chapter XVI). Fairbairn, one of the most influential of the theorists, regarded aggression, as had Freud in his earlier work, as a reaction to libidinal frustration and not an inevitable, unmotivated aspect of human behaviour.

The sociologist, Nancy Chodorow, in her important study, *The Reproduction of Mothering* (1978), was one of the first feminists to make use of object relations theory. In this book, following on from the work of Adrienne Rich (1976) and Dorothy Dinnerstein (1976), she seeks to explain and understand a key feature of women's psychology: their commitment to mothering, as well as the way this commitment is transmitted and reproduced over generations of women and its impact on men's psychology. In so doing Chodorow, like Rich and Dinnerstein, was reacting against the views of feminists of the second half of the 1960s and the first half of the 1970s who had been critical of women's commitment to their roles as wives and mothers, had stressed the negative consequences of these roles for women, and had urged them to escape from the cage of domesticity. She sees these arguments as oversimple and instead attempts to understand women's desire to mother and the institution of mothering (Segal 1987: 135).

Chodorow offers a mix of sociological and psychodynamic ideas. She employs sociological concepts, such as gender and role, but explicitly rejects sociological accounts of role learning (along with biological explanations of gender difference) as inadequate for understanding the reproduction of mothering – that is, for the acquisition of the appropriate self-definitions, self-concepts and psychological needs. For this she turns to the insights of psychoanalysis about the internal dynamics of the psyche, which she believes can provide a more adequate analysis of the ways in which 'family structure and process, in particular the asymmetrical organisation of parenting, affect unconscious psychic structure and process' (1978: 49). However, in her view, in the last instance, the external world determines male and female psychology:

> A child also comes to channel libido and aggression in patterned ways as a result of its relational experiences and its interactions with caretakers, that is, the id becomes patterned and constructed. Thus, society constitutes itself psychologically in the individual not only in the moral strictures of the superego. All aspects of psychic structure, character, and emotional and erotic life are social, constituted through a 'history of object-choices'. This history, dependent on the individual personalities and behaviour of those who happen to interact with a child, is also socially patterned according to the family structure and prevalent psychological modes of a society (ibid: 50).[7]

Of course, the relationship between internal and external is not simple, for 'Internalization is mediated by fantasy and by conflict' (ibid).

Because of the asymmetries of parenting and the importance of mothers and mothering, the development of femininity in girls and masculinity in boys follow different paths. Here Chodorow, while emphasising the mother–child relationship, departs from Freud in seeing the development of male identification and masculinity as more problematic than that of female identification and femininity:

> Because women are responsible for early child care and for most later socia- lization as well, because fathers are more absent from the home and because men's activities generally have been removed from the home while women's have remained within it, boys have difficulty in attaining a stable masculine gender role identification. Boys fantasize about and idealize the masculine role and their fathers, and society defines it as desirable (ibid: 185).

Gender identification and role learning are embedded in girls' relation- ships with their mothers. They are less likely to be embedded in boys' relationships with their fathers. And, as boys are parented primarily by their mothers, male identification and role learning involve rejection of dependence on, and attachment to, their mother, with a consequent devaluation of the feminine and an overvaluation of the masculine. The result is that men tend to deny their own feelings and attachments, and reject 'the world of women and things feminine' (ibid: 186) – they become 'the pseudo-independent organization man' (ibid: 190).

Chodorow's analysis of why men and women have different feelings and thoughts and behave differently (including differing in the expres- sion of psychological difficulties) gives, therefore, crucial weight to mothering – a weight she subsequently considered too great. In the Introduction to a collection of her papers a decade later, she commented that whereas she had once argued that 'women's mothering was *the* cause or prime mover of male dominance' (1989: 6), she now thought that 'An open web of social, psychological, and cultural relations, dynamics, practices, identities, beliefs, in which I would privilege neither society, psyche, nor culture comes to constitute gender as a social, cultural and psychological phenomenon' (ibid: 5).

Luise Eichenbaum and Susie Orbach, who founded the Women's Therapy Centre in London in 1976, have also developed a feminist analysis of the development of women's distinctive psychology grounded in object relations theory and have specifically tied it to issues of mental health. The best known of their books is Orbach's specific text on women's relation to eating, diet and obesity, *Fat is a Feminist Issue* (1978). This was followed by a second volume on fatness (1984) and by two more general books with Eichenbaum about women, *Outside In ... Inside Out: Women's Psychology, A Feminist Psychoanalytic Approach* (1982) (revised as *Understanding Women* in 1985), and *What do Women Want?* (1984). Eichenbaum and Orbach, who indicate an indebtedness both to object relations theory and to Chodorow's and Rich's work, write for a wider, less academic audience. Their objective is to construct an account of women's psychological development and, as the title of their general texts indicate, they pay far less explicit attention to men than Chodorow. As with Chodorow, the development of women's psychic life is viewed as a social rather than a biological process and again their approach combines sociological and psychodynamic ideas. Drawing on sociology they employ the concept of social role to describe women's situation in the external world – a situation that requires an appropriate, gendered psychology which has to be acquired:

> These features of women's social role – growing into a woman (with attendant conditioning), finding a mate, becoming a wife, learning to take care of babies, and making a home involve extensive social preparation. They are not inevitable consequences of women's biology. To find a man, a woman has to present herself in a certain way. She has to develop her sexuality along particular lines; she has to create an image of herself that a man will find pleasing. This is a complex social matter, not at all a straightforward, natural process (1985: 5).

The psychological demands on women, given their social role, are considerable. First, 'she must *defer* to others – follow their lead, articulate her needs only in relation to theirs' (1985: 7). Consequently, women may be reluctant to speak for themselves and even hide their desires from themselves. Second, 'she must always be *connected* to others and shape her life in accordance with a man's' (ibid: 8). An important corollary is that a woman has to learn to anticipate the needs of others, whilst her own needs remain largely hidden. And, since she does not have an emotional caregiver to turn to, she herself '*then carries deep feelings of neediness*' (ibid: 9). The situation for men is rather different, since their dependency needs are usually met by women throughout their lives: first, by their mothers and then by their wives. For this reason men can be independent: for independence can only be properly achieved when dependency needs are met.

In this analysis, it is women's sense of neediness in comparison with men's that accounts for their higher level of psychological symptoms – particularly somatic symptoms and symptoms of phobia. Women's psychological development is shaped through their relation with their mothers in childhood. Their sense of loss of maternal nurturance and the fact that it is not replaced by nurturance from men leads to strong feelings of neediness and to behaviour symptomatic of mental ill-health:

> But the psychic preparation for this social role leaves a woman with a legacy of unmet needs, frustrated desires, deep feelings of unentitlement, and a fragmented, malleable, or incomplete sense of self. These experiences in turn generate feelings of anger, despair, and hopelessness. Women unable to reconcile themselves with their confinement attempt to break out. Such attempts may be conscious and purposeful, or unconscious, or both. An unconscious expression of such protest, rage, or desperation often manifests itself in a somatic or phobic symptom (ibid: 158).

There are a number of problems with Chodorow's and Eichenbaum and Orbach's account of the development of female psychology and of gendered individuals. First, they tend to conceptualise gender as a role. For instance, although Chodorow explicitly rejects sociological accounts of role learning, she still uses concepts of gender role and gender role learning. Similarly, Eichenbaum and Orbach readily talk of women's social role. Yet as I noted in Chapter 2 when discussing theories of gender, theorising gender itself as a social role is problematic.

Second, despite the assumption of the impact of the social environment on psychological development, which should allow for the diversity of psychological experience, these writers tend to generalise rather too freely about female psychology, taking little cognisance of differences in women's experiences, such as those of age, class, ethnicity, time or place. In this respect they seem to revert to a form of essentialism which is almost a mirror-image of accounts which stress the biological and psychological inferiority of women, only this time, *contra* Mitchell, it is the shared superior characteristics of women that are affirmed. There is still, as Segal puts it, an 'exaggeration of sexual difference' (Segal 1987: 145). The tendency to essentialism arises from the emphasis on mothering as a universal social phenomenon: the belief that women manifest a capacity for caring that men cannot meet. This time the psychological difference is more a product of society than biology, but the essentialist tendency is the same. It is a tendency that arises from the attempt to generalise about the characteristics of women and, in the process, sets aside historical and cultural variation.

Third, in Eichenbaum and Orbach's account, the subtlety of object relations psychology is rather lost in the tight match they suggest between women's social roles and their psychic structure. The problem is the extent to which 'their generalisations about individual psychologies simply mirror the generalisations they make about social phenomena' (Segal 1987: 140). In so doing they not only forego 'a more complex, contradictory and conflict-ridden view of society', they also forego 'a more autonomous and more conflict-ridden dynamic to the psychic than that of mere conformity to social pressures' (ibid: 140). In other words, they end up with an 'over-socialised' conception of the individual – a standard failing of sociological interpretations of psychodynamic theorising (Wrong 1963). The complexity of the dynamics of personality and of the possibilities of resistance and non-conformity have been left out.

Other writers have produced accounts of female psychology (see, for instance, Miller 1986). Most, however, fall into the trap of essentialism in their desire to produce a general psychology of women. Clearly what is needed is an analysis of both male and female psychology that gives more weight to social and cultural diversity. The need both to build on, and move beyond, feminist psychologies can be illuminated if we explore feminist analyses of anorexia nervosa.

The Case of Anorexia Nervosa

Feminists have shown an especial interest in the eating disorder of anorexia nervosa because of its distinctive place as a female mental disorder in late twentieth-century Western societies. Estimates vary but, as I noted in Chapter 2, most studies indicate an overwhelming (more than 90 per cent) female preponderance. The disorder is also considered to be more common among young, middle and upper-class women, although as we would expect, claims as to the exact social distribution of the disease vary. So, too, do estimates of its overall prevalence. Anorexia nervosa is frequently said to be reaching 'epidemic' proportions (Gordon 1990: Chapter 3), claims often backed up by figures from selected samples (usually teenagers or university students). The American Psychiatric Association (1994: 543) suggests prevalence rates for clinically defined anorexia somewhere between 1 in 100 and 1 in 200 amongst females in late adolescence and adulthood. It also reports that 'Of individuals admitted to university hospitals the long-term mortality from Anorexia Nervosa is over 10%' (ibid: 543). However, these samples typically maximise those at risk by virtue of age, class and gender.

There is no consensus on the exact symptoms of anorexia nervosa or how it should be differentiated from the eating disorder of bulimia nervosa. The 1992 Glossary to the WHO's Classification of Mental Disorders describes anorexia nervosa as follows:

> a disorder characterized by deliberate weight loss, induced and/or sustained by the patient. The disorder occurs most commonly in adolescent girls and young women, but adolescent boys and young men may be affected more rarely, as may children approaching puberty and older women up to the menopause (World Health Organisation 1992: 176).

This characterisation focuses on symptoms such as refusal to eat, and weight loss, locating the illness at a particular stage of the life cycle. The American DSM-IV's characterisation of anorexia differs in important respects: the description of symptoms does not specifically refer to the social characteristics of patients, though this information is provided separately, the manual noting that the disease is far more common in females and the mean age of onset is 17 years (American Psychiatric Association 1994: 543). It concurs in listing weight loss and amenorrhoea as symptoms, but offers a more motivational characterisation, with fear of becoming fat a key feature as well as distortions of body image:

> The essential features of Anorexia Nervosa are that the individual refuses to maintain a minimally normal body weight, is intensely afraid of gaining

weight, and exhibits a significant disturbance in the perception of the shape or size of his or her body. In addition, postmenarcheal females with this disorder are amenorrheic. (The term *anorexia* is a misnomer because loss of appetite is rare) (ibid: 539).

The DSM's description of anorexia nervosa appears to have been influenced by Hilde Bruch's work on anorexia. Bruch, a psychiatrist and psychotherapist who worked in the States, published a number of influential studies of the condition (1973, 1978, 1988). In her view the psychological features of anorexia – 'the relentless pursuit of thinness through self-starvation' (1973: 4) and the 'panicky fear of gaining weight' (1978: 4) – are primary, and physical features such as weight loss are secondary (1978: 4). She identifies three key areas of disordered psychological functioning. First, the anorexic shows a *'disturbance of delusion proportions in the body image and body concept'* (1973: 251–2). The anorexic stubbornly defends her thinness. Second, she shows a *'disturbance in the accuracy of the perception or cognitive interpretation of stimuli arising in the body'* (ibid: 252). In particular she does not recognise she is not eating enough for her body's needs and there is a denial of hunger. There may also be hyperactivity and a denial of fatigue. Third, there is 'a *paralysing sense of ineffectiveness*, which pervades all thinking and activities of anorexic patients (ibid: 254). There is an overriding sense of passivity and helplessness, and a lack of initiative and autonomy.

There is some uncertainty as to whether bulimia nervosa, a more recent addition to the psychiatric lexicon, is to be regarded as a subtype of anorexia or a separate disorder.[8] The 1978 Glossary to the WHO Classification did not use the term, but the 1992 edition included it as a variant of anorexia:

Bulimia nervosa is a syndrome characterised by repeated bouts of overeating and an excessive preoccupation with the control of body weight, leading the patient to adopt extreme measures so as to mitigate the 'fattening' effects of ingested food. The term should be restricted to the form of the disorder that is related to anorexia nervosa by virtue of sharing the same pscyhopathology... The disorder may be viewed as a sequel to persistent anorexia nervosa (although the reverse sequence may also occur) (World Health Organisation 1992: 178).

The DSM-IV, however, lists bulimia nervosa as a distinct illness, characterised as follows:

The essential features of Bulimia Nervosa are binge eating and inappropriate compensatory methods to prevent weight gain. In addition, the self-evaluation of individuals with Bulimia Nervosa is excessively influenced by body shape and weight. To qualify for the diagnosis, the binge eating and the inappropriate compensatory behaviours must occur, on average, at least twice a week for 3 months (American Psychiatric Association 1994: 545).[9]

Anorexia nervosa was developed as a disease category in the 1870s. The term's first use is usually attributed to Sir William Gull, a British physician, in a paper published in 1874, who had described a form of hysterical anorexia some six years earlier. His contemporary, Charles Lasègue, Professor of Clinical Medicine at the University of Paris, also identified cases of hysterical anorexia and, unlike Gull, asserted a more thoroughly psychogenic origin. Both Gull and Lasègue associated anorexia with women. Joan Jacobs Brumberg (1988), in her history of the condition, points to somewhat similar cases of 'fasting girls' in the sixteenth, seventeenth and eighteenth centuries which by Gull and Lasègue's criteria might well have fallen into the category of anorexia. Some cases were described in medical texts; for example, in 1669 one John Reynolds produced *A Discourse upon Prodigious Abstinence*, and in 1689 Richard Morton, a physician, in a text on consumptions, described a case of nervous atrophy or nervous consumption whose symptoms included loss of appetite, amenorrhoea and extreme wasting. Both were women; however, in 1790 a physician Robert Willan described 'A remarkable case of abstinence' in a young man (Hunter and MacAlpine 1963: 230). Nonetheless, although the existence of instances of prolonged abstinence and fasting prior to the mid-nineteenth century cannot be doubted, their identification as cases of anorexia nervosa ignores important cultural differences that can exist in apparently similar behaviours (see Brumberg 1988: 2–3; MacSween 1993: 17–23).

Explanations of anorexia nervosa are diverse. Lasègue's view that anorexia had psychic rather than physical origins is shared by psychoanalytic theorists, who tend to portray it as a regression to infantile sexuality in which problems over food symbolically express internal sexual conflict, precipitated by the need to adjust to adulthood (more specifically the rejection of food is a rejection of phantasies or oral impregnation) – hence the gender bias of the condition (see Bruch 1973: 216–7). What is important about this type of theorising is its focus on the psychological dynamics of the disorder and the symbolic importance of being thin.

By the end of the 1960s the pace of publications on anorexia was beginning to increase, paralleling the increasing use of the category, although Bruch in her 1973 book still emphasised the rarity of the condition. Much of this work, in line with psychodynamic theorising of family relations, which were a feature of the 1950s and 1960s, concentrated on the particular familial constellation associated with anorexia, with some attention given to the social location of the condition. Bruch herself regarded anorexia as a disease of affluence and abundance – 'food refusal would be an ineffectual tool in a setting of poverty and scarcity' (1973: 13) – and she located it almost exclusively in upper-middle and upper-class families, arguing that of the few cases coming from lower-middle or lower-class backgrounds the families 'were upwardly mobile and success-oriented'(1978: 24). In addition, both parents tended to be older than average at the child's birth and were more likely to have daughters and no sons (ibid). She considered the dynamics of family relationships vital, especially the relationship between mothers and daughters.[10] The mothers were usually 'of superior intelligence and education' had 'often been career women, who felt they had sacrificed their aspirations for the good of the family' (ibid: 26). Some consciously regretted this and tended to focus on the physical appearance and achievement of their daughters. In this context their expectations of their daughters were high, there was a considerable emphasis on academic achievement, and daughters felt they had to be especially concerned about their parents' feelings, responding to their needs rather than their own. Mothers not only transferred their own desires for achievement onto their daughters, but also did not encourage them to develop their own sense of identity and to differentiate their needs from those of others – either by being neglectful or over-solicitous – so that daughters could not discriminate between being hungry and being sated (ibid: 40-41). The result was daughters engaged in a 'desperate struggle for a self-respecting identity' (Bruch 1973:250) – the core of the disorder.

Feminist theories of anorexia nervosa have built on Bruch's foundations adding a distinctively feminist gloss to the analysis, in which the exploitation and oppression of women are emphasised and the meanings of food and thinness are analysed in relation to the social situation of women.[11] In this process, anorexia is portrayed less as a matter of individual pathology and more a result of women's oppression. In Britain, Susie Orbach's account of anorexia, which developed out of her study of obesity, has been especially influential. In *Fat is a Feminist Issue* (1978) and a companion volume first published in 1982, Orbach, like Bruch, argued that obesity is the product of 'compulsive' eating: that is, there is a pattern of eating which is psychologically motivated.

Consequently, dieting cannot deal with obesity because it does not tackle the psychological addiction to food. Since fatness, Orbach contends, is a more common problem in women than men it is necessary to unravel the special meanings both of food and the body in women's lives.

On the one hand, food is linked with women's role as nurturers both practically and symbolically:

> Beyond getting the nutritional requirements right, the woman is encouraged to express her unique personality through the food she prepares. Food becomes a medium through which she communicates many feelings. It demonstrates her love, her caring and her concern for her family. A woman's value rises with her ability to produce prettier, more economic, more wholesome and at the same time delectable meals, snacks and picnics (1984: 19–20).

On the other hand, a woman's body is the means whereby she has to present herself as attractive and appealing:

> A woman's body can always use improving; our legs, our hair, our bustline, our skin, our cellulite are all in danger of being unseemly unless attended to in a feminine way. Encouraged to see ourselves this way, it is not surprising that we grow up alienated and scared of our bodies. A woman's body is one of the few culturally accepted ways a woman has to express herself and yet the scope of this expression is limited by a contradiction: the pressure to look a certain way, to conform to today's slim image (ibid: 21).

It is the convergence of women's focus on nurture and body image that makes food so significant: 'Food is about health for *others*, but about beauty for herself '(ibid: 21). In this situation it might seem that the easy solution would be slimness as an expression both of woman's concern to give to others and for her own appearance (in a culture where beauty and slimness are equated). However, as we have seen earlier, Orbach takes the view that women's own needs are considered illegitimate. As a result their natural hunger mechanism becomes socially and psychologically distorted and they may unconsciously desire to be fat, despite consciously desiring, in conformity with cultural prescription, to be thin. Food can, therefore, become a way of expressing protest against the expectations and images of women: an individual rebellion against an imprisoning social role. 'Food, therefore, can become a way to try to give to herself. Her fatness can become a way to express a protest at the definitions of her social role... For many women, fatness feels like a rejection of the packaged sexuality around us' (ibid: 22).

A similar set of ideas combining a strong emphasis on the cultural significance of food and eating with her ideas on female psychology developed with Eichenbaum, underpin Orbach's analysis of anorexia in *Hunger Strike*, first published in 1986.[12] In her view anorexia, too, is another form of protest and rebellion. It is not, as might seem at first sight, an act of simple conformity with the injunctions on women: to deny themselves and to appear slim, though self-denial is at its centre. For the anorexic's relation to food is one of active rejection and refusal. It has the defiance of the suffragettes' hunger strikes, albeit that the cause for which she makes her protest is not clearly articulated: it is 'an attempt at empowering' (Orbach 1993: 83). This rejection of food stems from feelings common in women 'as wrong, as unentitled and at the same time needy' (ibid: 86). The objective of the anorexic is to create 'an apparently needless self – a self that has the possibility of being accepted' (ibid: 87); it is an attempt to establish control and autonomy and a sense of self:

> The control over food and the particularly complicated way she relates to it is linked with a need to have something uniquely her own, something under her control, something she fashions. Throughout her life she has felt herself to have been on a path shaped by others. Who *she* is has been ignored and dismissed. She hasn't had a chance to develop herself. She has responded to the desires of others and tried to fit herself to their projections. Unable to do this anymore, she must do her own thing at any cost. She has designated her body as the arena for the struggle. Treating it like an enemy, she wrestles with it, trying to defeat its needs. She puts all of her energy into trying to conquer it, to make it submit to her will. Paradoxically and tragically in this struggle with her body, she perpetuates the very denial of self that she is fighting against. But as we have seen, she gains a measure of self-respect and peace, for she has shown herself that she can be more in charge of her life than anyone else (ibid: 94).

Orbach's accounts of compulsive eating and anorexia have a number of positive features. Patterns of eating are viewed as motivated conduct, albeit often unconsciously, which have meaning for the women in question and are linked to the social and cultural context in which they live. Consequently, not only can the individual be helped by therapy, there are also prescriptions for social and political change in the position of women. However, her accounts also raise a number of problems. In the first place, they tend to fall into the type of essentialist thinking we have already criticised. As in her general discussion of female psychology with Louise Eichenbaum, Orbach tends to make statements about women's situation and women's psychology that are assumed to hold across time and place. It is true that she takes account of the fact that anorexia is a relatively new disease and links its emergence to the development of a culture preoccupied with food and body-image. This culture affects the way in which psychological difficulties are expressed, for 'psychological symptoms express the ideas a culture has at any given time about itself' (ibid: 47). In a different culture, a different form of protest would have emerged. Thirty years ago, for example, problems of self-esteem might have led to obsessional rather than anorexic symptoms. Yet, despite this recognition of the cultural and temporal specificity of anorexia, we are offered an account embedded in ideas about women that generalise across time and place.

Second, and related to this, she tends to view the construction of the key cultural categories with which she operates as relatively unproblematic. Diamond argues that in *Fat is a Feminist Issue*, Orbach starts with the 'presumption that actual fatness and compulsive eating are the problem' (1985: 48). By so doing Orbach avoids any analysis of the way fatness is constructed as a social problem for women:

> The terms 'fat', as well as 'thin', are both assumed as given and are used repeatedly throughout the text. This repetition has the effect of solidifying a social opposition (which poses female 'fat' as the problem and 'thin' as the ideal) set up by forms of media practice and the diet industry. In providing no definition for the terms 'fat' and 'thin', these terms are consequently left open to definitions set by the aforementioned practices (which relatively fix the imagery and meanings of these terms) (1985: 48).

Neither fat nor thin have fixed referents and the images and meanings of these terms vary in different social contexts. Orbach's analysis of culture and meanings is too restricted. On the one hand, following psychoanalytic principles of psychic determinism, she treats fatness (or 'excessive' thinness) as a symptom which has a meaning for the individual that must be examined. On the other hand, she uses a simple notion of culture to account for the particular focus on food and body weight. But this still treats the key concepts themselves as unproblematic. Part of the problem, Diamond argues, is that Orbach seems to assume a natural, biological order independent of and separable from social ideas, feelings and needs. Orbach seems to want to get the individual back in touch with that natural order and experience only the physiological hunger with its own self-regulatory mechanism. Yet 'the experience of "hunger" cannot be freed from meaning, since it is meaning that defines the experience as such' (ibid:58). There can be no experience of need, as of emotion without the attributions of social meaning.

Finally, it is important to note the tension in Orbach's work between a view of women as constrained and controlled by oppressive social forces with their symptoms an expression of unconscious desires and impulses, and a view of their 'symptoms' as acts of deviance and rebellion. Women are portrayed both as the victims of uncontrollable internal and external forces, and as active creatures engaged in protest and resistance. Of course, this tension can be regarded as either a defect or a virtue of the approach. What might appear to be a lack of consistency and a potential contradiction, can equally be considered an accurate portrayal of women's attempt to struggle against powerful forces both within and without: a reflection of the female condition. Nonetheless, the parallel she explicitly draws between anorexia nervosa and the hunger strikes of the suffragettes, too readily attributes a political motivation to actions whose element of resistance does not have an equivalent conscious political intent.

Orbach, in line with her tendency to generalise about the female condition, says rather little about the social location of women with eating disorders and, although she appears to have partly derived her ideas about inadequate rearing and subsequent psychological needs from Bruch, has ignored Bruch's concern about issues of class and pressures to achieve. These issues have, however, been explored by other writers. Marilyn Lawrence (1984, 1987), another member of the Women's Therapy Centre who draws on Eichenbaum and Orbach's work, focuses on education. Noting that anorexia is common in young middle-class women, she argues that the key variable is education not class. Education, she suggests, creates conflicts in identity formation for women: 'To take education seriously not only contradicts the injunction that motherhood is the primary component of female sexuality, it actually threatens the girl with a sexual identity which is negative and almost universally disapproved of' (1987: 214). In certain respects the formulation parallels Hannah Gavron's argument in *The Captive Wife* (1968), about the conflicts women face when taking on subordinate, low-status domestic roles in a society that stresses social equality (see also Chapter 8 below). However, in Gavron's account domestic roles are the problem. The danger of Lawrence's account is the implication that women's education is the problem (with unfortunate resonances with late nineteenth-century ideas about women's unsuitability for advanced education). Lawrence is aware of the danger of mis-interpretation but, *contra* Gavron, she lays herself open to this by sug-gesting the conflict is generated by education not the ideology that defines motherhood and domesticity as women's natural place. We should not, she argues, deny that education places women in a difficult situation or 'prevent them giving voice to it'. ' "Symptoms", only occur when difficulties cannot be acknowledged for what they are' (ibid: 223).

More recent feminist scholarship, much of it influenced by a post-modernist theorising, has shifted away from the development or psy-chologies of women, and has focused instead on the gap noted by Diamond concerning the cultural constructions of bodily shape.[13] For example, Susan Bordo, herself a strong critic of postmodernist theory (see Bordo 1993), has analysed the changing construction of the cul-tural ideal of 'slenderness', which now means not just thinness but the avoidance of flabbiness. Slenderness, she argues, has come to symbo-lise what she calls the state of the soul — the level of moral and per-sonal adequacy and will-power. This significance is only possible in a culture of over-abundance and it arises, she suggests, when there are 'instabilities in the "macro-regulation" of desire within the system of the social body' (1990:96) which generate a preoccupation with the internal management of the body. Tensions within the broader society are reflected in individuals' struggles for control over their own bodies.

For Bordo the tensions in question are those of consumer capital-ism in which we have to be both producers, capable of sublimating, delaying and repressing gratification, and also consumers who have to 'capitulate to desire and indulge in impulse' (ibid: 96). The affinities here with Kovel's argument (see pp. 67–8 above) are striking; both postulate an individual moulded by capitalism's needs of production and consumption to have the necessary subjectivities. The post-modernist focus on cultural construction (and deconstruction) are given a distinctively Marxist gloss. There are also interesting echoes of Freudian theorising in Bordo's work with the tension between desires and impulses (the id) and the need to delay and defer gratification (the superego), although psychology is no longer at the forefront of the analysis.

The initial stages of Bordo's argument are cast in gender-neutral terms. She then introduces gender, arguing that bodies are always gendered and slenderness is an ideal of distinctively female attractiveness. The management or female desire is a problem in 'phallocentric' (patriarchal) cultures and may be especially problematic where there is disruption and change in gender relations. Male anxieties may lead to the regulation of women's desires (fleshiness in women may symbolize women's maternal power). Equally, however, women may themselves see slimness as a liberation from their domestic reproductive identities – softness and bulges evoke in women 'helpless infancy and symbolize maternal femininity as it has been constructed over the last hundred years in the West' (ibid: 104). Like Orbach she suggests that anorexia may constitute a form of rebellion against femininity (again the Freudian echoes are strong). Consequently the axis of consumption–production is overlaid by a gendered hierarchical dualism 'which constructs a dangerous, appetitive, bodily "female principle" in opposition to a masterful "male" will' (ibid: 105).

Bordo's analysis provides, therefore, an account not only of why anorexia should be more common in women, but also suggests why it should have become something of an epidemic in Western societies, for not only do we live in a culture of over-abundance (and since over-abundance is class related this can account for the distinctive class location of the condition), but we also live in a period where gender relations are undergoing change. This is not to say that the analysis is unproblematic. Her argument, like Orbach's, is almost too powerful and pays too little attention to differences between women of class, age and ethnicity. If slenderness is such a strong cultural imperative (Bordo) and women's needs are so inadequately catered for (Orbach), we might expect to find rather higher proportions of woman from all social groups suffering from anorexia or bulimia than we do. In particular we might expect a peak in incidence rather later in the lifespan. Anorexia usually develops in the teenage years, yet the pressures on women concerning their appearance, and the lack of response to their emotional needs, are arguably not at their height in this period. Women have, for instance, to use food to nurture others rather than themselves when they have their own families, and their appearance is arguably more important after rather than before they leave school. Nonetheless, despite these problems there can be no doubt that feminists' analyses, with their focus on the problematic character of female identity in patriarchal societies and on the structural and cultural contradictions which women face (MacSween 1994: 254), have greatly enhanced our understanding of anorexia nervosa.[14]

Conclusion

Feminist psychologies, grounded as they are in psychodynamic theorising, share both the strengths and limitations of a psychodynamic approach. The limitations are clear enough. There is a tendency to generalise too freely about human psychological development which, when applied to gender differences, leads to forms of psychic essentialism. There is also a tendency to attribute too much to the inner world (albeit often held to be socially generated) and too little to external situational pressures and events, as in the classic psychodynamic focus on phantasy rather than reality (with the attendant danger of denying the reality of external events). And there is a related tendency to end up pathologising individuals, rather than focusing on the deficiencies of the society in which they live.

Yet feminist accounts of the development of gendered psychologies cannot be dismissed so readily. Their strength lies first, in their recognition of the complexity of human mental life – of the importance of inner conflicts, tensions and feelings, often unconscious, and of the role they can play in human thought and action, including their role in the generation or feelings and behaviours considered symptomatic of mental disorder. Second, and linked to this, they provide ways of understanding differences in gender identity and in the gendered expression of inner difficulties and conflicts, which are germane not just to levels of identified mental disorder (as currently constituted), but also to the form of disorder. Such ideas provide understandings which can help to complement sociological theorisations of the acquisition of gendered behaviour. Third, their strength lies, as in Freud's theorising, in the importance that is attached to childhood experience. For, whilst psychodynamic theorists may have been prone to over-emphasise the importance of early childhood experiences and their implications for personality, sociologists have arguably tended to forget or ignore their importance and the way in which they can make individual behaviour, including behaviour symptomatic of mental disorder, so resistant to change.

What, however, of the external social pressures and cultural factors? As we have seen, these are often incorporated into feminist accounts of gendered psychological development and are frequently given even more weight in feminist analyses of anorexia nervosa. We need, however, to examine some of the key social and cultural factors that can have a differential impact on men's and women's mental state –

either because they impinge unevenly on men and women or because of socially generated differences in response. In this chapter we have explored a number of factors that may differentially affect men's and women's mental states, including the extent to which dependency needs are met, the asymmetries of parenting and the psychological requirements of gender roles. In the next I consider the impact of situational stress and the gender division of labour.

Chapter 10

Stress and the Gender Division of Labour

If a physician of high standing, and one's own husband, assures friends and relatives that there is really nothing the matter with one but temporary nervous depression – a slight hysterical tendency – what is one to do?

My brother is also a physician, and also of high standing, and he says the same thing.

So I take phosphates or phosphites – whichever it is, and tonics, and journeys, and air, and exercise, and am absolutely forbidden to 'work' until I am well again.

Personally I disagree with their ideas.

Personally, I believe that congenial work, with excitement and change, would do me good.

But what is one to do?

I did write for a while in spite of them, but it *does* exhaust me a good deal – having to be so sly about it, or else meet with heavy opposition (Charlotte Perkins Gilman, *The Yellow Wallpaper* [1892] 1981: 10)

The studies of anorexia nervosa considered in the previous chapter indicate the way in which any adequate understanding of the impact of gender on the origins of mental disorder needs to locate differences in the psychological development of men and women within the context of the structural and cultural features of particular societies at particular moments in time. Socially generated male and female psychologies are linked both to gendered cultural requirements and to the gender division of labour.[1] In this chapter I want to examine the features of the

188

individual's more immediate social situation which may be directly conducive to mental disturbance, and consider whether we can detect any clear gender differences in the influence of these situational features. I begin by examining the notion of stress since it provides the most popular conceptualisation of the link between present or recent situational factors and mental disorder. I then consider studies examining the relationship between the gender division of labour and mental disorder. I argue that the concept of stress has important drawbacks as a means of analysing the impact of situational features on psychological states, and it is better to examine specific situational features without grouping them together via some synthesising notion such as stress.

Much of the work I consider in this chapter is grounded in social epidemiology. Taking gender differences in mental disorder (quite frequently alongside other measures of health) as its starting point, it endeavours to relate them to other variables, usually using quantitative techniques, and often obtaining measures for individuals at a single point in time. As will become apparent, the methodology of the studies raises a range of problems concerning the adequacy of the measures of the different variables. Moreover, the epidemiological approach often generates a rather individualistic, static picture for, notwithstanding the emphasis on the social, too little attention is usually given to the structural and cultural features of the society. This is particularly true of epidemiological studies of stress.[2]

Stress and Mental Disorder

The idea that certain recent or ongoing social circumstances or occurrences in an individual's life might be stressful to them and generate mental disorder, long predates twentieth-century epidemiology. As I indicated in Chapter 7, Michael MacDonald, in his study of anxiety and madness in the seventeenth century, points to the way in which madness was believed to result from an interaction of inherited predispositions and environmental 'stresses'.[3] He cites a physician and demonologist writing in 1665 who catalogued typical disturbing experiences as 'Sadness, fears, and scares, jealousy, discontents betwixt man and wife (the most lacerating of all grief) ... loss of love, and disappointment in a marriage, destiny of friends and loss of estates' (quoted in MacDonald 1981: 73).[4] Similar ideas were reiterated throughout subsequent centuries with lists of environmental causes rehearsing much the same factors, such as business and financial losses, the death of a child or spouse, and marital difficulties and conflicts.

The twentieth-century contribution has been twofold: first, to bring together the diversity of distressing experiences as possible causes of mental disorder under the potentially all-encompassing notion of stress; second, to try and measure, using empirical studies, the precise nature and extent of the association between stress and mental disorder. A major influence on this reformulation was Hans Selye's book, *The Stress of Life* (1956), which helped to give scientific legitimacy to the study of stress. In the mental health field the concept was initially deployed largely in the context of studies linking social class and mental disorder, which in the second half of the 1950s and the 1960s was the major focus of the social epidemiology of mental disorder. Repeated studies showed that rates of mental disorder, measured both by patient statistics and community surveys, were higher in the lower social classes (Hollingshead and Redlich 1958; Srole et al. 1962; Dohrenwend and Dohrenwend 1969) and the concept of stress was invoked to account for this association. Stress, it was suggested, was greater for those towards the bottom of the social structure – they were more likely to become unemployed, have poor housing, get divorced and so forth and, as a result, were more likely to become disturbed. It was but a simple step to extend the same idea to observed gender differences in mental disorder. Since women have lower status within society than men and face oppression and discrimination they, too, are more likely to become disturbed. Indeed, given the ready elision between notions of stress and oppression, it seems very easy to shift from claims about stress and mental disorder to claims about women's oppression and mental disorder (and vice versa). A similar argument was subsequently deployed in discussions of ethnicity and mental disorder (see King et al. 1994).

Part of the attraction of the concept of stress is the easy way in which a diversity of experiences – bereavement, unemployment, financial difficulties, marital troubles, pressures at work – can be brought into the fold. Moreover, the concept can be used to link features of the individual's *social* situation to mental disorder, so offering the potential for a genuinely social (environmental) explanation of psychological disorder that focuses not on events or circumstances in early childhood but on an individual's more immediate situation. It is no doubt these advantages that have made the idea of a link between stress and psychological disorder so popular and so pervasive. Yet, precisely because the link is so widely accepted it needs to be examined with care. Explanations of mental disorder in terms of stress raise many problems, as do claims that this is an area where there are important gender differences.

First, and very importantly, the notion of stress, which has affinities with concepts such as strain, pressure and trauma, is imprecise. That it can encompass so much, whilst an attraction, is also a potential disadvantage, for the term is used in diverse, contradictory ways. Much epidemiological research employs the concept to refer to certain features of the individual's social situation – 'stressful situations' or 'stressors'. This use of the concept needs to be clearly distinguished from its use to refer to the physical or psychological *responses* to difficulties – stress responses. Although widespread, this latter usage is of little explanatory value, since the differentiation of stress responses from mental disorder *per se* is difficult. This is particularly true where disorder is measured by some single-scale symptom inventory of distress, since there is little analytical distinction between stress as a response and psychological distress.

Second, even if we only use the term to refer to stressful situations not stress responses, we still have to decide which features of the individual's situation are likely to prove stressful – in other words, to identify the 'domain of the stressful'. Potentially the domain is infinite; in practice researchers limit the range quite considerably, incorporating varying assumptions as to what is stressful into their research. Epidemiological research tends to focus on relatively common, everyday aspects of people's lives in present-day society rather than more extraordinary occurrences. Divorce and unemployment are included in the standard lists but not war, or sexual abuse, although changing ideas about the frequency of abuse could lead to its inclusion in future lists.[5] These less common stressful experiences or traumas do feature in clinical work and are considered in the next chapter. The exclusion of childhood sexual abuse from the lists of the stressful is not only a matter of the presumed exceptional nature of the occurrence, but also because of another common limitation on the domain of the stressful: it is generally restricted to recent occurrences – usually the previous year or six months – rather than to more distant events. The substantive and temporal restrictions on the spectrum of events are important when considering gender differences, since the events included in standard inventories may under-represent some of the important events likely to be experienced by women, even in a recent period – including abortion and miscarriage as well as sexual attack, let alone being abused as a child. Some may be picked up under a heading such as 'major personal injury or illness' (Holmes and Rahe 1967), but only if they are so defined by the respondent.

Third, as the phrase 'stressful life events' indicates, much of the research has tended to focus on events rather than on 'ongoing difficulties' or 'chronic hassles' (Lazarus and Cohen 1977:89), though there are important exceptions to this, such as Walter Gove's work on marital roles, which was partly theorised in terms of stress, and George Brown and Tirril Harris's (1978) work on class differences in depression, which included both major events and severe difficulties.[6] When the focus is only on events then becoming unemployed during the period in question is included, being unemployed throughout the period is not. This distinction is also relevant to many features of women's situation which may only feature as stressors if ongoing difficulties are included. This applies not only to the possible ongoing stress of domestic labour and child care or managing household tasks alongside full-time work outside the home. It also applies to the quality of relations within the family – a sphere of much interest in other work on the causes of mental disorder, but largely excluded here (see Laing and Esterson 1964; Wynne et al. 1958), and to the experience of discrimination.[7] Fourth, much of the research has tended to assume it is undesirable events or circumstances, such as losing your job or getting divorced, that are stressful, although some researchers have argued that any change, even if desired, is stressful: for instance, starting a new job or getting married (Holmes and Rahe 1967; Dohrenwend 1973).

In practice, therefore, the range of what is regarded as stressful and included in particular studies is quite diverse and is often determined empirically rather than theoretically. Methodologically the studies also vary considerably and researchers face major problems both in measuring mental disorder and in determining how to assess the stressfulness of particular events or circumstances. Given the epidemiological underpinnings of much of the research in this area, and the desire to measure mental disorder across populations, it is usual to measure disorder using either single-scale symptom inventories or multiple-disorder scales, rather than by direct clinical evaluation. This means that most research links stressful events or difficulties either to self-reported psychological distress or to one or more psychiatric conditions based on self-assessed symptoms, not to clinically assessed disorder. This is an important feature of the research and means that we need to be very cautious about broad-ranging claims linking stressful circumstances to clinical disorder.

The measurement of stressful events and circumstances also raises numerous problems. A common strategy has been to try to standardise the measurement of stress by asking people to rank the stressfulness of a series of events; on this basis a scale of stressful events of different degrees of severity is constructed. Individuals are then assigned scores for the stressfulness of the events they have experienced over a particular period. Typical of this approach is the Holmes and Rahe (1967) Social Readjustment Rating Scale (SRRS) which includes over forty items involving change, ranging from death of a spouse (assigned a unit value of 100), divorce (with a unit value of 73) and separation (65), through to Christmas (12), a vacation (13), and a major change in eating habits. The full scale is given in Table 10.1.

Other researchers, notably Brown and Harris (1978), have suggested that highly standardised scales of stress are misconceived and some attempt must be made to measure the stressfulness of a particular event or difficulty for the individual in question. The major danger with this more subjective approach is that of contamination. An individual's retrospective assessment of the stressfulness of an occurrence is unlikely to be independent of their subsequent psychological state – that is, if depressed, a person is more likely to rate a prior event as having been stressful. Brown and Harris attempt to circumvent this problem, whilst retaining a concern with the significance of the event for the particular individual, by the researcher determining the stressfulness of events on the basis of information obtained about the individual's relevant aspirations, values and actions, and not subjective reports, using their Life Events and Difficulties Schedule (LEDS). In other words, the death of someone where the attachment has been shown by words and action to be strong is assessed as highly stressful, whether or not the respondent claims to have experienced it in this way.

Empirical support for the existence of a link between stressful events or circumstances and psychological distress is reasonable (see Totman 1990), but more complex models are needed than simple, additive ones that merely hypothesise that for every extra quantum of stress, psychological disorder becomes more likely. In the first place, the evidence indicates that stress is positively associated not only with psychological distress but also with other adverse outcomes such as physical sickness, accident rates, delinquent behaviour and a range of pathological

TABLE 10.1   *The Holmes–Rahe 'Social Readjustment Rating Scale'*

Rank	Life event	Mean value
1	Death of spouse	100
2	Divorce	73
3	Marital separation	65
4	Jail term	63
5	Death of close family member	63
6	Personal injury or illness	53
7	Marriage	50
8	Fired at work	47
9	Marital reconciliation	45
10	Retirement	45
11	Change in health of family member	44
12	Pregnancy	40
13	Sex difficulties	39
14	Gain of new family member	39
15	Business readjustment	39
16	Change of financial state	38
17	Death of close friend	37
18	Change to different line of work	36
19	Change in number of arguments with spouse	35
20	Mortgage over $10,000	31
21	Foreclosure of mortgage or loan	30
22	Change in responsibilities at work	29
23	Son or daughter leaving home	29
24	Trouble with in-laws	29
25	Outstanding personal achievement	28
26	Wife begin or stop work	26
27	Begin or end school	26
28	Change in living conditions	25
29	Revision of personal habits	24
30	Trouble with boss	23
31	Change in work hours or conditions	20
32	Change in residence	20
33	Change in schools	20
34	Change in recreation	19
35	Change in church activities	19
36	Change in social activities	18
37	Mortgage or loan less than $10,000	17
38	Change in sleeping habits	16
39	Change in number of family get-togethers	15

TABLE 10.1   *Cont ...*

Rank	Life event	Mean value
40	Change in eating habits	15
41	Vacation	13
42	Christmas	12
43	Minor violations of the law	11

SOURCE   Holmes and Rahe (1967) *Journal of Psychosomatic Research*, 11: 213–18.

indices. Mental disorder is only one of a number of possible responses and we need to identify the factors that produce differences in response. This issue is particularly salient when considering gender since, as I noted (see Chapters 5 and 8), men and women often handle psychological difficulties in different ways: men, at least in Western societies, tend to express their feelings outwards, for instance, in aggression or violence; in contrast, women tend to turn them inwards, for instance, in depression (commonly said by psychodynamic theorists to be a product of internalised, suppressed aggression). Adequate models need, therefore, to account for the way in which individuals express inner tension and stress, whether by reference to early psychological development (see the previous chapter), or to features of the individual's social situation, including the particular character of the stressful events or circumstances.

One suggestion in the latter mould (see Jackson 1962) is that where achievements rank higher than ascribed statuses individuals tend to blame others for their problems and feelings are turned outwards; where achievements do not match ascribed statuses then individuals are more likely to blame themselves (the attribution of blame to oneself is one of the psychological features of depression: see, for example, Abramson et al. 1978).[8] Extended to gender, this would suggest that women are more likely to turn feelings generated by stress and tension inwards and to blame themselves because on 'standard' measures their achievements are more limited.[9] Put another way, judged by male standards women are less successful than men and tend to blame themselves for this. Brown and Harris's approach is not dissimilar in that they link symptomatology with the character of events. On the one hand, they argue that clinical depression is particularly linked to events involving loss, such as the death of a spouse or child or marital separation (1978:105). On the other hand, they include in their model a category of 'symptom formation factors', factors designed to explain the different patterns of depressive symptomatology including the severity of depression (ibid: 1978: 254–63).[10] The idea of a linkage between the character of events and the character of the response has been pursued by others. For example, Andrews and House (1989), also in a study using the LEDS, found that patients with functional dysphonia ('a difficulty in voice production that cannot be explained by any demonstrable structural lesion of the larynx or any neurological lesion' – ibid: 343) had experienced situations where there was a conflict over speaking out (they faced situations where many would want to protest or complain, but there were obstacles to so doing).[11]

Second, whilst various forms of illness, deviance or under-performance may result from stressful experiences, an adequate model also needs to allow for the possibility of 'coping' with stress (Mechanic 1978: 11; Totman 1990: Chapter 8). Indeed, under some circumstances stress may enhance performance. Theoretical models like Brown and Harris's (1978) incorporate such a variable. In their model, the impact of stressful events and ongoing difficulties is mediated by a variable termed 'vulnerability' – which they indicate is interchangeable with coping. Vulnerability for them is not a matter of inherent capacities, but is a *situationally generated* capacity that is itself a function of certain features of the individual's circumstances. Amongst the women they studied, four factors were of importance: the presence or absence of an intimate relationship (the most important factor); work outside the home; having three or more children under fourteen at home; and the loss of their own mother before the age of eleven (the latter is the only factor that refers to a past event rather than an aspect of the immediate situation). According to Brown and Harris the four are vulnerability factors rather than additional events or difficulties, because they only have an impact in the presence of events or difficulties and do not exert an independent force (this claim has been hotly contested, see McKee and Vilhjalmsson 1986). The key components of their model are set out in Figure 10.1.

Brown and Harris's research showed that differences in vulnerability played a significant part in accounting for class differences in women's levels of depression. Although some of the class difference was due to differences in the number of major events and ongoing difficulties experienced, with working-class women facing more events and difficul-

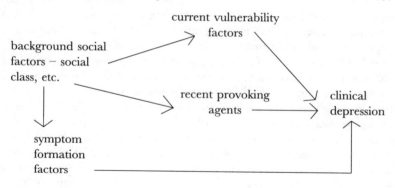

SOURCE Brown and Harris (1978: 48).

FIGURE 10.1   *Causal Model of Depression*

ties, class differences were only fully accounted for when situationally generated vulnerability was incorporated into the analysis. Working-class women were more likely than middle-class women to be in situations where they were vulnerable to severe events and major difficulties. An intimate confiding relationship was a key factor protecting women when faced by various adversities.

This latter finding has been confirmed by a range of subsequent studies which have shown that what has come to be known as 'social support' plays an important role in mediating the impact of stressful events and circumstances (see Totman 1990: Chapter 6). Other research has also suggested the importance of positive events in raising self-esteem and facilitating individuals' capacity to cope with stress (Phillips 1968)[12]

Brown and Harris's study is of considerable importance. First, it provides a more complex model for the analysis of the impact of stressful events and circumstances on individuals, although admittedly the incorporation of a separate set of vulnerability factors is its most disputed feature. Second, it provides, via the vulnerability factors, important insights into variables that may be particularly salient to understanding depression in women. The significance lies not only in listing factors such as the importance of the lack of a supportive, confiding relationship or the demands of having several young children at home, but in attempting to specify their mode of operation. Third, and perhaps most importantly, the study provides strong evidence of the importance of situational factors in explaining the origins of depression (biochemical changes may be necessary, but are not sufficient to account for the occurrence of depression).[13] If we are to understand why women and men become depressed we need to move beyond the realm of biology to explore social issues.

One problem with the study, as with other epidemiological studies, is that, notwithstanding both the attention to meaning in the study of stressful events and major difficulties and the focus on the situational features of individuals' lives, it takes the structural arrangements and culture of the society as given. Clearly, the demands of having three young children depend on the social, material and cultural context. Where there is ready access to nursery and child care outside the family then we would not expect the number of young, dependent children to be a vulnerability factor and subsequent research has indicated some change in the salience of this factor (Brown and Harris 1989). We cannot, therefore, readily generalise from this study across time and place. Moreover, the study was not designed to explore gender differences in the origins of depression (the use of a sample of women was contingent) and, as no men were included, gender comparisons are not possible.[14]

Direct comparisons of either the character or the levels of stress faced by men and women are limited in number. One early study by Barbara Dohrenwend (1972), using a relatively small sample, focused on events requiring readjustment that were assigned standard ratings. She found that women tended to have higher life change scores. This was true both of events the individual did not control as well as those they did, but the former seemed to be more closely linked to symptom levels 'suggesting that their psychological distress tended to be associated with the lack of power to control their lives' (ibid: 232). However, other studies have shown little difference between the levels of stress faced by men and women, and more recent authors have tended to conclude that 'men and women do not differ greatly in the number of undesirable life events they experience' (Kessler and McLeod 1984:620). This conclusion must, however, be treated with caution. It is based on a relatively small number of studies carried out over a limited period of time in a restricted range of social contexts, with a restricted and arguably gender-biased set of events, and typically excludes ongoing difficulties. Consequently, it largely leaves untapped precisely the sort of structural and cultural features which most feminists would see as the *sine qua non* of women's oppression. We need, therefore, to recognise that the assumption of a ready elision between stress and oppression is mistaken. It should also be noted that writers like Brown and Harris (1978:106–11; 1989:71–81) explicitly reject the view that stresses are *additive*, with each additional stress making mental ill-health more likely, unless the events are unrelated to one another.

Interestingly, some research appears to support the view that whether or not women face more stressful circumstances they are more vulnerable to them. A number of suggestions have been put forward to account for this possible difference. One is that women have fewer supportive relationships to help them cope with stress (see Berkman and Breslow 1983: 128–9). Such an idea goes against the evidence that women generally have more close relationships than men and are more able to talk about their problems (Allan 1979, 1989), though we should note that there are a higher proportion of divorced, separated and widowed women than men).[15] However, in couples women provide more emotional support for their partner than men (Duncombe and Marsden 1993). Another possibility raised by Kessler and McLeod (1984) focuses on the consequences of women's involvement with others (which is linked to the support they provide). Women, they argue, are not generally more vulnerable to undesirable events, but they are more vulnerable to events of a certain type: those involving someone in their close network. They not only report more of these types of event but also seem more affected by them (see Belle 1982). The claim is that women's emotional involvement with others, and their support and caring for others, is potentially stressful and accounts for the higher levels of psychological distress they report (whilst at the same time it may reduce the vulnerability of those they support, including their spouses, to stress). For example, women's typically closer emotional attachment to their children leaves them more vulnerable to any severe adversities that may befall them. This may be one factor making depression more common in women, since emotional losses are particularly associated with depression. Taken together, therefore, the data suggest a gender gap in the level of social support men and women provide that increases women's vulnerability to mental disorder and reduces men's.

I would argue, however, that exploration of specific factors affecting men's and women's mental health is more fruitful than attempts to make quantitative comparisons between the aggregate levels of stress experienced by men and women, given the difficulty of formulating gender-neutral measures of stress. Indeed, while the concept of stress may be useful in an examination of the processes mediating *between* situational factors and mental disorder, it is the situational factors which need explicit attention. To describe these situational factors as stressors or stressful life events and group them together is not a very useful strategy. What is needed is a careful examination of the key structural and cultural features of society that are conducive to mental disorder. In this respect the conceptual and theoretical strategies adopted in feminist analyses of anorexia nervosa are of more potential value, with their attention to the structural divisions within the society that underpin gender relations and the related cultural meanings attached to food and the body. In the remainder of the chapter, therefore, I want to focus on one key feature: the gender division of labour both in the domestic sphere and in paid employment.

The Gender Division of Labour

The image of the trapped housewife suggested by three of Brown and Harris's vulnerability factors has frequently been invoked by feminists and psychiatrists to explain mental disorder in women, especially to try and account for the association between women and depression. The image takes many forms. One variant was given powerful voice by Charlotte Perkins Gilman in her brief novel, *The Yellow Wallpaper* (1981), first published in the United States in 1892, which subtly and effectively conveys the view that it is women's domestic situation, not inherent predispositions, that leads to mental disturbance. In passages like the one at the beginning of this chapter she beautifully evokes an image of a woman trapped into passivity and patienthood by her marital role.

Gilman, who became an active feminist, was writing in a period when the cult of domesticity generally restricted the activities of middle-class women in the US and Britain to the home – a home in which their job was to ensure the smooth regulation of the household, although much of the labour, including the care of children, was carried out by servants. In order to counter the reduction in the labour of housework, resulting in part from the increasing commercialisation of many activities, middle-class women were encouraged to develop and systematise their expertise in housewifery (Davidoff 1976). Many, including some feminists, expounded the virtues of domestic education and the importance of preserving the home. Others, like Gilman, saw the home as the source of women's oppression from which they must liberate themselves: they were like birds trapped in a 'gilded cage', forced into sickness and neurosis by the narrowness, boredom and constraints of their lives.

Similar themes were articulated by 1960s feminists in response to the idealisation of the home and family during the late 1940s and the 1950s following the Second World War. In *The Feminine Mystique* (1963) Betty Friedan identifies 'the problem that has no name'. The problem is women's sense of dissatisfaction and discontent with their role as housewives, which, in Friedan's view, is evidenced by high rates of divorce, and by women's high levels of anxiety and depression and their increasing resort to psychiatric help. The voice of these women, she suggests, can no longer be ignored. It is a voice which says 'I want something more than my husband and my children and my home' (1963: 32). Of course, the situation of middle-class women in the 1950s differed in important respects from that of their nineteenth-century counterparts. With the expansion of the middle classes they had become a far larger group within the society. And although few women with children had paid employment outside the home, more middle as well as lower-class women worked prior to marriage and in the period between marriage and having their first child. And proportionately fewer, even of the middle-class women, had servants. Running the household 'properly' consequently entailed more direct domestic labour for middle-class women – an increase not entirely compensated for by the new domestic consumer durables, which were restricted to the most affluent households in the 1950s, or by the reduction in family sizes (Busfield and Paddon 1977: 9). Indeed, despite all the demographic and social changes, middle-class women were still largely confined to the home. The married woman was still 'the captive wife' (Gavron 1968). Subsequent researchers investigated and analysed the nature of domestic work in some detail. Anne Oakley (1976), for instance, contended that being a housewife should be viewed as a form of employment and the work compared with various jobs in the labour market. Her research, along with that of others (see Lopata 1971), pointed to the routine, monotonous, and fragmentary nature of housework and the social isolation it involved. She also pointed to the difficulty of being both a good wife and a good mother – Anna Davin (1978) contending that the relative importance of these two roles had changed over time, with the role of mother replacing the Victorian focus on that of wife as the key marital role of women.

Feminist ideas like this provided an important underpinning of the work of Gove and his co-workers (Gove 1972; Gove and Tudor 1972) on marital roles and psychological disorder.[16] In turn both Gove's work on marital roles and mental disorder, like the feminist writing of the late 1960s and early 1970s, is indebted to the intellectual tradition of sociological functionalism and more specifically to the role analysis of Talcott Parsons (Parsons 1951; Parsons and Bales 1956).[17] In Gove's work, the substantive concerns of the feminist writing of the end of the 1960s and early 1970s and the theoretical approach of functionalism were combined with a further element: an essentially epidemiological methodology.

Gove's studies of the early 1970s are well-known. His starting point was his observation that women's higher overall level of mental disorder was mainly due to the higher levels of mental disorder amongst married women when compared with married men (Gove 1972; Gove and Tudor 1972). Amongst the single, the situation is reversed and levels of diagnosed disorder are far higher amongst men than women. Indeed, rates of mental disorder are considerably higher amongst the single than the married, but the married constitute such a high proportion of the adult population that this gender difference determines the aggregate picture. These epidemiological observations provided the basis for Gove's argument about marital roles. For, if the key gender difference is amongst the married, *prima facie* it must be tied to differences in marital role. Hence, Gove postulates that women's marital role is 'more frustrating and less rewarding' than men's (Gove and Tudor 1972: 816) and, on the assumption 'that stress may lead to mental illness' (ibid: 1972: 814), the result is more mental disorder in women.

Gove initially listed five differences between men's and women's marital roles which he considered unfavourable to women. First, a married woman's structural base is typically more fragile than a man's, since women generally occupy only one major social role, housewife, whereas men usually are both household head and paid worker, and if one role is unsatisfactory they can focus on the other. Second, many married women find their major role as housewife frustrating: it does not demand much skill and has low prestige. Third, a housewife's role is relatively invisible: she can put things off, let things slide and brood on her troubles. Fourth, if a woman has a paid job she is in a less satisfactory position than a man because of discrimination at work and the tensions between the demands of work and home, since women are still required to do the bulk of the household chores. Fifth, the expectations confronting women are unclear and diffuse, and the uncertainty and lack of control over the future is frustrating – for instance, the problems when their children leave home.[18]

According to Gove, these differences in marital role account for the higher level of mental disorder in married women, and are further supported by the fact that the gap between the rates of disorder in married and single men is greater than in women. Whilst marriage has positive benefits for both men and women it appears to benefit men more than women, an argument developed by Emile Durkheim in his classic study, *Suicide* (1951). However, Gove contends that women's level of mental disorder has only been higher since the 1940s, for it is only in this period that women's marital role has become especially stressful (Gove and Tudor 1972). Until then their role was more meaningful: families were larger, child care took up most of a woman's adult life and 'housework required more time and skill and was highly valued' (ibid: 816).[19]

Theoretically, Gove subsequently distinguished between 'fixed roles' and 'nurturant roles' to illuminate the contrasting dimensions of men's and women's roles. His concept of a fixed role is a reformulaton of his idea of the invisibility of women's marital role which means they can easily let things slide. The point is that fixed obligations – 'obligations that are not easily rescheduled' (1984: 78) – are more typical of male than female roles. Consequently, there is also likely to be a stronger societal reaction to men who show signs of mental disorder than to women. Gove's nurturant role is arguably a redescription of women's usual marital role since it is one in which someone has to carry out 'the *essential* household tasks' and take on 'the major responsibility for the care of children, spouses and aged relatives' (ibid: 80). These obligations mean that 'women will find it more difficult to adopt the sick role completely', and 'will tend to experience the demands of others as excessive and as impairing their ability to rest and relax' (ibid: 80). Gove contends these claims are not incompatible with his fixed role hypothesis, for in his view housewives are in a situation where it is easier to adopt a sick-role partially but more difficult to adopt it fully (ibid: 81).

Gove's arguments have attracted attention from feminists and others because of their emphasis on the negative features of women's marital

situation, and the strong support they appear to provide for claims as
to women's oppression. They have also been widely criticised. One
problem concerns his conceptualisation of mental disorder. The Doh-
renwends (1976) noted that Gove (Gove and Tudor 1972: 812–3)
employs a narrow definition of mental disorder in his early work that
embraces the neuroses and (non-organic) psychoses, but excludes
organic and behaviour (personality) disorders, where male rates tend to
be higher.[20] This biases the data towards female over-representation, as
well as ignoring issues arising from the fluidity of the concept of mental
disorder. It also ensures a poor correspondence between the theoretical
definition and those embodied in the substantive data. Gove recognises
this problem and excludes cases of organic or personality disorders
where a diagnosis is given. Where it is not, he makes the questionable
assertion that 'the measures of mental illness relate very well to our
conception of mental illness' (Gove and Tudor 1972: 818)[21]

Gove's reliance on patient data is another limitation of his early
work. In his initial paper, only three of seventeen studies listed are
community surveys (Gove 1972: 37); the rest use service statistics. Yet if
we restrict our attention to community surveys it is clear that the data
on the link between gender, marital status and reported symptoms are
far from consistent. Cochrane, reviewing the evidence from community
surveys, argued that it did not confirm the finding that marriage provides less protection for women than men (1984: 53). For example, a
study (Cochrane and Stopes-Roe 1980) of mental disorder in urban
areas of England showed no clear association between marital status
and mental disorder, and married women did not manifest higher
symptom levels than married men. Hence the observations on the link
between marital status, gender and mental disorder that Gove seeks to
explain are arguably an artefact of his measures of mental disorder.

This does not mean, however, that the differential demands of marriage on men and women are irrelevant to mental health. One of the
deficiencies of Gove's analysis is the theorisation of the impact of marriage through a notion of social role grounded in 1950s functionalism.
Not only does he talk at times of gender as if it were a social role (see
Chapter 3), but his analysis of marriage in terms of the marital roles
tends to be static and over-general. He assumes, for instance, that
women usually occupy one major social role, that of housewife. Yet,
even if we leave aside the issue of the high proportion of married
women in paid employment (more now than when Gove was writing),
it is not helpful to view married women as occupying a single major

role. Married women, even when they do not participate in the paid labour market, often have a diversity of roles as wife, mother, daughter, sibling, friend and so forth. Treating those monolithically as a single role is unsatisfactory. Moreover, Gove's analysis also reflects both its functionalist origins and its epidemiological methodology in the lack of attention to conflict, tension and struggle within the marital relationship. In his theorisation, the dynamic of power within the marital relationship, so patent in Gilman's *The Yellow Wallpaper*, disappears from the picture.

Subsequent work, including some by Gove (Gove and Geerken 1977), has examined the impact of different aspects of the gender division of labour more directly, some studies concentrating only on women, others comparing men and women. Much of it, adopting an epidemiological approach, still does little to capture the dynamics of power and conflict. Nonetheless, it has helped to clarify the complex relationships between gender, domestic labour, paid employment and mental disorder.

The research has largely centred on two competing models of women's marital roles. On the one hand, there is the argument found in Gilman's narrative that women's roles tie them to the house and that their lives need enhancing (the role enhancement model). [22] On the other hand, there is the argument that when women work outside the home they have to do too much, labouring both at home and in paid employment (the role overload model). The studies provide empirical support for both models, and indicate that both processes – overload and enhancement – need to be taken into consideration. In line with the role enhancement model, most studies find that the psychological health of women who work is better than for those who do not (Cochrane and Stopes-Roe 1981; Surtees et al. 1983); yet where a distinction is made between part-time and full-time work, studies usually indicate that the mental health of women who work part-time is better than that of full-time workers – a finding more consistent with the role overload model.

One problem with many of the studies is the lack of precision in the measurement of different variables (for instance, number of children is typically a surrogate measure for domestic responsibilities). Another is the lack of attention to the possibility that health status influences employment status, rather than employment status determining mental health (or physical). However, a recent study (Bartley et al. 1992) using data from the Health and Lifestyles Survey (Blaxter 1990), attempted to control for the selective effect of health status, and still found that women who worked were psychologically (and physically) healthier than those who did not.[24] It also confirmed earlier studies in finding that women who worked part-time had fewer psychological symptoms than full-time workers. The study employed a relatively complex measure of domestic conditions and found this was more strongly related to psychological symptoms than either employment status or socio-economic group. The measure took account of the following factors: the total number of dependent children in the household, the number of children under three, the presence of persons over 75 years, living density, lone parenthood, sharing accommodation, access to a garden, the type of area (built-up, rural, etc.) and the number of unemployed people in the household. It represents, therefore, a composite measure of a selected set of potentially stressful 'ongoing difficulties' (but not events), and provides further confirming evidence that the difficulties of women's social situation are conducive to mental ill-health.

Bartley et al.'s study focused only on women. Kate Hunt and Ellen Annandale (1993) have, however, recently considered whether the relationships between health (mental and physical) and domestic and paid work are gender-specific. Using data from the cohort of 35 year-olds in the West of Scotland Twenty-07 Survey, they found that domestic work had more impact on women than men (largely, they suspected, because so few of the men were engaged in a substantial amount of domestic work) and that paid work had stronger effects on health than domestic work, although combining the two increased the effect on health. Paid work generally had somewhat similar effects on men and women, with poorer conditions of work generally being associated with higher symptom scores. However, just as working conditions differed markedly between the genders (men were more likely to face noxious working environments and longer hours of paid work, women to have poor sickness and holiday arrangements), so which working conditions affected health differed (interestingly the length of working hours did not correlate significantly with health in either men or women).

However, the similarities in the effect of domestic and paid work on men and women should not blind us to the marked gender divisions reflected in patterns of working (42 per cent of women in the sample spent 23 hours or more on domestic labour, only 3 per cent of men; 33 per cent of men spent 50 or more hours on paid work, only 7 per cent of women). There is still a very high degree of gender segregation in the labour market and marked divisions in the allocation of domestic labour, which are reflected in the different working conditions of men and women. These differences are arguably more significant than the fact that if men and women do face similar working conditions they appear to respond in similar ways. In addition, it should be noted that Hunt and Annandale, like Bartley et al., use a malaise measure to screen for problems of mental health, with all the in-built gender bias of instruments in both the selection of symptoms to include and the reliance on self-assessments (see Chapter 5 above).

Conclusion

A number of points emerge from this discussion of stress, mental disorder and the gender division of labour. First, there is strong evidence that immediate situational factors do play a part in the aetiology of mental disorders, especially of the neuroses and affective disorders, and we cannot treat them simply as a matter of individual vulnerability and individual pathology. Second, whilst women's oppression is both a material and social reality, we cannot readily conclude on the basis of studies of stress that women face higher levels of stress than men and, by extension, of levels of oppression, not least because of the difficulty of constructing gender-neutral measures of stress.

Third, although similar adverse conditions of domestic and paid labour (where they do occur) may have equally adverse consequences on men's and women's mental health; gender segregation in the labour market and gender divisions in domestic labour ensure that their conditions of work are often very different. Moreover, women's emotional attachments may make them especially vulnerable to events involving someone in their close network. Regrettably there has, however, generally been relatively little work that tries to link types of events or circumstances to the precise type of response (the frequent use of malaise scales does not encourage the examination of differences in response).

Fourth and finally, rather than collapsing diverse experiences into aggregate measures of stress, more progress may be made by examining specific structural features of men's and women's lives and exploring their links with mental disorder. It is the distinctive features of the social circumstances in which people live that we need to explore if we are to understand the impact of gender on the origins of mental disorder. And in so doing we need to be more aware of changing structural and cultural arrangements of society than epidemiological studies have tended to recognise. In particular, we need to attend to a dimension only implicit in studies of stress – that of power. In the next chapter I explore two specific features which raise the question of power more clearly: war and sexual violence.

Chapter 11

Trauma and Powerlessness:
War and Sexual Violence

In traumatic neuroses the operative cause of the illness is not the trifling physical injury but the affect of fright – the psychical trauma. In an analogous manner, our investigations reveal, for many, if not for most, hysterical symptoms, precipitating causes which can only be described as psychical traumas. Any experience which calls up distressing affects – such as those of fright, anxiety, shame or physical pain – may operate as a trauma of this kind; and whether it in fact does so depends naturally on the susceptibility of the person affected . . . (Breuer and Freud [1893] 1974: 56).

It would be an exaggeration if I were to describe Slateford as a depressing place by daylight. The doctors did everything possible to counteract gloom, and the wrecked faces were outnumbered by those who were emerging from their nervous disorders. . .

But by night they lost control and the hospital became sepulchral and oppressive with saturations of war experience. . . One became conscious that the place was full of men whose slumbers were morbid and terrifying – men muttering uneasily or suddenly crying out in their sleep. Around me was that underworld of dreams haunted by submerged memories of warfare and its intolerable shocks and self-lacerating failures to achieve the impossible. By daylight each mind was a sort of aquarium for the psychopath to study. In the daytime, sitting in a sunny room, a man could discuss his psycho-neurotic symptoms with his doctor, who could diagnose phobias and conflicts and formulate them in scientific terminology. Significant dreams could be noted down, and Rivers could try to remove repressions. But by night each man was back in his doomed sector of a horror-stricken Front Line, where the panic and stampede of some ghastly experience was re-enacted among the livid faces of the dead. No doctor could save him then, when he became the lonely victim of his dream disasters and delusions (Sassoon 1937: 556–7).[1]

The connection frequently made between trauma and mental disorder has its twentieth-century foundations in psychoanalytic theorising. In their first paper on hysteria, Breuer and Freud outlined a traumatic theory of the disorder, contending that the concept of traumatic hysteria – that is, hysteria provoked by some physical accident – could be extended to include hysteria provoked by a psychic event or series of events. Their delineation of the notion of trauma was broad and was formulated in terms of the reaction to certain events. A trauma was any experience provoking distressing affect, such as fright, anxiety, shame or physical pain. Consequently, the term potentially embraced a domain of experiences little different from that now encompassed by 'stressful events'. However, their theoretical focus in analysing individual cases was more restricted, concentrating on sexual experiences and on the sexual dynamics of family relations. Of the five cases (all women) presented in *Studies in Hysteria* (Breuer and Freud 1974), only Breuer's Anna O, whose hysteria was said to have its origins in the illness and death of her father, was not directly attributed to sexual trauma.

Breuer and Freud postulated that it was the memory of the traumatic event – a memory that is repressed but 'acts like a foreign body which long after its entry must continue to be regarded as an agent that is still at work' (1974: 56–7) – that produced the symptoms of disorder. It was only by bringing that memory into consciousness that the disorder would disappear. In Freud's theorising, memory was soon to be transformed into phantasy, at least as far as instances of sexual abuse were concerned. This vital shift, which has rightly been widely criticised by a range of scholars in recent decades (see Masson 1984), was undoubtedly facilitated by Freud's focus on ideas. It was not so much what actually happened to people but their mental life which was decisive, and the relationship between the external and the internal – the event and the experiences of it – was less important. The inner world of the individual had primacy over the material reality of the social (see Chapter 9 above).

Despite Freud's potentially broad definition of the domain of the traumatic, which appears to make it more or less coterminous with the stressful, in everyday discourse a distinction, albeit not very exact, is commonly made between stress and trauma. This is that, whereas a stressful event (or ongoing difficulty) is a pressure which may produce a range of responses, including coping, it is the character of the response that defines whether an experience is traumatic or not. Only events producing a severe psychological reaction belong to the domain of traumas. This means that in practice the term trauma refers to more extreme, severe and exceptional experiences which are more over-whelming in their psychological consequences. They often involve threats to life or bodily integrity, or a close personal encounter with violence and death (Herman 1992: 33). In contrast, stressful experi-ences have a more mundane, routine character and their effect, though it may be insidious, is less catastrophic. However, the domains of stress and trauma are set by convention and often overlap: what is a stress for one person may be traumatic for another.

Academics' definitions and measures reflect and contribute to these conventions. I noted in the last chapter that measures of stressful events typically encompass a range of quite common events (common, that is, within a population) such as unemployment, sickness or the death of close family members which, though they may be very traumatic for certain individuals, are culturally normal and less shocking. In contrast they tend to exclude sexual abuse or domestic violence or certain experiences of war or torture. Such occurrences are by no means always uncommon and this constitutes a strong ground for including them in measures of stress. However, domestic violence and sexual abuse are often highly traumatic, especially certain forms, most obviously rape and incest. I have therefore chosen to discuss them under the heading of trauma rather than stress to reflect their more extreme and overwhelming character.

Whereas Freud emphasised the inner world in his traumatic theory of the neuroses, others, influenced by feminist analyses of domestic vio-lence and sexual abuse, have emphasised the dimension of power in understanding trauma. Judith Herman in her study *Trauma and Recovery* views psyhological trauma as 'an affliction of the powerless', adding that:

> At the moment of trauma, the victim is rendered helpless by overwhelming force. When the force is that of nature, we speak of disasters. When the force is that of other human beings, we speak of atrocities. Traumatic events overwhelm the ordinary systems of care that give people a sense of control, connection, and meaning (1992:33).

This gives a much more structural dimension to the analysis of trauma than Freud's theorisation. It allows us to consider the ways in which individuals or groups are rendered powerless – as well as the ways in which, in a situation of powerlessness, they are threatened or treated with harshness and violence. This is necessary if we are to look at the linkages between gender, trauma and mental disorder. Certainly there can be no simple claim that women are treated with greater physical harshness or brutality than men, as the literature on sexual abuse and violence might seem to suggest. As Connell claims, 'So far as the official and semi-official figures go, then, it appears that men are more commonly than women the victims of serious interpersonal violence', adding, 'and even more commonly the perpetrators' (1987:14). This is because much violence is inflicted by men on other men. However, violence inflicted by men on women may be particularly traumatising both because of its specific character (often from someone they know) and because of women's high degree of powerlessness.

In order to explore some of these issues further I want to examine two areas: first, the link between violence in war and mental disorder through the concept of shell-shock; and second, the link between sexual abuse and mental disorder.

War, Masculinity and Shell-Shock

War represents the ultimate exercise of power. It involves coercion through the deployment of military power − a form of power which some sociologists have regarded as distinctive (see Mann 1986) and which in most countries has long been concentrated in the hands of the state.[2] This power takes the form of violence and threats of violence, a violence which is authorised and legitimated by the state and is institutionalised and 'impersonal' in that the military personnel who exercise violence do so on behalf of someone else rather than acting directly for themselves. Consequently, their motivations to act violently are subject to complex mediations, and their violent actions may be more detached and calculated.

Historically, military activity has been almost exclusively male (see Connell 1987: 14). During this century, women have come to be employed in the armed forces in a number of countries, but have been largely excluded from active combat and the dangers of the front line.[3] Not surprisingly military activity, especially active service in times of war, is strongly linked to notions of masculinity. Indeed, the ideal requirement for the conduct and characteristics of the military man constitute nigh on a roll call of idealised masculinity: bravery, courage, strength, endurance, discipline. Of course, what is expected of the military varies across time and place and according to rank. Whereas leadership, tactical skills, responsibility and judgement are required of officers; discipline and obedience are considered essential amongst the lower ranks. Moreover, the large scale, ground-based combat typical of say First World War battles imposes different requirements from say guerrilla warfare or airborne combat.

The standards and qualities required of the military in the conduct of war requires both the tight regulation of conduct and special training in which discipline and toughness are key elements. Though war may harness 'natural' tendencies to aggression, it is highly dependent on socially acquired skills and characteristics. The strategies used in military training – the harsh regimes, the humiliation and 'mortification of self' (Goffman 1961), the victimisation, coercion and punishment have been well-documented, notably in biographical and autobiographical accounts. Departures from the expected standards of conduct are treated harshly, whether informally or via formal procedures such as the court martial – a harshness that is no doubt a reflection in part of the difficulties of maintaining the required levels of order and obedience. Those who become sick are, not surprisingly, often treated with suspicion and are liable to charges of malingering.

The requirements of military activity and the techniques for training soldiers and controlling deviance need to be born in mind in any consideration of the phenomenon of 'shell-shock' – a condition whose delineation recognises that the harsh realities of war can have a traumatic effect on the psychological health of the men.[4] Shell-shock is of particular interest to an examination of the linkages between gender and mental disorder. In the first place, it belongs to the group of 'male mental disorders' – that is, disorders more commonly diagnosed in men than women – a group that now includes alcoholism, drug addiction and various types of sexual disorder, and formerly included GPI and hypochondriasis (see Chapter 2).

Second, as a male disorder, shell-shock is unusual in that it was located in the emerging group of psycho-neuroses, a group of disorders especially associated with women rather than men. It therefore stands out as fracturing the standard gender linkages. Third, it is of particular interest because it requires us to confront very directly issues of masculinity, a domain where we might expect, other things being equal, problematic behaviour to be treated as wrongdoing rather than illness (see Chapter 6). It raises very directly, therefore, the question of the conditions under which male behaviour comes to be constituted as mental disorder. Fourth and finally, it is of interest because of the salience of class in the differentiation of cases of shell-shock. Consequently, it allows some examination of the complex interaction of class and gender in relation to mental disorder. Although there were far fewer officers than privates, and in absolute terms far more cases of shell-shock in the latter rather than the former, rates of mental breakdown were higher amongst officers than privates. Some suggested the discrepancy was very considerable: 'Officers are affected in the proportion of five to one as compared with privates and non-commissioned officers' (MacCurdy 1918:9). Another put the over-representation rather lower but still estimated it as two to one (see Wittkower and Spillane 1940:15).

Shell-shock

The term shell-shock was introduced by a British doctor, Charles Myers, serving in the Royal Army Medical Corps in France, in a brief article published in *The Lancet* in 1915.[5] In it he described three cases of what he regarded as a nervous disorder in soldiers who had been at the front line. The key symptoms were loss of memory and disturbances of vision, smell and taste, and he pointed to the close relation between the three cases and cases of hysteria. Myers was presumably referring to so-called conversion hysteria in which some physical malfunction such as paralysis or anaesthesia was held to be of psychogenic rather than physical origin (psychic processes being 'converted' into some physical symptom or sign (Batchelor 1969: 146)). What was distinctive in his view was the association of these symptoms with being under direct fire from shells and he gave the syndrome the label 'shell-shock', reflecting its specific aetiology.[6] The treatment he prescribed for the three soldiers included rest, suggestion and hypnosis.

The concept of shell-shock rapidly entered public consciousness in Britain, a consciousness increasingly horrified by the slaughter of large numbers of young men in the trenches in France, and the number of cases identified was relatively high (by the end of the war some 80,000 cases had passed through the army medical services (Stone 1985: 249)). The loss of memory noted as severe in two out of Myers's three cases became the hallmark of the condition and was reflected in the literature of the period. Rebecca West's (1988) vivid portrait of a soldier returning home unable to remember his wife and marriage in *Return of the Soldier*, first published in 1918, makes amnesia the defining symptom. Yet medical characterisations of the condition broadened (and loosened) the symptom list. G. Elliot Smith and T.H. Pear, a doctor and a psychologist, in their book, *Shell Shock and Its Lessons* (1917), first mention disturbances of sensation and movement such as blindness, deafness and mutism as key symptoms; they then list a range of what they term subjective disturbances which they assert are 'frequently more serious than the objective', including:

> loss of memory, insomnia, terrifying dreams, pains, emotional instability, diminution of self-confidence and self-control, attacks of unconsciousness or of changed consciousness, sometimes accompanied by convulsive movements resembling those characteristic of epileptic fits, incapacity to understand any but the simplest matters, obsessive thoughts, usually of the gloomiest and most painful kind, even in some cases hallucinations and incipient delusions (1917: 12–13).

The lack of specificity of symptoms was widely noted as was the fact that none were new to the psychiatric repertory: 'shell-shock involves no *new* symptoms or disorders. Every one was known beforehand in civil life' (ibid: 24–5).

The widening of the symptom list went alongside a growing tendency to differentiate two major types of what were increasingly called war neuroses by professionals, if not by the lay public. First, there was the hysterical form initially outlined by Myers and held to be common amongst the non-commissioned ranks (Myers's three cases all fell into this group – two were privates, one a corporal). Second, there was a form closer to anxiety states and neurasthenia, which was the type more commonly identified amongst officers.[7] For example, John Mac-Curdy, an American doctor who visited Britain in 1917 to carry out a study of war neuroses, distinguished between conversion hysteria and anxiety states. He contended the former were 'confined almost entirely to privates and non-commissioned officers' (1918: 87), asserting that, 'Although in absolute numbers they are more frequent in occurrence than pure anxiety states, yet they are so much simpler in mechanism that it is less difficult to understand them and to treat them' (1918: 87).[8] The frequent use of the term war neuroses to embrace both hysteria and anxiety states is of some interest since, when the label psychoneuroses began to enter psychiatric classifications, hysteria was not usually included in the list.[9]

Yet, although the term shell-shock quickly caught the popular imagination, the existence, nature and character of the disorder was widely contested. On the one hand, there was considerable anxiety amongst the military establishment including some military doctors, who were presented with what seemed to be a new phenomenon of rather startling proportions, that recognition of the condition would lead to a flood of cases from those who wanted to get away from the front. They were also concerned that the soldier's state of fear, which often preceded the breakdown for some length of time, served to 'weaken, or tend to weaken the morale of his group' (MacCurdy 1918: 9). Some argued it was impossible to separate shell-shock and malingering – a view that found its way into the official medical history of the First World War (Stone 1985: 250); others that shell-shock cases 'should be court-martialled and shot' (ibid: 250); yet others that shell-shock cases lacked courage and suffered from 'funk' (Smith and Pear 1917: 19), or that they were mad and should be certified and shut up in asylums.[10] As a result, whilst the term was accepted by the War Office who set up an inquiry into the condition, it was officially banned by the Army Medical Services in 1917.

On the other hand, those willing to accept the existence of some sort of disorder, offered very varying accounts of its character and aetiology. Some saw the disorder as primarily organic in nature and offered physical explanations of its occurrence. MacCurdy noted that, 'Those who had emphasised physical factors in peace times were able to demonstrate to their satisfaction that all cases were suffering from extreme physical fatigue, concussion from high explosive shells, or poisoning with gases from explosives' (1918: 3). However, apart from the issue of fatigue, which was widely noted by many commentators, such explanations, including those focusing on the effects on the central nervous system of exploding shells, suffered from the fact that immediate proximity to bursting shell was not necessary to the condition's occurrence.

Influenced by the hereditarian views that tended to predominate amongst asylum psychiatrists at the end of the nineteenth and beginning of the twentieth centuries, others emphasised the importance of hereditary predispositions claiming that 'the soldiers who become affected by shock were weaklings or were descended from mentally afflicted or nervous parents' (Smith and Pear 1917: 88–9). However, this theory came up against the fact that mental breakdown occurred more frequently amongst officers than those from the lower ranks. The idea that those who broke down were men with 'tainted family histories' (ibid: 89) was viewed as a 'slur on the noblest of our race' (quoted in Stone 1985: 252). Anyone could suffer from shell-shock: 'it would be a gross misrepresentation of the facts to label all the soldiers who suffer from mental troubles as weaklings', for even 'The strongest man when exposed to sufficiently intense and frequent stimuli may become subject to mental derangement' (Smith and Pear 1917: 89) – a point that was frequently reiterated.

Increasingly, a number of clinicians employed by the military contended that shell-shock had to be understood in psychodynamic terms, through an analysis of the emotions, even though such views were often anathema to the military establishment. Unconscious motivations were considered crucial and in the words of one contemporary the disorder was 'an escape from an intolerable situation' (quoted in Showalter 1987: 170). The Freudian influence was strong in the understandings that were offered. Even so, most concurred with MacCurdy's view, reiterated by Rivers, that 'sexual factors take a comparatively small place in the production of war neuroses' (Rivers 1918: vii). Instead they emphasised the conflict between fear and duty which generated the 'flight into illness' (see Wittkower and Spillane 1940: 12).

Many accounts, taking cognisance of what appeared to be a new phenomenon reaching close on epidemic proportions and of the over-representation of officers, emphasised both the particular conditions of First World War battlefields, the first industralised war, and the differing demands of officers and other ranks. The special conditions of trench warfare which imposed long, continued strain with lack of sleep and exposure to 'cold and wet, hunger and the irritation from vermin' (Smith and Pear 1917: 7), and the need to suppress fear, were used to account for the emergence of shell-shock. There were few satisfactions in such situations:

> In previous wars the soldiers, it is true, were called upon to suffer fatigue and expose themselves to great danger. In return, however, they were compensated by the excitement of more active operations, the more frequent possibility of gaining some satisfaction in active hand to hand fighting, where they might feel the joy of personal prowess. Now, the soldier must remain for days, weeks, even months, in a narrow trench or a stuffy dugout, exposed to a constant danger of the most fearful kind; namely, bombardment with high explosive shells, which come from some unseen source, and against which no personal agility or wit is of any avail (MacCurdy 1918: 14).

As this passage indicates, enforced inactivity was considered a major problem: 'Inactivity under harassing fire is said to affect the mental health of the soldier more than active warfare'; so, too, was the 'prolonged uncertainty and fear of a land-mine' (Wittkower and Spillane

1940: 5). Both were characterised by a high degree of powerlessness and lack of control which seem crucial to understanding the psychological breakdowns of the soldiers.

Officers who were in positions of responsibility were considered especially vulnerable:

> The officer on the other hand has to a large measure the responsibility of individual decision. He has to make up his mind whether he is or is not going to give a certain order – whether he will or will not expose himself to danger. Moreover, it is his duty not only to be courageous himself and to prevent the thought of his personal danger from disturbing his judgement, but he must also act before his men as to inspire them and given an example of indifference to all the hazards of war (MacCurdy 1918: 123).

The difficulty of acting decisively, in a situation in which they had little control, arguably created especial tensions for officers. Typically their breakdowns took the form of neurasthenia or anxiety states in which there was often a wish for death and suicidal tendencies (MacCurdy 1918: 23). In contrast, lower ranks, whose 'responsibilities begin and end with obedience to orders' (MacCurdy 1918: 88), wished to be wounded in a way that would release them from active service. Consequently, they produced hysterical symptoms that would achieve that effect such as mutism, deafness and motor disturbances.

The Acceptance of Shell-Shock

That shell-shock or war neuroses were eventually accepted as psychiatric disorders, and not as forms either of madness, malingering or wilful 'funk', is significant in view of the harsh attitudes and strict values of the military and the threat shell-shock posed to military strength and morale, to conceptions of masculinity and to assumptions of male agency. Why was it that this male disorder was formulated and accepted in this particular period? The reasons relate to the difficulties with, and unattractiveness of, alternative accounts when faced with a situation in which the overall numbers of men manifesting these problems were relatively high and officers were over-represented. In the first place, the sheer number of cases made it very difficult to maintain that those who manifested the symptoms should be treated as cowards or malingerers and court-martialled. To have defined the cases in this way would have involved claims that a high proportion of men could not face up to war, which would have threatened notions of masculinity.

Whilst the notion of cowardice helps to construct masculinity and allows, even requires, the identification of some instances of cowardly behaviour, a more wholesale application to military personnel has a very different significance and was not a real option.

Second and related to this, the fact that officers were apparently more prone to shell-shock than the lower ranks, posed an especial threat to conceptions of masculinity and manliness and to assumptions about the strength and quality of British fighting men. It also posed immediate practical problems when so many were being killed on the battlefields. It required serious investigation and encouraged a more sympathetic response, rather than accusations of cowardice and malingering. Officers could not be expected to face the stigma of the asylum as cases of insanity, and as a group they could not be assumed to be 'weaklings', lacking in masculine qualities of courage and endurance.[11] Yet it was precisely the officers rather than privates who displayed, in the symptoms of shell-shock, more fearfulness and anxiety (neurasthenia rather than hysteria), emotions more commonly associated with women and children than men. Such behaviour had to be explained, and explained in a way that did not threaten existing conceptions of masculinity and the standing and courage of officers. And here no doubt part of the popularity of the concept of shell-shock was that it suggested a clear physical source for the problems (the disclaimers of many psychiatrists notwithstanding), just as in popular parlance the concept of 'nerves' with its physical connotations found favour over more psychological terminology.

Third, the construction of categories such as shell-shock and war neurosis had the advantage that agency and rationality were denied – the soldier was not responsible for his behaviour – and questions of his possible resistance to fighting were not brought centre-stage. Here there was a specific situation where it was for once advantageous to challenge the standard assumption of male agency and rationality. It is true that, as we have seen, psychodynamic theorists, whose ideas became more influential as the war progressed, suggested the existence of unconscious resistance to war, and it was widely recognised that many soldiers did not want to fight. But fighting was considered a duty, and the construction of a disease category of shell-shock served both for the soldier and for the military as a way of denying any refusal to fight – a refusal that could not be admitted. In this context, Robert Graves's actions in ensuring that his friend, Siegfried Sassoon, was sent to a shell-shock hospital following his definite expression of pacifism, showed clear recognition of the value of shell-shock to both soldiers and the military establishment. That Rivers, his psychodynamically inclined physician, described his condition as an 'anti-war complex', and Sassoon himself did not believe he was suffering from shell-shock, shows just how conscious resistance to war was in this case. It was, however, a resistance interwoven with considerable ambivalence; Graves commented that Sassoon 'varied between happy warrior and bitter pacifist' (quoted in Fussell 1975: 98). Significantly, Sassoon decided that the only solution to his dilemma was to return to the war front, influenced no doubt by the paternal Rivers, whom Sassoon believed saw it as his duty to 'cure me of my pacifist errors' (Sassoon 1937: 541). Sassoon came to feel that as a soldier, conscious defiance of military authority was intolerable and returned to the front line.[12]

The case of shell-shock shows how a male mental disorder was constructed in circumstances in which alternative designations for the phenomenon in question posed considerable problems, threatening as they were both to conceptions of masculinity and to conceptions of class. Shell-shock was preferable to the alternatives, even though it meant an increasing recognition of the anxieties and fears war could generate even in the toughest and most disciplined of men and a denial of male agency and rationality. Consequently, whilst it helped to ensure that issues of mass resistance and mass cowardice could be avoided, the concept still called the masculinity of its recipients into question: 'The Great War may have demonstrated beyond doubt that psychological agents can, by themselves, utterly disrupt the body's functions, but the lesson did nothing to mitigate the certainty that nervous breakdown unmanned men' (Oppenheim 1991: 152).

As I noted in Chapter 7, the impact of shell-shock on psychiatric thought and practice was considerable.[13] However, although the number of cases diagnosed amongst soldiers actually increased after the war ended, shell-shock itself gradually disappeared from the psychiatric lexicon. When Emmanuel Miller, prompted by the outbreak of the Second World War, published a collection of papers on mental health in war-time he entitled it *The Neuroses of War* (1940) and included a discussion of the psychological consequences of war on the civilian population as well as on soldiers. Significantly, the text retains the contrast between anxiety states and conversion hysteria as the two major types of breakdown which MacCurdy's text had done much to popularise. However, whilst mental breakdowns in the Second World War were not uncommon, they do not seem to have been quite so frequent or to have attracted so much public attention, although there is reference in the literature to so-called 'battle fatigue'.

One group of the military vulnerable to mental breakdowns were the members of the air force squadrons whose missions were highly dangerous, but who had to spend long periods of inactivity waiting for the call to action – again a situation characterised by powerlessness. Another were prisoners of war, a problem of greater importance in the Second than the First World War. Here as with shell-shock or battle fatigue, the problem was not a single traumatic event, but the build-up of psychological tension in a situation of continuing powerlessness that was traumatising. In the years following the end of the war it was the traumas of prisoners, especially those in concentration camps, which received much of the attention.

Within psychiatry an attempt to bring together the reactions to various extreme stresses and traumas came in 1952 in the American Psychiatric Association's first version of the DSM with the concept of 'gross stress reaction' – a conceptualisation replaced in the 1968 DSM-II with the broader concept of 'temporary situationual disorder' (Gersons and Carlier 1992). In 1980, following the Vietnam War and pressure from anti-war veterans for proper recognition of the psychological consequences of war on Vietnam veterans, the concept of 'post-traumatic stress disorder' (PTSD) was introduced into the new DSM-III under the general heading of anxiety disorders; its 'essential feature is the development of characteristic symptoms following a psychologically traumatic event that is generally outside the range of usual human experience' (American Psychiatric Association 1980: 236). The DSM-III listed its characteristic symptoms as: 'reexperiencing the traumatic event; numbing of responsiveness to, or reduced involvement with, the external world; and a variety of autonomic dysphoric, or cognitive symptoms' (ibid). The possible traumas, which 'would evoke significant symptoms of distress in most people' (ibid) and are generally outside the range of usual experiences such as simple bereavement, chronic illness, business loss or marital conflict, include rape, military combat, torture and earthquakes. The disorder is said to be more severe and longer lasting if the stress is 'of human design' (ibid).

Significantly PTSD, which still features in the DSM-IV, breaks the convention underpinning the DSM's classification of psychiatric disorders of not defining conditions in terms of aetiology (except where this is very clearly established). Indeed, PTSD provides an excellent example of the way in which social and political factors shape the con-

struction of diagnostic categories – that it is included as a separate disorder is a way of diminishing the stigma of psychiatric disorder: 'This
construction made it possible for victims of war and violence to be
recognised as psychiatric patients, without the stigma of their being
classified among the more serious psychiatric conditions such as hysteria, depression or psychosis' (Gersons and Carlier 1992: 742). The
construction also facilitated compensation claims (ibid).

PTSD is, of course, a potentially far broader psychiatric category
than shell-shock and could equally be applied to those who are victims
of domestic violence, as well as of military violence. However, while the
DSM–IV's list of traumatic events includes rape, it does not include
continuing domestic violence. The evidence suggests that sexual and
domestic violence are implicated in the aetiology of a far broader range
of mental disorders than PTSD, a category more likely to be invoked
for those involved in major disasters, such as plane crashes or fires,
than the more 'routine' sexual and domestic violence.

Sexual Violence

There is no doubt that sexual violence is often traumatic, even though
it occurs more frequently than often assumed and so can less readily be
viewed as falling 'outside the realm of usual human experience' where
traumatic events are supposedly located. However, accepting that the
occurrences are more frequent than generally assumed, does not
remove them from the domain of the potentially traumatic, since they
are often associated with the intense fear, terror and powerlessness that
also characterises traumatic events. Liz Kelly in *Surviving Sexual Violence*
(1988) develops the idea of a 'continuum of sexual violence', but argues
that we should not view the continuum as one of severity or seriousness
of violence; all forms of sexual violence are serious and 'it is inappropriate to create a hierarchy of abuse within a feminist analysis' (ibid:
76). Her continuum refers to the *prevalence* of the forms of sexual violence from the more common threats of violence (sexual harassment) to
the less common (rape and incest). Certainly we should not assume that
severity (and the potentially traumatic effects) lies simply in the type of
sexual violence but in various features of its occurrence, such as the
characteristics of the relationship between perpetrator and recipient
including the distribution of power. However, Kelly's claim that the
distinction is one of frequency rather than severity is problematic.

Whilst an incident of 'flashing' may be as traumatic for one women as an incident of rape for another, it is less likely to be so (typically a women is more powerless when raped, and the bodily violence is greater).[14]

Equally, differentiating types of violence or abuse is far from easy. Most authors distinguish between sexual abuse and physical violence and would defend the distinction on the grounds that the two often differ in their motivation and in the typical social characteristics of perpetrators and recipients. However the domains undoubtedly overlap and authors like Kelly argue that male violence towards women almost always has a sexual dimension. Her definition of sexual abuse is broad:

> any physical, visual, verbal or sexual act that is experienced by the woman or girl, at the time or later, as a threat, invasion or assault, that has the effect of hurting her or degrading her and/or takes away her ability to control intimate contact (ibid: 41).

The attention to the woman's experience of the act and to its effects in this definition is significant. Kelly also implicitly restricts sexual violence to acts by men against women (no doubt it is this that readily allows the claim that there is always a sexual dimension). Other definitions of sexual violence make overt sexual activity more central and are more restrictive about the range of acts that are involved – threats in themselves would not, for instance, be sufficient to count as sexual abuse, or violence. For example, Jean La Fontaine restricts child sexual abuse to bodily contact such as 'fondling, genital stimulation, oral and/or anal intercourse as well as vaginal intercourse', explicitly excluding 'suggestive behaviour, sexual innuendo or exhibitionism ("flashing")' (1990: 41) and specifies that it is exclusively abuse by adults – that is, persons aged 18 or over.

Defining particular types of sexual violence is even more problematic and there may be significant discrepancies between researchers and lay definitions. Women, for instance, have often had very narrow definitions of rape and have been reluctant to define sexual intercourse with friends or spouses under coercion as rape (legally there was no rape within marriage in England until quite recently). What constitutes incest is also by no means straightforward. For example, in English law incest has been narrowly defined in terms of consanguinity (biological relatedness). It covers only parent–child and inter-sibling sexual relations (not grandparent–grandchild, uncle–aunt or nephew–niece) and excludes relations by marriage, such as stepfather–stepdaughter, or by adoption.

It also requires actual or attempted penetrative sex. In practice many people define incestuous relationships more widely.[15]

One of the major contributions of the feminist movement has been to provide a more complex vocabulary relating to physical and sexual assaults, such as domestic violence, sexual harassment, battered women, thereby 'making visible what was invisible, defining as unacceptable what was acceptable and insisting that what was naturalized is problematic' (Kelly 1988: 139). Perhaps even more important, has been its role in examining the ideological constructions surrounding sexual violence – constructions in which women are somehow held responsible for what has happened – through an emphasis on sexual enticement and sexual promiscuity, while men are exonerated by reference to the power of the male sexual drive, the lack of sexual alternatives and so forth. Feminists are in almost total accord on the importance of analysing sexual violence in terms of issues of power and social control and not as a matter of individual pathology. Connell comments:

> Rape, for instance, routinely presented in the media as individual deviance, is a form of person-to-person violence deeply embedded in power inequalities and ideologies of male supremacy. Far from being a deviation from the social order, it is in a significant sense an enforcement of it (1987: 107).

Since definitions are so varied, establishing the precise extent of sexual violence – what can be called its epidemiology – is no easier than other epidemiological endeavours, and we find the same tendency for the figures generated by one empirical study (often limited in its sample size and operating with one particular definition) to be repeated elsewhere with little qualification. Comparing data from different studies or over time is very difficult, given the different definitions employed, and responses are influenced by the precise focus of the study and the wording of the questions. Moreover, the fact that experiences may be repressed or, even when they are not, are usually considered very personal and private, makes good data hard to find.

Much of the data on the extent of sexual violence is, therefore, only fragmentary and it is difficult to piece together a comprehensive picture. For instance, estimates of the incidence of child sexual abuse vary. A range of studies in the 1970s in the USA, where most of the work has been carried out, showed between 17 per cent and 28 per cent of women were sexually abused by men prior to puberty (Herman

1981: 13). A large scale study (Finkelhor et al. 1990) of some 2,626 men and women in the USA in 1985 found 27 per cent of the women and 16 per cent of the men had been sexually abused prior to the age of 18. Although the highest percentages reported touching, grabbing or kissing that they 'would now consider sexual abuse', some 14.6 per cent of women and 9.5 per cent of men reported 'someone trying or succeeding in having any kind of sexual intercourse with you or anything like that' (ibid: 20–1), which again they would now consider sexual abuse. The authors argue that the data are in line with those from other smaller scale studies on the extent of abuse. It could be argued, however, that the data collection method employed, that is, a telephone poll with standardised questions, was not designed to generate the confidence likely to facilitate revelations about any personal experiences which were remembered, or to bring into consciousness those that had been repressed. On the other hand, however, the very anonymity of the questioning may have made revelation easier.[16] (There is no indication of the gender of the telephone interviewers.)

As the Finkelhor survey shows, child sexual abuse is not confined to girls. However, the survey showed that girls were more likely than boys to be abused by a member of the family (29 per cent as against 11 per cent), less likely to be abused by a stranger (21 per cent versus 40 per cent) and more likely to have force used against them (19 per cent versus 15 per cent). As we shall see, these are precisely the factors that are likely to make the experience more traumatic. Significantly, most of the perpetrators of sexual abuse, whether of male or female children, were male (83 per cent of the offenders against boys; 98 per cent against girls). This contrasts with data on the physical abuse of children where, no doubt because they typically have more child care responsibilities, women are usually at least equally represented amongst the perpetrators (Stark and Flitcraft 1988).

The extent of female violence against men in domestic contexts in adulthood is contested. Early feminists tended to emphasise that men were the perpetrators and women the 'victims'. However, some studies have shown quite high levels of female violence, although the interpretation of these findings is open to debate. On the one hand, there is the question of whether violence is recognised – a number of studies have shown that male perpetrators tend to deny they are violent; on the other hand, there is the question of whether women's violence is primarily a matter of self-defence. Certainly the data on violent deaths in the family show men to be the typical perpetrators.

Sexual violence is not, of course, a new phenomenon, although feminist politics have brought it to public attention over the past two decades or more. Linda Gordon (1989) contends that the attention to family violence is more variable than the phenomenon itself, although we should not assume it is constant across time and place. Some writers claim that sexual abuse of children is more likely where the family is more privatised and its activities less subject to external controls (La Fontaine, 1990: 208). There has also been a tendency to see it as more common in marginal groups, including the lower rather than higher social classes. However, the evidence suggests it extends across the social spectrum (ibid: 58–60) and is not specific to more marginalised groups. The belief that it is more common in such groups is part of the mythology surrounding sexual abuse. Incest, for instance, is often seen as a practice of isolated communities (ibid: 103–4), but the evidence does not support this proposition.

Much feminist attention has focused on revealing the extent of sexual violence, especially against women, and on analysing its character (both theoretically and empirically). Rather less attention has been given to its consequences. Kelly (1988: Chapter 7) argues very convincingly that it is important to consider the way in which we study the precise consequences of sexual violence (including the psychological consequences). In particular we should not view women who have been abused as victims but as 'actively engaged in a struggle to cope with the consequences of abuse' (ibid: 159). She advocates an approach in which the focus is on three dimensions which she terms as 'coping', 'resistance' and 'survival', instead of the more usual approach in which women tend to be viewed as passive victims both of the assault itself and/or of the consequences of the assault. In her account resistance is especially salient in the situation itself, and coping and survival when it is over. The danger, she contends, is that by analysing the psychological consequences simply in terms of negative 'effects' we reinforce the perception of women as victims and ignore the active role they play in dealing with the situation. For instance, she argues that the act of forgetting, which is one of the responses to trauma, needs to be viewed as a way of coping with the trauma – an adaptive process that facilitates survival. Even more obviously a child's decision to leave home at the earliest possible opportunity in the face of sexual abuse within the family is clearly a survival strategy. Consequently, attention to resistance and coping can and should be applied to children as well as adults.

Kelly is surely right in emphasising the importance of the way we conceptualise the responses to sexual abuse and the need to avoid confirming stereotypes of women as victims. Equally, however, it is important, as she shows herself, to recognise the traumatic nature of sexual violence and the long and short-term consequences it may have for individuals. Even positive coping strategies, such as forgetting, may themselves have some adverse effects. If, for instance, forgetting takes the form of a more active repression or denial it may prevent the individual working through their experiences of sexual violence, so that short-term survival is secured at the price of longer-term difficulties. What then are the adverse consequences and the factors that heighten them?

Studies vary in the consequences they identify. A number of the most common effects noted in Kelly's own study of 60 women who had been the recipients of some form of sexual violence (all a year or more previously) do relate quite closely to the typical symptoms of the old category of shell-shock or the newer one of post-traumatic stress disorder. 78 per cent of her sample reported 'flashbacks', 69 per cent dreams or nightmares of the events; 61 per cent described how they tended to forget or 'cut off' the experience and 47 per cent spontaneously described their enhanced sense of vulnerability or fear (1988: 190). This does not mean, of course, that those who survive sexual violence are very likely to be identified as having a post-traumatic stress disorder. Many survivors do not have contact with psychiatrists, and even if they do, they are just as likely, for a range of reasons, to receive other diagnoses. Other 'symptomatic' responses may, for instance, seem more dominant. Along with the fear and vulnerability noted by Kelly and mentioned by many other researchers, often as a consequence of child sexual abuse, are feelings such as anxiety, anger, hostility, and depression. Kelly also notes changed attitudes to men, especially an increased distrust of them, which in some cases was clearly linked to fear: 'I think my attitude to men changed an awful lot. I'm very aware of ... the power they can have over you ... I still feel very wary' (ibid: 202). In other instances the distrust was experienced more in the form of hatred and anger than fear. One woman said of men 'They have to work very hard to prove themselves to me as being people. I hate men but I don't mind people' (ibid: 203).

Browne and Finkelhor's (1986) survey of the impact of child sexual abuse reports that anger and hostility are common responses (they do not discuss against whom they are directed). But they are not included either by them or by Beitchman and his co-workers (1991) as a long-term consequence. All, however, mention either depression or suicidal tendencies. Eight of Kelly's sample of 60 spontaneously mentioned they had made a suicide attempt and a high incidence of suicide attempts is reported as a long-term consequence in samples of those who have experienced child sexual abuse (see Browne and Finkelhor 1986: 69). One recent suggestion is that suicide attempts are specifically associated with the use of force in child sexual abuse (Beitchman et al. 1992: 107–8). Depression is also a well-established short and long-term response to sexual violence, including child sexual abuse (Browne and Finkelhor 1986: 69) and some form of depression is a likely psychiatric label for survivors of child sexual abuse who become psychiatric patients as adults.

However, by no means all recipients of sexual violence become clinically depressed, suicidal, or even fearful. As far as child sexual abuse is concerned four key factors make an adverse impact more likely: first, the length of abuse. As we might expect, abuse occurring over a longer period of time is likely to have more adverse consequences. The second factor is the threat or use of force. Russell (1986), for instance, found that all those in her sample (a general population sample) who had experienced violent abuse reported extreme or considerable trauma, against 74 per cent of those who had experienced 'forceful' abuse and 46 per cent who had experienced 'non-forceful' abuse. Third, where the abuser is the father or stepfather the impact is typically more severe than in other forms of incestuous (inter-familial) abuse. There are a number of reasons for this including the betrayal of trust, the fracturing of cultural norms and taboos, the more disruptive consequences for the family as a whole, including possible family conflict and break-down. Fourth, and finally where the sexual abuse involves penetration, whether in the form of intercourse, or oral-genital contact, the consequences tend to be more severe – especially those assessed in terms of the perceived trauma or harm (Beitchman et al., 1992: 113–14).

It should be noted, however, that few studies look for more positive aspects of adjustment following the trauma of sexual violence, although Kelly (1988: 188) refers to one which found that survivors 'tended to be more independent and self-accepting than the control group'. She found that around a third of her own sample felt more independent and/or stronger as a result of their experience; almost as many reported more feminist attitudes. Equally, few studies have attempted to assess separately the impact of sexual violence on male survivors. There is some evidence that the impact may differ, with the adverse effects for boys who experience sexual abuse as children falling especially into the area of 'sexual dysfunction'. (Since men are the usual perpetrators the typical sexual abuse of women and girls is heterosexual whereas that of men and boys is homosexual.) Sexual disturbance is also a consequence for girls, especially, of father–daughter incest (see Herman, 1981). Confusions of sexual identity, problems concerning masculinity, and homosexuality have been noted amongst samples of male survivors. However, studies comparing effects by gender are too limited to permit firm conclusions (Beitchman et al. 1992: 111), although differences seem likely.

What conclusions can we draw from this evidence? It is clear that sexual violence is often traumatic and can have long-term consequences for the individual. It also appears that if we consider sexual abuse of both children and adults, abuse of women is more common than of men and is by its nature more likely to be traumatic, not least because of the relative powerlessness of women. The reaction to abuse may also differ with gender, with men more commonly showing some form of sexual disturbance, women some emotional disturbance. This means, of course, given existing boundaries and practices, that male reactions are less likely than female to be treated as mental health problems.

Conclusion

Studies of the psychological impact both of war and sexual violence point to the importance of powerlessness in helping to determine the extent to which particular events are traumatising. It is this structural inequality that helps to shape the meanings attached to particular events, meanings which themselves play an important mediating process in the linkages between events and psychological experiences. It is women's relative powerlessness and the form violence often takes – that is, sexual violence – that is likely to make violence particularly traumatic for them.

Chapter 12

Conclusion

Feminist writers have adopted a range of approaches in seeking to cast light on the relationship between gender and mental disorder or, more specifically, between women and mental disorder. Early feminist analyses were typically constructed on the dual foundations of anti-psychiatry and feminist theory: to the anti-psychiatrists' claim that psychiatry served as an institution of social control was added the feminist gloss of patriarchy: the repressive control of the psychiatric apparatus was typically exercised by men over women. The work of Ehrenreich and English in the 1970s (1974; 1976; 1979), which viewed male doctors as usurping the powers and responsibilities of female healers and women as the ideal patients, was an influential exemplar, as was that of Chesler (1972) and, more recently, Showalter (1987).

The strength of the work of writers like Chesler is, as I have argued in Chapter 6, the emphasis they place on the way in which gender permeates constructs of mental disorder. Categories of mental disorder, though usually formally delineated is gender-neutral terms, are by no means gender-free. Yet, despite bringing both women and gender squarely into the centre of the analysis, this type of feminist theorising is doubly flawed, manifesting the failings of both anti-psychiatry and its own theorising of gender. On the one hand, conceptualising mental disorder as a form of deviance, it does not acknowledge the distinctiveness of the terrain occupied by 'problems of mind' in contrast to problems of body or behaviour, and also, rather automatically, assumes individual agency. On the other hand, the analysis of gender, stemming as it does primarily from a concentration on the position and experiences of women, is over-simple. The problem is not the use of the concept of patriarchy, but of using it to suggest that psychiatry (or the mental health services more broadly) is primarily constituted through the male control of female patients. What this leaves out is the extensive regulation of men both outside the sphere of psychiatry and mental health and within it.

It is easy enough to point to areas in which the regulation of male behaviour is extensive and often repressive – a male regulation that is strongly associated both with class and ethnicity. Obvious instances are provided by the criminal justice system and the military where control is frequently harsh and coercive, as well as the regulatory processes that operate in the labour market. The discipline of labour, whether it takes the form of harsh repression or more subtle, ideological forms of control, is all-pervasive and has been illuminated through the analysis of class relations. Equally, within the mental health system men, especially working class men and men from certain ethnic groups, have at times been subject to as much control and coercion as women, if not more. The asylum system has its origins in the desire for places of confinement for awkward and disruptive lunatics – including criminal lunatics – many of whom were men, and direct physical as well as legal controls have been key features or institutional life. The use of chains and later of strait-jackets, solitary confinement and drugs, along with compulsory detention, have been, and continue to be, incarcerative components of the mental health system, and historically have often been used to control men at least as much as women, especially those considered dangerous and disruptive.

It is clear that any neat opposition that posits male power and regulation over powerless, female patients within the mental health system provides a distorted picture. This is not to say that gender never enhances male power over female patients. It obviously does; nor is it to deny that men often have more power than women. But we need more subtle and complex forms of analysis that fully allow for the presence of male as well as female patients within the mental health services.

Penfold and Walker's analysis in *Women and the Psychiatric Paradox* (1984) is in many respects more effective than earlier analyses, since they begin with an examination of the character of psychiatry and psychiatric practice before moving on to a detailed consideration of the place of women. Moreover, drawing on a Marxist theoretical framework, they clearly position psychiatry in relation to the state and other institutions, such as business and the legal system. And they also point to the contradictory nature of the psychiatric system with its explicit objective of helping women as patients alongside its simultaneously coercive, constraining role, through the way it views distresses as personal pathology, its stereotypical images of women, and so forth. Yet Penfold and Walker still tend to concentrate only on women and in so doing, like earlier feminist writers in the field, are in danger of providing a one-sided, even distorted picture.

The same is true of Jane Ussher's analysis in *Women's Madness* (1991). Ussher, like earlier feminists, explicitly argues that a concentration on women's madness is justified, since there has in the past been a concentration on men and men's experience. Such a position is further justified by the fact that men's 'madness' largely falls outside the psychiatric system. Ussher claims 'that often men's madness takes a different form in our society. It may have different roots. It certainly exists in a different framework' (1991:9), and contends, following Chesler, that 'Whilst women are positioned within the psychiatric discourse, men are positioned within the criminal discourse. We are regulated differently' (1991:10). However, while there is certainly a need to redress the balance and bring women into the picture, and while differential regulation of men and women is often a reality – if by that we mean regulation through different social institutions and practices – for analytic purposes the exclusion of men from discussions of mental disorder is just as problematic as the earlier, long-established exclusion of women, since men do feature quite prominently in certain psychiatric patient populations. Information about women and women's experiences in the mental health system needs to be set against, and compared with, information about men and men's experiences.

An Alternative Approach

The sociological approach developed in this book, which builds on the work of numerous other authors, concurs with Penfold and Walker's argument that any examination of the place of women and men within psychiatry or the mental health services more generally needs to offer an analysis of these institutions themselves, including the concepts with which they operate, and which are embedded in their practice.

Madness and mental disorder, I have argued, drawing on Foucault, are concepts that set the boundaries of 'unreason'. Precisely what counts as unreason is socially variable: changing over time and differing between societies. But the concept of mental disorder groups together as disturbances of mind a range of 'disruptions' of the everyday social order, including failures of task and role performance, which are viewed as being grounded in deficiencies of reasoning but are not regarded as wilful, and in that respect are not to be treated as forms of deviance or wrongdoing. Historically, these forms of unreason have come largely to be viewed as types of illness, but they differ from other illnesses in that it is mind not body that is judged to be disordered. However, like other illnesses they embrace a diversity of types, ranging from intellectual incapacities (such as senile dementia) to obvious irrationality (such as the delusions and hallucinations which may underpin violent behaviour), through to the personal miseries and unhappiness commonly diagnosed as depression or anxiety.

In setting the boundaries of unreason concepts of mental disorder clearly play a part in, and contribute to, social order. On the one hand, they are part of the categorical map through which social behaviour is classified and given meaning. On the other hand, through the institutions in which they are embedded – most obviously the mental health services – they are part of the machinery which orders that behaviour for practical purposes in a way that may simultaneously be both humane (since any behavioural deviations are not assumed to be wilful and efforts may be made to help the individual) and regulatory. Regulation is, indeed, inherent in the very constructs of mental disorder, given their evaluative character and implicit, though changing, recipes for action. Care and control in mental health services – Penfold and Walker's 'psychiatric paradox' – are not, however, mutually exclusive alternatives as too many writers have often seemed to assume, for control is integral to caring. The key issue is not the absence or presence of regulation, but on what grounds, for what purposes and in whose interests any regulation occurs, the degree of voluntarism involved, and so forth. Where the individual's interests are to the forefront then any regulation is usually considered acceptable and the dimension of care is more likely to be emphasised. Restoring a sick person to health through help, support and treatment is likely to be seen as an instance of care not control, if it is considered in line with the individual's wishes and interests. Yet the support is, nonetheless, likely to be highly regulatory. In contrast, we tend to talk of control and regulation when it is less clear that the individual's interests are satisfied.

The sociological use of concepts of social control and regulation is itself often ambivalent. Whilst recognising the pervasiveness of social control, its functional necessity to society and, consequently, its positive value, sociologists have frequently deployed the language of regulation and control in a way that plays on their negative imagery (this is especially notable in writings on surveillance and regulation influenced by Foucault). What is needed, however, is a much more explicit consideration of the values at stake in such judgements and their relation to the individual's interests and power.

The major ground for disquiet concerning the present day regulatory apparatus surrounding mental disorder, lies in the very marked focus on the individual in contrast to the wider social order. The tendency to pathologise the individual is not restricted to medical theories and interventions in relation to mental disorder, which concentrate on the body. They equally apply to many psychodynamic theories and practices as well as to work in the field of family therapy, where it may be parents, especially mothers, who receive the blame for the problems experienced by their children. These individualising tendencies, which stem from the nature of the clinical enterprise – healing individuals who are already sick – blind many of those involved in the care of people with mental disorders to the importance of the social and material conditions of individuals' lives that are often conducive to mental disorder.

Where, however, does gender fit into this analysis? First and most obviously, gender, like social class and ethnicity, shapes judgements of unreason and, consequently, the way in which the boundaries of mental disorder are determined for men and women, both in relation to the construction of categories of mental disorder and the identification of individual cases. I have argued that men's 'disruptions' and difficult behaviour have typically been viewed as the product of agency and, consequently, as behaviour for which they are to be held responsible. In contrast, women's disruptions have often been seen as something outside a women's control for which agency has been denied. Similarly men's behaviours, especially white, middle class men's behaviour, have been more commonly seen as rational, as grounded in reason – whereas women's behaviours have more often been seen as irrational and grounded in emotion and impulse. And this applies even to problems such as anorexia nervosa where issues of control are frequently held to be central. For this highly controlled pattern of behaviour is, nonetheless, held to be grounded in unreason, and is viewed as an expression of feelings and impulses the individual cannot control. Men's and women's behaviour is all too often seen through the lens of social stereotype. Yet this generalisation about the impact of gender on judgements of unreason should not blind us to the way in which men's behaviour can, under certain circumstances, be treated as indicative of irrationality and treated harshly and repressively within the psychiatric system.

The linkages between men, masculinity, agency and rationality and women, femininity, passivity and irrationality are themselves interconnected with the issues of power. The inequities in the distribution of power between men and women help to ensure that women are more likely to be seen by both men and women as passive, emotional, and irrational, and these cultural characterisations in turn help to legitimate and justify male power (similar patterns can be observed in relation to class and ethnicity with assumptions about intelligence playing a crucial role). But the importance of inequities in power more generally also ensures that, where there are differences in power between men, the relative powerlessness of some men may make judgements of their conduct as irrational more likely.

As this analysis implies, judgements of mental disorder are, as we have seen, particularly likely to be involved when there is some failure of what Parsons called role performance. Consequently, gender is also salient to considerations of mental health because social order is itself gendered. It is not, therefore, only that constructs of mental disorder are gendered, but so, too, is the social order they help to regulate.In so far as mental health services fit people to return to their particular place in society, this is a gendered location; and though individuals may be better equipped (or no less well equipped) to attempt to change the gender relations of society as a result, it is a gendered set of social relations that is sustained by this restoration, no less than other aspects of the social order such as class and ethnicity – an order in which women typically have less power than men (of equivalent class and ethnicity) both in the wider society and in closer inter-personal relations. Here, too, the individualising tendencies of mental health theorising on the origins of disorder and their treatment play their part. For, instead of encouraging an increased awareness of social conditions and social relations, including gender relations, such theorising, at least in its biomedical and psychodynamic guises, often actively discourages social consciousness.

The third way in which gender fits into the analysis of mental disorder is through the way, by virtue of its salience to so many social institutions and arrangements, gender inevitably structures and shapes the origins of mental disorder in men and women. I have argued that it would be wrong to make any simple equation between women's oppression and mental ill-health and to assume, as some feminists have done, that where higher levels of mental ill-health in women are observed they are necessarily evidence of their oppression. Nonetheless, the different structural and material circumstances of men and women and the differences in power and status are highly pertinent to understanding the genesis of men's and women's mental disorder (as defined in specific times and places). Power is clearly a key dimension here as it is in relation both to gender and judgements of mental disorder and gender and the regulation of social order. I have suggested, for instance, that whether events or experiences are traumatic for the individual is linked to issues of powerlessness. This area is however, as yet, under-explored and needs further examination.

The fourth and final way in which gender is salient to the analysis of mental disorder is through the gendered norms and rules governing the ways of behaving and expressing emotion themselves, which vary across time and place. These different forms of expression, which structure individuals' responses to difficulties and problems in their lives, help to ensure that there is a gendered patterning of forms of psychological disturbance and distress, not all of which are identified as 'symptomatic of mental disorder'. These forms of expression are themselves shaped by material resources and social opportunities. The classic contrast noted in Western societies between male anger and violence – a turning of feelings outwards – and female anxiety, misery and hopelessness – with feelings turned inwards – relates to the gender division of labour and material circumstances, as well as to cultural expectations. Here, too, issues of power play their part in shaping the response (violence may be an attempt to reassert and re-establish power).

Highlighting the importance of power to the analysis of gender and mental disorder points to the links between the denial of agency (power) that is often involved in judgements of mental disorder and the importance of powerlessness in understanding gender differences in the genesis of mental disorder. Women's relative lack of power in many situations in comparison with men, and the perceptions surrounding their lack of power, means they are doubly disadvantaged. On the one hand, their lack of power makes it more likely that their behaviours may be viewed as indicative of mental disorder. And, on the other hand, it makes certain experiences more traumatic or distressing.[1] We cannot, however, make broad generalisations about which of these processes is more important where women are over-represented in patient populations since their relative importance will vary across time and place. Nor should we forget the regulation of male as well as female behaviour both through definitions of mental disorder and by a variety of other means.

Policy Implications

No simple solutions follow from this analysis of gender and mental disorder. The implicit panacea in the writings of the 1960s anti-psychiatrists: that if one abandoned the label of mental illness altogether, leaving patients, whether male or female, with only their somehow less burdensome 'problems in living' (Ssasz, 1960) or their 'voyages of discovery' (Laing 1967), the world would be a better place, seems to display an optimism harder to sustain in the harsher light of the 1990s. Relabelling men's and women's disorders of mind hardly seems to offer much in the way of improvement for them as individuals; nor does it offer any real advantages theoretically and analytically. Equally, if we conceptualise mental disorder not as illness but as forms of unreason generating incapacities of social performance, we should not believe that we can somehow change the boundaries of reason and irrationality in some simple emancipatory gesture.

There is relatively little to be gained, I would argue, from abandoning concepts such as madness, mental disorder or mental illness. For, while these concepts do assert the existence of some individual 'pathology' that characterises the individual's present mental state, they do not require us to make any assumptions about individual pathology in the *causation* of that state. Recognition of some individual pathology – that is of a degree of mental distress and unreason which is, for a range of reasons, problematic – may, in some cases, be necessary and appropriate. However, two things are essential. First, that we are aware of the way in which factors such as gender (or social class or ethnicity) help to set the boundaries of mental disorder and the judgement of individual cases. We need, therefore, continually to question any judgements of disorder, examining how appropriate they are and whether they are in the individual's interest. Second, we have to move beyond the body and the individual psyche both in analysing the causes of any mental disorder or distress and in providing any help. The limitation of psychiatry has too often been the narrowness of its vision and an exclusion of any real concern with the structure of people's lives. Community care, for all its inadequacies, drawbacks and under-resourcing has the potential advantage of drawing on a broader range of professional ways of thinking, expertise and types of care. As such it is to be welcomed, even though the focus is still too frequently more on the individual than the wider structural and cultural features of society.

Once we accept these two important points the possibilities for action begin to emerge. They come, as I have already implied, both from recognising the way in which gender permeates categories of mental disorder, and from recognising that our knowledge of the origins of mental disorder is actually far better than is frequently acknowledged. On the one hand, changes in gender relations and in the gender division of labour will affect the boundaries of mental disorder and the identification of individual cases. On the other hand, the clear evidence that individuals can often be 'driven mad' by destructive and difficult experiences in their lives suggests many possibilities for action. We only need to look at the cases of shell-shock in the First World War, or the empirical support for the linkage between major difficulties and depression (as in the work of Brown and Harris 1978, 1989), or the evidence that adverse experiences in childhood – such as being brought up in an institution – may general subsequent mental disorder, to find empirical support for the importance of social processes in the genesis of mental disorder and to identify strategies for social intervention. To assert the importance of social processes in the causation of mental disorder is not to claim that the linkages with disorder are direct and unmediated, or that psychological and biological factors play no part in the genesis of mental disorder, or to deny that some individuals may be more likely to succumb to traumas and difficulties, perhaps in part because they attach a different meaning to them. Consequently, whether as a result of physically, psychologically or socially generated processes, not all individuals will be equally vulnerable to material and social circumstances.

Yet to focus on individual vulnerability to disorder, though it may be important in some contexts, is to blind ourselves to the knowledge that we have of the power of social situations and experiences, which are linked to the structural and institutional arrangements of society, to generate unreason, and to the possibilities for action and change. The most obvious source of action is to shift mental health practice away from its strongly individualising mould in which the individual is pathologised, to a frame of reference which accepts and recognises the importance of social and material circumstances in shaping men's and women's lives and their mental health. This recognition may occur in cases where some obviously traumatic event such as a major disaster – an airline crash, a severe fire or a terrorist attack – precipitates psychological problems, and counselling is provided to those who survive.[2] Yet, when it comes to persons suffering some psychological difficulty which is less clearly related to any single traumatic experience, too often the remedy is simply brief reassurance and a prescription for some psychotropic medication – some tranquilliser, anti-depressant or anti-psychotic. And if the problems persist and become chronic, long term medication becomes almost a *sine qua non*, whether the individual is living in some institution or 'in the community'.

Both women and men are affected by these deficiencies in the mental health system. But the character of current mental health practice is particularly pertinent to women, not only because they are more likely to feature as patients than men, but also because women are over-represented amongst patients diagnosed as suffering from anxiety or depression, where the evidence of the importance of social origins to the condition is especially strong. And they are also more likely to be prescribed psychotropic medication, and to receive ECT.

Mental health services themselves, both private and public, also need to be better regulated. In this context the increasing privatisation of mental health series in Britain gives cause for concern since private services tend to be less well regulated by outside inspectors than public services and less directly accountable to patients and the public.[3] The need for greater regulation applies to individual practice no less than to institutional care. Yet the emphasis on competitive free-market models has created a climate generally antithetical to such regulation – indeed, to state support for professional practice. The arguments for increased regulation stem from the frequent evidence of the exploitation of patients, many of whom are women, whether this takes the form of sexual abuse by therapists, or the harshness and cruelty to the elderly (women, for instance, make up a very high proportion, by virtue of their longevity, of those living in homes for the elderly mentally disturbed). The fact that in Britain talk of the quality of health and social care is currently high on the political agenda does not vitiate these concerns. Regrettably the focus on quantifiable performance indicators helps to ensure that quality is interpreted very narrowly and essential aspects of care receive little attention. It is the quantity of interventions, the number of patients treated, and how long they have to wait (not, of course, an unimportant issue) that count, not whether they are receiving the most appropriate treatment, whether they are being cared for in a humane manner, or indeed, whether staffing levels are adequate. Moreover, the focus on quality draws attention away from restrictions in the range of services that are provided and the concentration on those who are most disturbed.

The wider project is, of course, to try and create a society in which social conditions, which can so adversely affect mental health, are improved and enhanced. In its *The Health of the Nation* report (1992) the government set as two of its targets the reduction of suicide and the improvement of mental-health. However, like so many other official documents with a preventive focus, its strategies were largely individual. Social changes such as reductions in unemployment, improvements in housing and education, more adequate neighbourhood facilities, or better and more extensive child care provision and education, were not on the agenda. Yet it is precisely these sorts of changes that could contribute to overall improvements in mental health. To argue this is not to call for a return to the mental hygiene movement of the early decades of the twentieth century and an increasing surveillance by professionals of all aspects of our daily lives. Rather it is to contend that men's and women's mental health is closely connected to social conditions and social arrangements. It is only if we can manage to create a better society that we are likely to enhance the mental health of the population as a whole. The complete eradication of mental disorder in both women and men is a utopian dream; some reduction in disorder through making our social institutions and social arrangements less destructive and difficult is not. It is not knowledge that is lacking but political will.

Notes

1. I have chosen to use the term mental disorder instead of mental illness throughout the remainder of this book, except where the definite medical connotations of the latter are appropriate. This is not because I wish to argue for a complete rejection of medical ways of thinking about mental disorder, but because I want to adopt a more neutral, analytic stance that does not take the medical framework for granted. Such a language is arguably more in line with the diversity of the approaches that inform the practice of community care. Some would argue that even the term mental disorder treats as too unproblematic the categorisation of phenomena as symptomatic of mental disturbance. It should be clear from what I say in the rest of the book that I regard the processes of categorisation as always open to contestation. I do, however, accept that certain phenomena can appropriately and properly be viewed as constitutive of disorder (see Chapter 4). I also use the term patients throughout the book since this best describes the status of individuals within the existing mental health services.
2. Some theorists reject causal language because of its positivist connotations. I would contend the concept of cause does have analytic value and needs to be grounded in a realist philosophy or science (see Keat and Urry 1975:27–36).
3. The confusion between the terms empirical and empiricist is very regrettable.

Chapter 1

1. Age and sex were usually basic variables in data collection in epidemiological studies, but quite commonly the data were not presented or analysed in ways that highlighted sex (gender) differences. The differences were not thought to merit detailed attention.
2. This tendency to prescribe psychotropic medication to women patients undoubtedly relates to the greater tendency to assign diagnoses of depression and anxiety. However, studies of psychotropic drug use do not tend to

control for diagnosis. It is also important to note that in primary care settings, where most psychotropic medication is prescribed, default rates are high (Johnson 1974).

3. The assumption of the family as a set of interrelated elements forming a functioning system on which family therapy is based tends to be blind to the inequalities of power between husbands and wives (Morgan 1985: Chapter 7). Yet because of the gender division of labour, women are usually held responsible for problems that arise in families.

4. Her reading of representations of madness is selective and she has little to say about male images of madness in the nineteenth and twentieth centuries (see Busfield 1994 and Chapter 2).

5. Ussher's use of the term misogyny is interesting, given her background in psychology. It suggests an analysis at the level of individual feeling and attitude rather than at the level of social structures and institutional practices.

6. This work draws heavily on the work on stress and mental disorder (see Chapter 10). Most of it has not developed the analysis in terms of gender very far, with the exception of studies of specific features of women's situations such as their employment patterns.

7. Showalter's reluctance to engage with the quantitative data may be due to her literary background; it cannot be adequately explained by her historical focus.

8. Showalter (1987) does, following Foucault, equate madness and irrationality, but makes no attempt to argue the case for this equation.

Chapter 2

1. The extract here is from a translation by John Swan published in London in 1742 (see Hunter and MacAlpine 1963: 221−2).

2. As we shall see, this association is especially grounded in the strong ties between women and diagnoses of anxiety and depression. Showalter's claim that schizophrenia is typically a female malady finds little support (see Scull 1989: 279).

3. In so doing I use medically defined categories of disorder which are considered more fully in Chapter 3.

4. I use the concept of a case − meaning simply an instance − because of its widespread use in psychiatric epidemiology, although it has somewhat objectifying overtones (a case, not a person). Its medical usage dates back at least to the eighteenth century. The issues concerning 'treated' and 'untreated' cases are discussed in Chapter 5.

5. There is a striking tendency for textbooks to merely repeat the same figures and for them to take on the status of established truth, without any reference to the methodological limitations of the studies or how few and far between they are.

6. Goldstein (1987: Chapter 9) links the emergence of this golden age in France with an expansionist movement in French psychiatry to capture the intermediary zone of 'demi-fou' – half-madness.

7. The concept of neurosis is now avoided in official psychiatric classifications because of its aetiological (and psychodynamic) associations (see American Psychiatric Association 1987: xxiv). I use it here and elsewhere, not only when referring to earlier conceptualisations, because of its continuing widespread use by lay people and by clinicians in their day-to-day practice.

8. An important distinction in epidemiology is between measures of incidence and of prevalence. Incidence refers to the numbers of *new* cases occurring during a particular period of time (often a year); prevalence to the number of cases, whether new or old, identified either at a single point in time or in a fixed period. Admissions data or episode rates yield a measure of incidence; residence data a measure of prevalence. The epidemiological approach is examined more fully in Chapter 10.

9. The data for the study were obtained from surveys carried out in New Haven, Baltimore and St Louis over the period 1980–2. The final sample contained over 9000 adults. The main diagnostic instrument was a Diagnostic Interview Schedule (DIS), an adaptation of the Schedule for Affective Disorders and Schizophrenia (SADS) and the Renard Diagnostic Interview.

10. Goldberg and Huxley (1992: Chapter 5) argue that anxiety and depression should be viewed as two dimensions not categories of disease and provide evidence that the two dimensions correlate quite highly.

11. The ECA study based their measure of cognitive impairment on Mini-Mental State Examination (MMSE) scores.

12. The gender difference in GPI is of considerable interest. It is unlikely that it was primarily due to gender differences in diagnosis or detection. One can only infer that syphilis itself was more common in men than women and this may well have been the result of gender differences in sexual behaviour. Women's sexual behaviour in the Victorian period was more closely controlled and regulated, so there must have been a smaller pool of women at considerable risk of syphilis – mainly prostitutes. Since men were more promiscuous they were more at risk (the greatest risk to most women was from their husband's contracting syphilis).

13. The ECA survey yielded six-month prevalence rates for antisocial personality for men close on double those for women (Myers et al. 1984).

14. Goldstein (1992) points out that some recent studies using current diagnostic criteria have found a higher incidence of schizophrenia among men than women. Studies also show gender differences in the age of onset, premorbid history and in the expression of illness. Phrases such as 'less severe' or 'more minor' are problematic since they seem to suggest the conditions

are trivial and not very distressing which they often are. It is, however, hard to avoid them.

15. Unfortunately MacDonald does not provide a very detailed examination of male–female differences. He also has a tendency to interpret the case notes he analyses in twentieth-century terms as in his whole use of the notion of stress.

16. This is a criticism of Gove's study (1972) which excluded organic conditions and behaviour and personality disorders from its definition of mental disorder (see Dohrenwend and Dohrenwend 1976). The study is discussed in Chapter 10.

17. A former example is so-called involutional melancholia – melancholia associated with the involutional period, that is, the period of the menopause (see Chapter 8).

18. Unfortunately official statistics on mental health services in England do not routinely include information on marital status, and these are the most recent data available. They specify the marital status of residents.

Chapter 3

1. Even these two terms suggest a different theoretical stance: gender divisions implies a structural approach; gender relations a more interpersonal perspective.

2. The terms masculinity and femininity are themselves used in a variety of ways (see Penfold and Walker 1984: 95).

3. As Sandra Harding notes a 'feminist standpoint may encourage us to attend to these differences between women or between men' (1992: 176–7)

4. Both binary and dimensional conceptualisations are employed in lay understandings.

5. The concept of gender identity is briefly discussed below (p 40).

6. When women are studied on their own, some comparison with men is often implicit (i.e. a knowledge of men is assumed).

7. Opposition to dualisms is fashionable, but they are valuable ordering devices.

8. The sociological origins of role analysis, of course, predate 1950s structural functionalism.

9. The concept of role has been variously defined by sociologists.

10. Foucault has been appropriated by postmodernists as one of their founding theorists, yet his own work departs in some key respects from postmodernist assumptions.

11. The characterisation of contemporary advanced industrial societies as postmodernist has been criticised by a range of writers (see, for instance, Woodiwiss 1993).

12. There are, of course, a range of feminisms rather than a single feminism.

Chapter 4

1. In this it follows medical convention, since medical practitioners rarely attempt general definitions of illness (see Busfield 1989: 35). The DSM-IV (following the DSM-III) defines a mental disorder as 'a clinically significant behavioural or psychological syndrome or pattern that occurs in an individual and that is associated with present distress (e.g. a painful symptom) or disability (i.e. impairment in one or more important areas of functioning) or with a significantly increased risk of suffering death, pain, disability, or an important loss of freedom' (American Psychiatric Association 1994: xxi).

2. There is an increasing ambivalence about the assumption of discrete categories of disorder. The DSM-IV, whilst adopting a categorical approach to classification, qualifies this by asserting that 'there is no assumption that each category of mental disorder is a complete discrete entity with absolute boundaries dividing it from other mental disorder or from no mental disorder' (American Psychiatric Association 1994: xxii).

3. It is notable that attempts to eradicate it have failed.

4. The evaluative nature of the concept of illness has been widely discussed (see, for instance, King 1954; Sedgwick 1982).

5. Once convicted of a crime he was soon transferred to Broadmoor on grounds of mental disorder.

6. A number of writers have argued that these behaviour and personality disorders should not be part of the domain of mental illness (see Wootton 1959; Chapter 8).

7. Goldberg and Huxley argue for a dimensional view of neurosis but not psychosis.

8. A number of studies indicate that psychiatrists tend to focus on what is wrong and presume disorder (Scheff 1963; Rosenhan 1973)

9. This was shown very clearly in Jeffrey Blum's (1978) study comparing the diagnoses assigned patients discharged from a single psychiatric hospital in 1954, 1964 and 1974. The proportion of patients treated for affective disorders increased from 7.4 per cent of the 1954 population to 21.9 per cent in 1974. The corresponding figures for neuroses showed a decline from 25.2 per cent to 4.5 per cent.

10. There are links between the American DSM and the ICD classifications (see American Psychiatric Association 1994: xx–xxi).

11. In that respect psychiatrists and other professionals are the administrators of the mental health system, though they play an active part in shaping it (see Navarro's claim 1977: Part II).

12. Psychiatrists do try and disentangle the reasoning underlying a belief from the belief itself, but this is not easy and what is culturally normative (for the psychiatrist) is more likely to be regarded as rational.

13. It is commonly argued (see, for instance, Turner 1987: 47) that Parsons's theorisation of the sick-role cannot handle chronic sickness and incapacity. Gerhardt (1987: 32–3) argues, very convincingly, that it can.

14. Szasz (1981) rejects the label of anti-psychiatrist, claiming that he is not against all psychiatry. Adolf Meyer had earlier conceptualised mental illness as 'problems of living' (see Prior 1993: 95)

15. In 'Insanity of Place', Goffman (1971) offers an interesting analysis in which he argues that the behaviour regarded as symptomatic of mental disorder is 'out of place'. This analysis, though drawing on symbolic interactionism, arguably has more affinities with the focus of reason and rationality discussed below.

16. Radden (1985: Chapter 4) persuasively argues that the notion of unreason is broader than that of irrationality encompassing unreasonableness as well as irrationality. Other authors emphasising unreason and irrationality as constitutive of mental disorder include Edwards (1981); Fingarette (1972); and Breggin (1974).

17. Although Laing shows quite effectively that the thoughts and actions of the supposedly mad person can be made intelligible and rational, if only we bother to try and understand them, this does not mean they are as intelligible/rational as the thoughts and actions of persons considered sane (see Busfield 1989a: 99–105; Radden 1985: Chapters 5 and 6)

18. Edwards lists a number of features of rationality. The first five are: '(1) being able to distinguish means from ends and being able to identify processes and manifest behaviours which likely will result in the realisation of consciously envisioned goals; (2) thinking logically and avoiding logically contradictory beliefs; (3) having factual beliefs which are adequately supported by empirical evidence or at least avoiding factual beliefs which are plainly falsified by experience; (4) having and being able to give reasons for one's behaviour; (5) thinking clearly and intelligibly and avoiding confusion and nonsense!' (1981: 314–5)

19. To focus on the reasoning underlying emotions is to recognise a cognitive dimension to emotional states (see Radden 1985: Chapter 7)

20. Althusser (1971), who employed the ideological/repressive contrast, used the latter term quite narrowly, treating physical coercion as its defining element.

Chapter 5

1. A number of commentators both within and outside psychiatry have questioned the value of the categorical model for some or all mental disorders (see Eysenck 1975; Goldberg and Huxley 1992; Bentall 1990). As I noted earlier (Chapter 4, note 2) its use is even being questioned in psychiatric classifications.

2. Attempts to cut back public expenditure in Britain in recent years have reduced the range of official statistics on mental health services that are published.

3. Recent health service changes, as well as changes in community care policies, are shifting some responsibilities from health to social services and, as a result, narrowing the boundaries of health problems (see Chapter 7).

4. Some writers argue (see Prior 1993) that the whole idea of untreated cases is problematic.

5. There are three main reasons for this. First, because of the continuing pressure to improve diagnostic schema. Second, because the complexity of schema developed at least in part for statistical purposes is likely to be simplified in clinical practice. And third, clinicians are likely to operate with schema with which they are familiar (usually ones used when they trained) and may be slow to adopt new ones.

6. Some psychiatrists argued that the introduction of the DSM-III-R (the revision to the DSM-III) would reduce biases in diagnosis. However, as Loring and Powell's (1988) study indicates they have not been eradicated.

7. See Chapter 3.

8. The problem, as with measuring mental disorder itself, is the operationalisation of concepts in the research situation. See Mechanic (1970) for an interesting discussion of this issue.

9. Angst and Dobler-Mikola (1984) showed that recall of depressive illness of longer than two weeks duration within either four weeks or the previous three months was not affected. However, men's recall of depression within the previous year was affected.

10. I use the term objective here to refer to the material components of illness – subjective to refer to the inner world of feeling and experience.

11. In many research contexts there is considerable pressure to use short screening instruments because of cost and time and this is particularly true where mental health status is being measured as part of a broader study.

12. For example, in their discussion of gender and mental disorder Gove and Tudor (1972), having defined mental illness to exclude organic and behaviour disorders, then proceed to work with statistics that typically include them.

13. Blum (1978) argued that the availability of new drugs for the treatment of depression were a key factor in the increase in the diagnosis of affective disorders in the psychiatric population between 1954 and the decline in the diagnoses of neuroses.

14. In the DSM-IV the term melancholia exists only as 'melancholic features', a characterisation that can be used to qualify a Major Depressive Episode where there is a 'loss of interest or pleasure in all, or almost all, activities or a lack of reactivity to usually pleasurable stimuli' (American Psychiatric Association 1994: 383).

15. For the remainder of the discussion in the section I use the term depression to cover only uni-polar disorders, excluding bi-polar, manic-depressive disorder.

16. In a later paper, Weissman and Klerman (1985) argue that alcohol is not to be viewed as the equivalent of depression in women since studies of familial transmission show the two disorders to be independent disorders familialy. However, in my view this is not decisive to the case that cultural factors shape the way psychological difficulties are expressed.

17. The way in which clinicians pick on one factor is noted by Kathy Davis (1988) in her fascinating analysis of medical consultations.

18. The assumption that the epidemiological objective is to establish the true prevalence of a disorder is common.

Chapter 6

1. This is more true of discussions of gender and constructs of mental disorder than it is of the impact of gender on the processes of becoming disturbed.

2. The notion of 'acting out' comes from psychoanalysis. The model is one of inner conflicts and impulses (instincts/drives) which need to find some outlet.

3. Although Chesler's focus is on gender, in a footnote she claims that psychiatric categories are also typed by race and class (1972: 57).

4. Her exclusion of anxiety and depression as well as anorexia nervosa from this list is rather surprising (see Busfield 1989b: 358–60).

5. Cf. the contrast between the deep and surface structures of language developed by Chomsky (1957).

6. A recent example of this indirect bias is the proposal by a psychologist that 'compulsive shopping' should be regarded as a psychological disorder (see *The Observer*, 16 October 1994). Shopping is not, of course, a gender-neutral activity.

7. Chesler argues that when men act out the male role rather than depart from it they are 'usually incarcerated as "criminals" or as "sociopaths" rather than as "schizophrenics" or "neurotic" ' (1972: 57).

8. Men's control over their emotions may itself involve considerable emotional management and emotional work (Ramsay 1996).

9. It does not follow, however, that they should be rejected by women. What is involved is a set of exclusionary ideas and practices in which characteristics of humans which are, for instance, regarded as the *sine qua non* of citizenship are less likely to be attributed to women.

10. MacDonald's (1981) study shows the way in which such problems were brought to medical attention even in the seventeenth century, but they were not officially constituted as mental disorders.

11. It is interesting to note that Allen emphasises the in-built particularism of the criminal justice system (see *Justice Unbalanced*, 1987) rather more than that of the psychiatric system where she contends gender only enters on the margins and not the 'solid, middle ground' (1986: 97)

12. The history of the psychiatric use of case histories is only just beginning to be written (see Loughlin 1993). Prior (1993) refers to these normal cases as vignettes.

13. The willingness of GPs to identify mental health problems and the frequency with which they make referrals to specialist psychiatric care vary very considerably (Goldberg and Huxley 1992: Chapter 3). Significantly, women are less likely to be referred to a specialist than men (ibid: 48).

14. The WHO glossary notes that physical and psychological symptoms may not coincide (brain degeneration can occur without any apparent attendant intellectual loss and vice versa) (World Health Organisation 1992: 47).

15. There is some evidence of gender bias on intelligence tests, some of which are used by psychologists in assessing intellectual deterioration.

16. There is evidence that gender relations change in old age and that men are, for instance, more willing to take on domestic tasks (Arber and Ginn 1991).

17. Arber and Ginn (1991: 12) note that because of differences in mortality in the UK and US about 75 per cent of elderly men (65 and over) are married, whereas only 40 per cent of elderly women are (women are much more likely to be widowed than men).

18. Interestingly Allen argues that the shift to a focus on coping reduces the significance of gender role maintenance, since in this domain the criteria of 'social coping are modest, and in principle do not require of the individual anything as elaborate as a successful adjustment to gender role' (1986: 101).

19. Allen claims, mistakenly in my view, that Chesler assumes gender role maintenance (gender regulation) is *constitutive* of psychiatry, whereas in her (Allen's) view the relation between them is contingent.

Chapter 7

1. The determination and measurement of needs is by no means unproblematic (see Doyal and Gough 1991), but the concept remains a useful one.

2. This is an instance where lack of manliness (cf. Chesler's argument about the masculine role) is constructed as a mental disorder. There are echoes of 'wimp' which is constructed around notions of masculinity.

3. Napier's women patients mentioned marital troubles and bereavement as the cause of their distress more than twice as much as men.

4. The data on admissions and resident numbers prior to the nineteenth century are very limited. Some are given in Parry-Jones (1972: Appendix E).

5. Mortality rates in the private madhouses are discussed by Parry-Jones (1972: 212–3). See also Ripa (1990: 156–8) and MacKenzie (1992).

6. Whereas medical men had not generally been at the forefront of campaigns to establish the initial voluntary hospitals, they tended to play a more active role in campaigning for funds to establish the voluntary asylums because by then the value of hospitals to the profession was much clearer. For example, William Battie played an important part in the establishment of St Luke's in London which opened in 1751 and was the first of the new voluntary asylums funded from subscriptions.

7. Separate institutions for 'idiots' as they were then termed only began to be set up in the mid-nineteenth century and many were to be found in the asylums.

8. The first professional associations of what was to become the profession of psychiatry (a term first used in the mid-nineteenth century) were the associations of asylums doctors. The Association of Medical Officers of Asylums and Hospitals for the Insane was founded in England in 1841. In America the Association of Medical Superintendents of American Institutions for the Insane was established in 1844 in Philadelphia.

9. Mortality rates in the public asylums are discussed in the *49th Report of the Commissioners in Lunacy* (1885: 6).

10. Posts in voluntary asylums were not paid but attracted ambitious doctors who could enhance their social standing and private practice through the contacts they made.

11. See also Morantz (1974) for a more cautious analysis.

12. In 1986 some 57 per cent of all residents of psychiatric beds in England were 65 or over (Department of Health and Social Security, 1986, Booklet 1: Table A8).

13. The term suggests that their problems do not merit attention, and can be largely ignored.

14. It is difficult to determine a national picture of the impact of the 1990 NHS changes and the introduction of the internal market. The public focus has been on dangerous schizophrenics, as in the Christopher Clunis case (North East Thames Regional Health Authority 1994), and there are strong pressures on purchasers to concentrate their limited resources on these groups. Yet, working with less severe problems where the therapeutic prospects seem better is often more attractive to mental health professionals.

15. There may also be certain financial advantages if fewer staff with lower levels of training can be employed.

Chapter 8

1. The phrase *the* medical model suggests, mistakenly, that doctors adhere to a single model of mental disorder.

2. Those who talk of bio-social models or bio-psycho-social models tend to assume that integration of biological, psychological and social approaches is relatively easy. Such models have become quite fashionable within nursing, where they appear to represent a rejection of medicine's physical bias and an alternative basis for nursing's own claims to professional expertise.

3. Physical factors could be constitutional or environmental.

4. It is interesting, however, that the 1931 paper appeared in the *Archives of Neurology and Psychiatry*.

5. In the DSM-IV this list is quite lengthy.

6. The DSM-III-R does indicate that too great a reliance should not be placed on retrospective data which should be the basis only of a provisional diagnosis: 'daily self-ratings for at least two symptomatic cycles are required to confirm the diagnosis' (American Psychiatric Association 1987: 367). However, such ratings are still subject to biases from the patient's awareness of the purpose of the ratings (i.e. they are not 'blind').

7. The Introduction to the DSM-III-R claims that the approach to classification is descriptive and atheoretical with 'regard to aetiology or pathophysiologic process, except with regard to disorders for which this is well established and therefore included in the definition of the disorder' (American Psychiatric Association 1987: xxiii). Late luteal phase dysphoric disorders would therefore presumably be held to fall into this latter category, although the implicit claim that aetiology is well established would be hard to defend.

8. The concept was first introduced by Kraepelin in the 1896 edition of his textbook when he talked of three involutional psychoses: melancholia, presenile delusional insanity, and senile dementia' (Jackson 1986: 193).

Chapter 9

1. The importance of the castration complex and penis envy, which are linked with the dynamic interplay of desires, attachments and inhibitions of the Oedipus Complex, are detailed critically by Millett (1972: 172–90) and more sympathetically by Mitchell (1985: Chapter 8).

2. Millet notes that Freud's view that passivity, masochism and narcissism are the distinguishing characteristics of femininity has a certain merit 'taken as pure *description*', but contra Mitchell she argues that Freud asserted 'that the elaborate cultural construction we call "femininity" was largely organic (1972: 193–4).

3. A long section of the book is taken up with her reading of Freud's ideas on what she calls 'The Making of a Lady'.

4. Her objective is the overthrow of patriarchy (see Mitchell 1975: Conclusion, Chapter 6).

5. There is none of the emphasis found in Chodorow on the positive qualities of women.

6. We see here very clearly the way in which the focus of psychodynamic theorising shifts attention from the external world of social events and circumstances to the individual's inner world.

7. Chodorow here gives more emphasis to the external world than Klein.

8. The term 'la boulimie' was used in France for a pattern of overeating in the eighteenth century (Gordon 1990: 3).

9. The DSM-IV gives a prevalence in young females of 1 to 3 per cent (American Psychiatric Association 1994: 548).

10. This focus on the mother is consistent with psychodynamic theorising and is linked with a parallel tendency to blame the mother.

11. MacSween (1994:41) argues that Bruch's analysis cannot readily account for why the body and body weight are the main focus of the anorexic's problems. She also claims that Bruch operates with a gender-neutral concept of the individual which leads her 'to analyse feminine receptiveness in anorexia, not as a central part of being an adequate women in a patriarchal culture, but as "ego deficiency" arising from "an abnormal family" '(ibid: 43).

12. Orbach describes bulimia as a third syndrome with affinities with compulsive eating and anorexia but does not examine it (1993: xiii).

13. The fascination of sociologists who write about 'late modernity' and 'postmodernity' with anorexia is interesting. It is tied to their belief that the body is a key focus of the consumerism that characterises such societies. Yet it means that their discussions of anorexia abstract it from the wider context of issues concerning gender and mental health.

14. Morag MacSween's study *Anorexic Bodies* (1994) was only published when this chapter was already completed. It has not, therefore, been possible to take any detailed account of her arguments. It is significant that in a postmodernist vein she focuses on the cultural rather than structural contradictions facing women

Chapter 10

1. I use the term gender division of labour to refer to the allocation of roles and responsibilities between persons on the basis of their gender in both the labour market and domestic realm. This will differ according to the domain in question.

2. Some authors distinguish individual, social and societal levels of analysis, the latter embracing the macro-level of the social system. Interestingly, however, Turner (1987: 4–5) in using the framework locates cultural constructions of disease at the social not the societal level and the distinction between levels is not very precise.

3. As I noted earlier (Chapter 2, note 15), MacDonald uses the term stress, without describing the language in which the cases themselves were constructed.

4. The term friend here meant 'members of one's immediate family and well-wishers, rather than one's comrades' (MacDonald 1991: 73).

5. Though scales, once introduced, are often slow to change.

6. The study included both psychotic and neurotic depression.

7. Overt familial tensions might be picked up by instruments such as Brown and Harris's Life Events and Depression Schedule (1978), but given the emphasis in the work on family pathology on hidden tensions and denial much would not.

8. This has been linked to Seligman's (1975) concept of 'learned helplessness'.

9. Achievements are usually measured in terms of recognition in the public sphere.

10. Past loss was the key influence on the *severity* of depression at admission, past loss being defined as 'loss of mother or father before seventeen, loss of a sibling between one and seventeen, loss of a child at any age, and loss of a husband by death' (Brown and Harris 1978: 210).

11. There are interesting parallels here with shell-shock (see Chapter 11).

12. Phillips (1968) noted that positive experiences were greater in the higher than the lower classes and that the occurrence of positive and negative experiences were not themselves correlated.

13. Its methodological sophistication and use of quantitative techniques help to make this case more convincing to psychiatrists.

14. A study of vulnerability to depression in men (Roy 1981) identified the following vulnerability factors: parental loss before 17, poor marriage and unemployment.

15. This is due both to women's higher life expectancy and men's higher rates of re-marriage.

16. Gove footnotes the work of Betty Friedan, Cynthia Epstein, Hannah Gavron and Jessie Bernard, but gives it little explicit attention.

17. Significantly Gove (1975) is also a strident critic of labelling theories of mental disorder.

18. Gove uses the concept of marital role quite broadly to encompass not only expectations *vis-à-vis* activities within the home but also in the labour market. In early studies however, marital status was treated as a measure of marital role.

19. Such claims require a greater specificity of time and social class than Gove offers.

20. Gove (Gove and Tudor 1972) defines mental disorder as conditions involving person discomfort and/or mental disorganisation that are not caused by organic disorder. He excludes personality disorders because they involve

anti-social or asocial behaviour rather than *mental* disorder – an objection to their inclusion raised by many other authors (see Lewis 1953).

21. An obvious gap in the light of Gove's definition are symptoms of psychoses.

22. Brown and Harris's (1978) focus on the value of employment outside the home in protecting against depression where women lack an intimate confiding relationship is a variant of this argument.

23. This study used a malaise measure based on psychological symptoms experienced in the last month (Bartley et al. 1992: 323).

Chapter 11

1. Siegfried Sassoon, in writing his autobiographical account of his war time experiences, called the hospital where he stayed as a case of shell-shock, Slateford, rather than its actual name Craiglockhart.

2. Historically, the development of states is linked with military activities which initially take up a high proportion of the state's resources (Mann 1981).

3. This applies even in countries such as Israel which have female conscription, though it is being challenged.

4. Shell-shock was identified in a few women serving as nurses at the front.

5. Myers was what was then called a medical psychologist.

6. Psychiatric disorders were increasingly differentiated along symptomatological rather than aetiological lines.

7. One might argue that the term shell-shock should be restricted to cases where symptoms took the hysterical form, but most authors who used the label employed it more broadly. Showalter (1987: Chapter 7) implies that all cases fell into the hysterical category (see also Leed 1979: Chapter 5).

8. This may reflect the influence of psychoanalytic thinking which was especially applied to anxiety states.

9. For instance, the first edition of Henderson and Gillespie's *Textbook of Psychiatry*, which was published in 1927, did not include hysteria under the heading of psycho-neuroses.

10. In all cases, admission to a public asylum required a formal process of certification and those admitted were detained on a compulsory basis.

11. Public asylums catered almost exclusively for pauper patients and admission to other institutions still involved the stigma of certification if not of pauperisation.

12. Sassoon's period in Craiglockhart Hospital under Rivers's care has been fictionalised by Pat Barker in *Regeneration* (1992).

13. Showalter identifies shell-shock as the key to the transition to psychiatric modernism, noting that it was men's rather then women's illnesses that made this transition possible (1987: 18–19), but in line with this approach

does not attempt to analyse shell-shock in terms of gender divisions (see Busfield 1994: 256–60).

14. Kelly's rejection of a hierarchy is linked to her focus on a women's experience in defining sexual violence and to her theoretical assumption that different types of sexual violence are similarly grounded in the asymmetry of gender relations.

15. Woody Allen's sexual relationship with his wife Mia Farrow's adopted daughter, which many regarded as having incestuous elements, provided one such example.

16. Obtaining reliable data in this field is very difficult.

Chapter 12

1. I have already noted that Sedgwick's (1982) claim that feminists cannot both have their cake and eat it by arguing that mental illness is a social construct, and that it is women's oppression that drives them mad, is mistaken (see Busfield 1988). My argument here goes one stage further by indicating that rather than being mutually exclusive women's powerlessness underpins both processes.

2. The resort to counselling in these situations does recognise the external causes. Yet there is a danger that the ready resort to counselling treats counselling as the 'solution' to traumas and difficulties and there is still little attempt to effect actual changes that would make the traumas and difficulties less likely to occur.

3. Accountability is also a key problem with NHS trusts, which are accountable upwards within the NHS, but have rather few mechanisms of accountability to the general public.

Bibliography

ABRAMSON, L.Y., SELIGMAN, M.E.P. and TEASDALE, J.D. (1978) 'Learned Helplessness in Humans: Critique and Reformulation', *Journal of Abnormal Psychology*, 78: 40–74.

AL-ISSA, I. (1980) *The Psychopathology of Women*, Englewood Cliffs, N.J. Prentice-Hall.

ALLAN, G.A. (1979) *A Sociology of Friendship and Kinship*, London: Allen & Unwin.

ALLAN, G.A. (1989) *Friendship: Developing A Sociological Perspective*, Hemel Hempstead: Harvester Wheatsheaf.

ALLDERIDGE, P. (1979) 'Management and Mismanagement at Bedlam, 1547–1633', in C. Webster (ed.) *Health, Medicine and Mortality in the Sixteenth Century*, Cambridge: Cambridge University Press.

ALLEN, H. (1986) 'Psychiatry and the Feminine', in P. Miller and N. Rose (eds) *The Power of Psychiatry*, Cambridge: Polity Press.

ALLEN, H. (1987) *Justice Unbalanced: Gender, Psychiatry and Judicial Decisions*, Milton Keynes: Open University Press.

ALTHUSSER, L. (1971) *Lenin and Philosophy and Other Essays*, London: New Left Books.

AMERICAN PSYCHIATRIC ASSOCIATION (1987) *Diagnostic and Statistical Manual of Mental Disorders*, Third Edition – Revised (DSM-111-R), Washington: American Psychiatric Association.

AMERICAN PSYCHIATRIC ASSOCIATION (1994) *Diagnostic and Statistical Manual of Mental Disorders*, Fourth Edition (DSM-IV), Washington: American Psychiatric Association.

AMERICAN PSYCHOLOGICAL ASSOCIATION TASK FORCE (1975) 'Report of the Task Force on Sex Bias and Sex-Role Stereotyping in Psychotherapeutic Practice', *American Psychologist* 1169–75.

ANDREWS, H. and HOUSE, A. (1989) 'Functional Dysphonia', in G. Brown and T. Harris (eds) *Life Events and Illness*, London: Guilford Press.

ANGST, J. and DOBLER-MIKOLA, A. (1984) 'The Zurich Study, II: The Continuum from Normal to Pathological Mood Swings', *European Archives of Psychiatry and Neurological Science*, 234: 21–9.

ANNANDALE, E. and HUNT, K. (1990) 'Masculinity, Feminity and Sex: an Exploration of their Relative Contribution to Explaining Gender Differences in Health', *Sociology of Health and Illness*, 12: 24–46.

ARBER, S. and GINN, J. (1991) *Gender and Later Life*, London: Sage.

ARMSTRONG D. (1983) *Political Anatomy of the Body: Medical Knowledge in Britain in the Twentieth Century*, Cambridge: Cambridge University Press.

BARKER, P. (1992) *Regeneration*, Harmondsworth: Penguin.

BARRETT, M. (1980) *Women's Oppression Today*, London: Verso.

BART, P. (1970) 'Mother Portnoy's Complains', *Trans-action*, 8: 67–74.

BARTLEY, M., POPAY, J. and PLEWIS, I. (1992) 'Domestic Conditions, Paid Employment and Women's Experience of Ill-health', *Sociology of Health and Illness*, 14: 313–43.

BATCHELOR, I.R.C. (ed.) (1969) *Henderson and Gillespie's Textbook of Psychiatry*, Tenth Edition, London: Oxford University Press.

BATTIE, W. (1962) [1758] *A Treatise on Madness* (introduced by R. Hunter and I. MacAlpine), London: Dawsons.

BECK, A.T., WARD C., MENDELSON, M., MOCK, J. and ERBAUGH S. (1962) 'Reliability of Psychiatric Diagnoses: 2. A Study of Consistency of Clinical Judgements and Ratings', *American Journal of Psychiatry*, 119: 351–7.

BEECHEY, V. (1979) 'On Patriarchy', *Feminist Review*, 3: 66–82.

BEITCHMAN, J.H., ZUCKER, K.J., HOOD, J.E., DACOSTA, G.A., AKMAN, D. and CASSAVIA, E. (1992) 'A Review of the Long-Term Effects of Child Sexual Abuse', *Child Abuse and Neglect*, 16: 101–18.

BELLE, D. (1982) 'The Stress of Caring: Women as Providers of Social Support', in L. Goldberger and S. Breznitz (eds), *Handbook of Stress: Theoretical and Clinical Aspects*. New York: The Free Press.

BENTALL, R.P. (1990) 'The Syndromes and Symptoms of Psychosis', in R. P. Bentall (ed.) *Reconstructing Schizophrenia*, London: Macmillan.

BENTON, T. (1991) 'Biology and Social Science: Why the Return of the Repressed Should be Given a (Cautious) Welcome', *Sociology*, 25: 1–29.

BERGER, J. (1972) *Ways of Seeing*, Harmondsworth: Penguin.

BERKMAN, L.F. and BRESLOW, L. (1983) *Health and Ways of Living: The Alameda County Study*, Oxford: Oxford University Press.

BHASKAR, R. (1978) *A Realist Theory of Science*, Brighton: Harvester.

BHASKAR, R. (1989) *Reclaiming Reality: A Critical Introduction to Contemporary Philosophy*, London: Verso.

BIRKE, L. (1986) *Women, Feminism and Biology*, Brighton: Wheatsheaf.

BLAXTER, M. (1990) *Health and Lifestyles*, London: Routledge.

BLUM, J. (1978) 'On Changes in Psychiatric Diagnosis over Time', *American Psychologist*, 33: 1017–31.

BLUSTEIN, B.E. (1981) '"A Hollow Square of Psychological Science": American Neurologists and Psychiatrists in Conflict', in A. Scull (ed.) *Madhouses, Mad-Doctors and Madmen*. London: Athlone.

BORDO, S. (1985) 'Anorexia Nervosa: Psychopathology as the Crystallization of Culture', *The Philosophical Forum*, 17: 33–103.

BORDO, S. (1990) 'Reading the Slender Body', in M. Jacobus, E.F. Keller and S. Shuttleworth (eds) *Body/Politics: Women and the Discourse of Science*, London: Routledge.

BORDO, S. (1993) '"Material Girl": The Effacements of Post-modern Culture', in C. Schwichitenberg (ed) *The Madonna Connection*, Boulder: Westview.

BOWLING, A. (1991) *Measuring Health*, Milton Keynes: Open University Press.

BOX, S. (1984) 'Preface', in P. Schrag and D. Divoky, *The Myth of the Hyperactive Child*, Harmondsworth: Penguin.

BREGGIN, P.R. (1974) 'Psychotherapy as Applied Ethics', *Psychiatry*, 34: 59–74.

BREUER, J. and FREUD, S. (1974) [1893–5] *Studies on Hysteria*, Harmondsworth: Penguin.

BROVERMAN, I.K., BROVERMAN, D.M., CLARKSON, F.E., ROSENKRANTZ, P.S. and VOGEL, S.R. (1970) 'Sex Role Stereotypes and Clinical Judgement of Mental Health', *Journal of Consulting and Clinical Psychology*, 34: 1–7.

BROWN, G.W. and CRAIG, T.K.J. (1986) 'Psychiatric Cases in Community Studies: How Important an Issue?'. *Social Science and Medicine*, 22: 173–93.

BROWN, G.W. and HARRIS, T. (1978) *Social Origins of Depression: A Study of Psychiatric Disorder in Women*, London: Tavistock.

BROWN, G. W. and HARRIS, T. (1989) *Life Events and Illness*, London: Unwin Hyman.

BROWN, P. (1985) *The Transfer of Care: Psychiatric Deinstitutionalisation and its Aftermath*, London: Routledge & Kegan Paul.

BROWN, P. and JORDANOVA, L.J. (1981) 'Oppressive Dichotomies: the Nature/Culture Debate', in The Cambridge Women's Studies Group: *Women in Society*, London: Virago

BROWNE, A. and FINKELHOR, D. (1986) 'Impact of Child Sexual Abuse: A Review of Research', *Psychological Bulletin*, 99: 66–77.

BRUCH, H. (1973) *Eating Disorders: Obesity, Anorexia and the Person Within*, New York: Basic Books.

BRUCH, H. (1978) *The Golden Cage: The Enigma of Anorexia Nervosa*, New York: Vintage.

BRUCH, H. (1988) *Conversations with Anorexics*, New York: Basic Books.

BRUMBERG, J.J. (1988) *Fasting Girls: The History of Anorexia Nervosa as a Modern Disease*, Cambridge, Mass: Harvard University Press.

BUSFIELD, J. (1983) 'Gender, Mental Illness and Psychiatry', in M. Evans and C. Ungerson (eds) *Sexual Divisions: Patterns and Processes*, London: Tavistock.

BUSFIELD, J. (1988) 'Mental Illness as Social Product or Social Construct: a Contradiction in Feminists' Arguments?', *Sociology of Health and Illness*, 10: 521–42.

BUSFIELD, J. (1989a) *Managing Madness: Changing Ideas and Practice*, London: Unwin Hyman.

BUSFIELD, J (1989b) 'Sexism and Psychiatry', *Sociology*, 23: 343–64

BUSFIELD, J. (1994) 'Is Mental Illness a Female Malady? Men, Women and Madness in Nineteenth Century England', *Sociology*, 28: 259–77.

BUSFIELD, J. and PADDON, M. (1977) *Thinking about Children: Sociology and Fertility in Post-War England*, Cambridge: Cambridge University Press.

CANETTO, S.S. (1991) 'Gender Roles, Suicide Attempts and Substance Abuse', *The Journal of Psychology*, 125: 605–20.

CARPENTER, I. and BROCKINGTON, I. (1980) 'A Study of Mental Illness in Asians, West Indians and Africans Living in Manchester, *British Journal of Psychiatry*, 137:201–5

CASTEL, R. (1988) *'The Regulation of Madness: The Origins of Incarceration in France'*, Oxford: Basil Blackwell.

CHERNIN, K. (1983) *Womensize: The Tyranny of Slenderness*, London: The Women's Press.

CHERNIN, K. (1985) *The Hungry Self: Women, Eating and Identity*, London: Virago.

CHESLER, P. (1972) *Women and Madness*, New York: Doubleday.

CHODOROW, N. (1978) *The Reproduction of Mothering: Psychoanalysis and the Sociology of Gender*, Berkeley: University of California Press.

CHODOROW, N. (1989) *Feminism and Psychoanalytic Theory*, Cambridge: Polity Press.

CHOMSKY, N. (1957) *Syntactic Structures*, The Hague: Mouton.

CLANCY, K. and GOVE, W. (1974) 'Sex Differences in Respondents' Reports of Psychiatric Symptoms: An Analysis of Response Bias', *American Journal of Sociology*, 80: 205–16.

CLARE, A. (1976) *Psychiatry in Dissent: Controversial Issues in Thought and Practice*, London: Tavistock.

CLARK, M.J. (1981) 'The Rejection of Psychological Approaches to Mental Disorder in Late Nineteenth-Century British Psychiatry', in A Scull (ed.) *Madhouses, Mad-Doctors and Madmen*, London: The Athlone Press.

CLOWARD, R. and PIVEN, F.F. (1979) 'Hidden Protest: The Channelling of Female Protest and Resistance', *Signs*, 4: 651–69.

COCHRANE, R. (1984) *The Social Creation of Mental Illness*, London: Longman.

COCHRANE, R. and STOPES-ROE, M. (1980) 'Factors Affecting the Distribution of Psychological Symptoms in Urban Areas of England', *Acta Psychiatrica Scandanavica*, 61: 445–60.

COCHRANE, R. and STOPES-ROE, M. (1981) 'Women, Marriage, Employment and Mental Health', *British Journal of Psychiatry*, 139: 373–81.

COMMISSIONERS IN LUNACY (1897) *Special Report on the Alleged Increase of Insanity*, London: HMSO.

COMSTOCK, G.W. and HELSING, K.J. (1976) 'Symptoms of Depression in Two Communities', *Psychological Medicine*, 6: 551.

CONNELL, R.W. (1987) *Gender and Power*, Cambridge: Polity Press.

CONOVER, D. and CLIMENT, C. (1976) 'Explanations of Bias in Psychiatric Case Finding Instruments', *Journal of Health and Social Behaviour*, 17: 62–9.

COOPERSTOCK, R. (1981) 'A Review of Women's Psychotropic Drug Use', in E. Howell and M. Bayes (eds) *Women and Mental Health*, New York: Basic Books.

DALLY, P. and GOMEZ, J. (1979) *Anorexia Nervosa*, London: Heinemann.

DALTON, K. (1964) *The Premenstual Syndrome*, London: Heinemann.

DANIELS, A.K. (1970) 'The Social Construction of Military Psychiatric Diagnoses', in H.P. Dreitzel (ed.) *Recent Sociology No. 2: Patterns of Communicative Behaviour*, New York: Macmillan.

DAVIDOFF, L. (1976) 'The Rationalisation of Housework', in D.L. Barker and S. Allen (eds) *Sexual Divisions and Society*, London: Tavistock.

DAVIDOFF, L. and HALL, C. (1987) *Family Fortunes: Men and Women of the English Middle Class, 1780–1850*, London: Hutchinson.

DAVIN, A. (1978) 'Imperialism and Motherhood', *History Workshop Journal*, 5: 9–65.

DAVIS, K. (1938) 'Mental Hygiene and the Class Structure', *Psychiatry*, 1: 55–65.

DAVIS, K. (1988) *Power Under the Microscope*, Dordrecht: Floris.

DEPARTMENT OF SOCIAL SECURITY (1988) *Community Care: Agenda for Action* (The Griffiths Report), London: HMSO.

DIAMOND, N. (1985) 'Thin is a Feminist Issue'. *Feminist Review*, 19: 45–64.

DINNERSTEIN, D. (1976) *The Mermaid and the Minotaur: Sexual Arrangements and the Human Malaise*, New York: Harper & Row.

DOHRENWEND, B.P., CHIN-SHONG, E.T., EGRI, G. and STOKES, S. (1970) 'Measures of Psychiatric Disorder in Contrasting Class and Ethnic Groups', in E.H. Hare and J.K. Wing (eds) *Psychiatric Epidemiology*, London: Oxford University Press.

DOHRENWEND, B.P. and DOHRENWEND, B.S. (1969) *Social Status and Psychological Disorder: A Causal Inquiry*, New York: Wiley.

DOHRENWEND, B.P. and DOHRENWEND, B.S. (1976) 'Sex Differences and Psychiatric Disorders', *American Journal of Sociology*, 6: 1447–54.

DOHRENWEND, B.S. (1972) 'Social Status and Stressful Life Events', *Journal of Personality and Social Psychology*, 28: 225–35.

DOYAL, L. (1985) 'Women and the National Health Service: The Carers and the Careless', in Lewin, L. and Olesen, V. (eds) *Women, Health and Healing*, London: Tavistock.

DOYAL, L. and GOUGH, I. (1991) *A Theory of Human Need*, London: Macmillan.

DUNCOMBE, J. and MARSDEN, D. (1993) 'Love and Intimacy: The Gender Division of Emotion and Emotion Work', *Sociology*, 27: 221–41.

DURKHEIM, E. (1951) [1897] *Suicide*, New York: The Free Press.

DURKHEIM, E. (1964) [1895] *The Rules of Sociological Method*, New York: The Free Press.

EDWARDS, A. (1989) 'The Sex/Gender Distinction – Has it Outlived its Usefulness?', *Australian Feminist Studies*, 10: 1–12.

EDWARDS, R. (1981) 'Mental Health as Rational Antonomy', *The Journal of Medicine and Philosophy*, 6: 309–22.

EGELAND, J.A. and HOSTETTER, A.M. (1983) 'Amish Study I: Affective Disorders Among the Amish, 1976–1980', *American Journal of Psychiatry*, 140: 56–61.

EHRENREICH, B. and ENGLISH, D. (1974) *Witches, Midwives and Nurses: A History of Women Healers*, London: Compendium.

EHRENREICH, B. and ENGLISH, D. (1976) *Complaints and Disorders: The Sexual Politics of Sickness*, London: Writers and Readers Publishing Cooperative.

EHRENREICH, B. and ENGLISH, D. (1979) *For Their Own Good: 150 Years of the Experts' Advice to Women*, London: Pluto.

EICHENBAUM, L. and ORBACH, S. (1982) *Outside in ... Inside Out: Women's Psychology, A Feminist Psychoanalytic Approach*, Harmondsworth: Penguin.

EICHENBAUM, L. and ORBACH, S. (1984) *What do Women Want?*, London: Fontana.

EICHENBAUM, L. and ORBACH, S. (1985) *Understanding Women*, Harmondsworth: Penguin.

EISENSTEIN, Z. (1979) 'Developing a Theory of Capitalist Patriarchy and Socialist Feminism', in Z. Eisenstein (ed.) *Capitalist Patriarchy and the Case for Socialist Feminism*, New York: Monthly Review Press.

ELLIOT SMITH, G. and PEAR, T.H. (1917) *Shell-Shock and Its Lessons*, Manchester: The University Press.

ENDICOTT, J. and SPITZER, R.L. (1978) 'A Diagnostic Interview: the Schedule for Affective Disorders and Schizophrenia, *Archives of General Psychiatry*, 35: 837–44.

ENGEL, G.L. (1977) 'The Need for a New Medical Model: A Challenge for Biomedicine, *Science*, 196: 129–36.

ENGEL, G.L. (1980) 'The Clinical Application of the Biopsychosocial Model' *American Journal of Psychiatry*, 136: 535–44.

ENNEW, J. (1986) *The Sexual Exploitation of Children*, Cambridge: Polity Press.

ESSEN-MOLLER, E. (1956) 'Individual Traits and Morbidity in a Swedish Rural Population', *Acta Psychiatria Scandanavica*, Supplement 100.

ETTORÉ, E. and RISKA, E. (1993) 'Psychotropics, Sociology and Women', *Sociology of Health and Illness*, 15: 503–24.

EYSENCK, H.J. (1960) *Handbook of Abnormal Psychology*, New York: Basic Books.

FIGERT, A.E. (1992) 'The Three Faces of PMS: The Scientific, Political and Professional Structuring of a Psychiatric Disorder', paper presented at the American Sociological Association Annual Meeting, Pittsburgh..

FINCH, J. and GROVES, D.L. (eds) (1983) *A Labour of Love: Women, Work and Caring*, London: Routledge.

FINGARETTE, H. (1972) 'Insanity and Responsibility', *Inquiry*, 15: 6–29.

FINKELHOR, D. HOTALING, G., LEWIS, I.A. and SMITH, C, (1990) 'Sexual Abuse in a National Survey of Adult Men and Women: Prevalence, Characteristics and Risk Factors', *Child Abuse and Neglect*, 14: 19–28.

FIRESTONE, S. (1971) *The Dialectic of Sex*, London: Jonathan Cape.

FLEW, A. 1973 *Crime and Disease?*, London: Macmillan.

FOUCAULT, M. (1967) *Madness and Civilization: A History of Insanity in the Age of Reason*, London: Tavistock.

FOUCAULT, M. (1973) *The Birth of the Clinic: An Archaeology of Medical Perception*, London: Tavistock.

FRANK, R.T. (1931) 'Normal Causes of Premenstrual Tension', *Archives of Neurology and Psychiatry*, 26: 1053–7.

FREIDSON, E. (1970) *Profession of Medicine*, New York: Dodd Mead.

FREIDSON, E. (1994) *Professionalism Reborn*, Cambridge: Polity Press.

FREUD, S. (1935) *An Autobiographical Study*, London: Hogarth Press.

FREUD, S. (1973) 'Femininity', in *New Introductory Lectures on Psychoanalysis*, Harmondsworth: Penguin Books.

FREUD, S. (1976) *The Interpretation of Dreams*, Harmondsworth: Penguin.

FREUD, S. (1977) [1905] *Three Essays on the Theory of Sexuality*, in *Freud 7: On Sexuality*, Harmondsworth: Penguin.

FRIEDAN, B. (1963) *The Feminine Mystique*, New York: Dell.

FUSSELL, P. (1975) *The Great War and Modern History*, London: Oxford University Press.

GAVRON, H. (1968) *The Captive Wife*, Harmondsworth: Penguin Books.

GERHARDT, U. (1989) *Ideas about Illness: An Intellectual and Political History of Medical Sociology*, London: Macmillan.

GERSONS, B.P.R. and CARLIER, I.V.E. (1992) 'Post-traumatic Stress Disorder: The History of a Recent Concept'. *British Journal of Psychiatry*, 161: 742–8.

GILLIGAN, C. (1982) *In a Different Voice*, Cambridge, Mass: Harvard University Press.

GILMAN, C.P. (1981) *The Yellow Wallpaper*, London: Virago.

GLUCKSMANN, M. (1990) *Women Assemble*, London: Routledge.

GOFFMAN, E. (1961) *Asylums*, Harmondsworth: Penguin.

GOFFMAN, E. (1971) 'The Insanity of Place', Appendix to *Relations in Public*, London: Allen Lane.

GOLDBERG, D. (1972) *The Detection of Psychiatric Illness by Questionnaire*, London: Oxford University Press.

GOLDBERG, D. and HUXLEY, P. (1980) *Mental Illness in the Community: The Pathway to Psychiatric Care*, London: Tavistock.

GOLDBERG, D. and HUXLEY, P. (1992) *Common Mental Disorders: A Bio-Social Model*, London: Routledge.

GOLDSTEIN, J. (1987) *Console and Classify: The French Psychiatric Profession in the Nineteenth Century*, Cambridge: Cambridge University Press.

GOLDSTEIN, J.M. (1992) 'Gender and Schizophrenia: a Summary of Findings'. *Schizophrenia Monitor*, 2, No.2: 1–4.

GORDON, L. (1989) *Heroes of Their Own Lives: The Politics and History of Family Violence*, London: Virago.

GORDON, R.A. (1990) *Anorexia and Bulimia: Anatomy of a Social Epidemic*, Cambridge, Mass: Blackwell.

GOTTESMAN, I. and SHIELDS, J. (1982) *Schizophrenia: The Epigenetic Puzzle*, Cambridge: Cambridge University Press.

GOTTESMAN, I. (1990) *Schizophrenia Genesis*, New York: W.H. Freeman.

GOVE, W.R. (1975) 'Labeling and Mental Illness: A Critique', in W.R. Gove (ed.) *The Labeling of Deviance*, New York: Halsted.

GOVE, W.R. (1972) 'The Relationship between Sex Roles, Marital Status and Mental Illness, *Social Forces*, 51: 34–44.

GOVE, W. (1984) 'Gender Differences in Mental and Physical Illness: The Effects of Fixed Roles and Nurturant Roles', *Social Science and Medicine*, 19: 77–91.

GOVE, W.R. and GEERKEN, M. (1977) 'Response Bias in Surveys of Mental Health: An Empirical Investigation', *American Journal of Sociology*, 82: 289–317.

GOVE, W.R. and HERB, T.R. (1974) 'Stress and Mental Illness among the Young: A Comparison of the Sexes', *Social Forces*, 53: 256–65.

GOVE, W.R. and TUDOR, J.F. (1972) 'Adult Sex Roles and Mental Illness', *American Journal of Sociology*, 78: 812–35.

GOVE, W.R., McCORKEL, J., FAIN, T. and HUGHES, M.D. (1976) 'Response Bias in Community Surveys of Mental Health: Systematic Bias or Random Noise?', *Social Science and Medicine*, 10: 497–502.

GUNTRIP, H. (1961) *Personality Structure and Human Interaction: The Developing Synthesis of Psycho-dynamic Theory*, London: Hogarth.

HAMMEN, G.L. and PADESKY, C.A. (1977) 'Sex Differences in the Expression of Depressive Responses in the Beck Depression Inventory'. *Journal of Abnormal Psychology*, 89: 194.

HARDING, S. (1986) *The Science Question in Feminism*, Milton Keynes: Open University Press.

HARDING, S. (1991) *Whose Science? Whose Knowledge?*, Milton Keynes: Open University Press.

HARDING, S. and O'BARR, S.F. (eds) (1987) *Sex and Scientific Inquiry*, Chicago: University of Chicago Press.

HARRÉ, R. (1986) *Varieties of Realism*, Oxford: Blackwell.

HARRIS, R. (1989) *Murders and Madness: Medicine, Law and Society in the Fin de Siècle*, Oxford: Clarendon Press.

HARRISON, G., OWENS, D. and HOLTON, A. (1984) 'A Prospective Study of Severe Mental disorder in Afro-Caribbean Patients'. *Psychological Medicine*, 11: 289–302.

HART, H.A.L. and HONORÉ, A.M. (1959) *Causation in the Law*, Oxford: Oxford University Press.

HARTMANN, H. (1979) 'The Unhappy Marriage of Marxism and Feminism: Towards a More Progressive Union', *Capital and Class*, 8: 1–33.

HEARN, J. (1987) *The Gender of Oppression: Men, Masculinity and the Critique of Marxism*, Brighton: Wheatsheaf.

HEARN, J. and MORGAN, D. (eds) (1990) *Men, Masculinity and Social Theory*, London: Unwin Hyman.

HEATHER, N. and ROBERTSON, I. (1989) *Problem Drinking*, Second Edition. Oxford: Oxford University Press.

HENRIQUES, J., HOLLOWAY, W., URWIN, C., VENN, C. and WALKERDINE, V. (1984) *Changing the Subject: Psychology Social Regulation and Subjectivity*, London: Methuen.

HERMAN, J.L. (1981) *Father–Daughter Incest*, Cambridge, MA: Harvard University Press.

HERMAN, J.L. (1992) *Trauma and Recovery*, New York: Basic Books.

HOBSBAWM, E.J. (1969) *Industry and Empire*, Harmondsworth: Penguin.

HOCHSCHILD, A.R. (1983) *The Managed Heart: Commercialization of Human Feeling*, Berkeley: University of California Press.

HOLLINGSHEAD, A.B. and REDLICH, F.C. (1958) *Social Class and Mental Illness*, New York: Wiley.

HOLMES, T.H. and RAHE, R.M. (1967) 'The Social Re-adjustment Rating Scale', *Journal of Psychosomatic Research*, 11: 213–8.

HORWITZ, A. (1977) 'The Pathways into Psychiatric Treatment: Some Differences between Men and Women', *Journal of Health and Social Behaviour*, 18: 169–78.

HUNT, K. and ANNANDALE, H. (1993) 'Just the Job? Is the Relationship between Health and Domestic and Paid Work Gender-specific?', *Sociology of Health and Illness*, 15: 643–64.

HUNTER, R. and MACALPINE, I. (1963) *Three Hundred Years of Psychiatry. 1635–1860*, London: Oxford University Press.

ILLICH, I. (1977) 'Disabling Professions', in I. Illich, I.K. Zola, J. McKnight, S. Caplan and H. Shaiken (eds) *Disabling Professions*, London: Marion Boyars.

INGLEBY, D. (1982) 'The Social Construction of Mental Illness' in P. Wright and A. Treacher (eds) *The Problem of Medical Knowledge*, Edinburgh: Edinburgh University Press.

ISRAEL, S.L. (1938) 'Premenstrual Tension', *Journal of the American Medical Association*, 110: 1721.

JACKSON, E.F. (1962) 'Status Consistency and Symptoms of Stress', *American Sociological Review*, 27: 469–80.

JACKSON, S.W. (1886) *Melancholia and Depression*, New Haven: Yale University Press.

JACKSON, S.W. (1992) 'The Amazing Deconstructing Women', *Trouble and Strife*, 25: 25–31.

JAMES, N. (1989) 'Emotional Labour: Skill and Work in the Social Regulation of Feelings', *Sociological Review*, 37: 15–42.

JASPERS, K. (1963) *General Psychopathology*, Manchester: Manchester University Press.

JOHNSON, D. (1974) 'A Study of the Use of Antidepressant Medication in General Practice'. *British Journal of Psychiatry*, 125: 186–92.

JONES, L. and COCHRANE, R. (1981) 'Stereotypes of Mental Illness: A Test of the Labelling Hypothesis', *Journal of Social Psychiatry*, 27: 99–107.

JORDANOVA, L. (1982) 'Conceptualising Power over Women' (review of Barbara Ehrenreich and Deirdre English, *For Their Own Good), Radical Science Journal*, 12, 124–8.

JORDANOVA, L. (1989) *Sexual Visions: Images of Gender in Science and Medicine between the Eighteenth and Twentieth Centuries*, London: Harvester Wheatsheaf.

KEAT, R. and URRY, J. (1975) *Social Theory as Science*, London: Routledge & Kegan Paul.

KELLY, L. (1988) *Surviving Sexual Violence*, Cambridge: Polity.

KENDELL, R.E. (1975) *The Role of Diagnosis in Psychiatry*, Oxford: Blackwell.

KESSLER, R.C. and MCLEOD, J.D. (1984) 'Sexual Differences in Vulnerability to Undesirable Life Events', *American Sociological Review*, 49: 620–31.

KESSLER, R.C. and MCRAE, J.A. (1981) 'Trends in the Relationship Between Sex and Psychological Distress, 1957–1976', *American Sociological Review*, 46: 443–52.

KING, L.S. (1954) 'What is Disease?', *Philosophy of Science*, 21: 193–203.

KING, M., COKER, E., LEAVEY, A., HOARE, A. and JOHNSON-SABINE, E. (1994) 'Incidence of Psychotic Illness in London: Comparison of Ethnic Groups', *British Medical Journal*, 309: 29th October.

KOVEL, J. (1978) 'The American Mental Health Industry' in D. Ingleby (ed.) *Critical Psychiatry*, Harmondsworth: Penguin.

KREITMAN, N., SAINSBURY, P., MORRISSEY, J. and SCRIVENER, J. (1961) 'The Reliability of Psychiatric Assessment: An Analysis', *Journal of Mental Science*, 107: 887–908.

LA FONTAINE, J.S. (1990) *Child Sexual Abuse*, Cambridge: Polity Pres.

LAING, R.D. (1960) *The Divided Self*, London: Tavistock.

LAING, R.D. (1967) *The Politics of Experience and the Bird of Paradise*, Harmondsworth: Penguin.

LAING, R.D. and ESTERSON, A. (1964) *Sanity, Madness and the Family, Vol I: Families of Schizophrenics*, London: Tavistock.

LANGNER, T.S. (1962) 'A Twenty-Two Item Screening Scale of Psychiatric Symptoms Indicating Impairment', *Journal of Health and Human Behaviour*, 3: 269–76.

LAWRENCE, M. (1984) *The Anorexic Experience*, London: Women's Press.

LAWRENCE, M. (1987) Education and Identity: The Social Origins of Anorexia', in M. Lawrence (ed.) *Fed Up and Hungry: Women Oppression and Food*, London: The Women's Press.

LAWS, S., HEY, V. and EAGAN, A. (1985) *Seeing Red: The Politics of Pre-Menstrual Tension*, London: Hutchinson.

LAZARUS, R.S. and COHEN, J.B. (1977) 'Environmental Stress', in I. Altmann and J.F. Wohlwill (eds) *Human Behaviour and Environment, Advances in Theory and Research*, Volume 2. New York: Plenum Press.

LEED, E.J. (1979) *No Man's Land: Combat and Identity in World War I*, Cambridge: Cambridge University Press.

LEWIS, A. (1953) 'Health as a Social Concept', *British Journal of Sociology*, 4: 109–24.

LEWIS, A. (1967) *The State of Psychiatry: Essays and Addresses*, London: Routledge & Kegan Paul.

LEWONTIN, R.C., ROSE, S. and KANIN, L.J. (1984) *Not in Our Genes: Biology, Ideology, and Human Nature*, Harmondsworth: Penguin.

LOPATA, H.Z. (1971) *Occupation Housewife*, New York: Oxford University Press.

LOPATA, H.Z. and THORNE, B. (1978) 'On the Term "Sex Roles"', *Signs*, 2: 718–21.

LORANGER, A.W. (1990) 'The Impact of DSM-III on Diagnostic Practice in a University Hospital', *Archives of General Psychiatry*, 47: 672–5.

LORING, M. and POWELL, B. (1988) 'Gender, Race and DSM III: A Study of the Objectivity of Psychiatric Diagnostic Behaviour', *Journal of Health and Social Behaviour*, 29: 1–22.

LOUGHLIN, K. (1993) ' "Framing Disease": The Case of Schizophrenia', European Association for the History of Psychiatry Conference. London.

LOWE, C.R. and GARRATT, F.N. (1959) 'Sex Pattern of Admission to Mental Hospitals in Relation to Social Circumstances', *British Journal of Preventive and Social Medicine*, 13: 88–102.

MACCURDY, J.T. (1918) *War Neuroses*, Cambridge: Cambridge University Press.

MACDONALD, M. (1981) *Mystical Bedlam: Madness, Anxiety and Healing in Seventeenth-Century England*, Cambridge: Cambridge University Press.

MACDONALD, M. (1986) 'Women and Madness in Tudor and Stuart England', *Social Research*, 55: 257–81.

MACINTYRE, A. (1988) *Whose Justice? Which Rationality?* London: Duckworth.

MACKENZIE, C. (1992) *Psychiatry for the Rich: A History of Ticehurst Private Asylum*, London: Routledge.

MACSWEEN, M. (1993) *Anorexic Bodies: A Feminist and Sociological Perspective on Anorexia Nervosa*, London: Routledge.

MANN, M. (1981) 'State and Society, 1130–1815', *Political Power and Social Theory*, 1: 165–208.

MANN, M. (1986) *The Sources of Social Power*, Vol I, *A History of Power from the Beginning to AD1760*, Cambridge: Cambridge University Press.

MANNONI, O. (1971) *Freud: The Theory of the Unconsious*, London: New Left Books.

MARTIN. E. (1987) *The Women in the Body*, Milton Keynes: Open University Press.

MASSON, J.M. (1984) *Freud: The Assault on Truth, Freud's Suppression of the Seduction Theory*, London: Faber & Faber.

MASSON, J. (1990) *Against Therapy*, London: Fontana.

MATTHEWS, J.J. (1984) *Good and Mad Women: The Historical Construction of Femininity in Twentieth Century Australia*, Sydney: Allen & Unwin.

MAUDSLEY, H. (1873) *Body and Mind*, London: Macmillan.

McGOVERN, D. and COPE, R. (1987) 'The Compulsory Detention of Males of Different Ethnic Groups with Special Reference to Offender Patients', *British Journal of Psychiatry*, 150: 505–12.

McKEE, D. and VILHJALMSSON, R. (1986) 'Life Support, Vulnerability and Depression: A Methodological Critique of Brown et al.', *Sociology*, 20: 589–99.

MECHANIC, D. (1970) 'Problems and Prospects in Psychiatric Epidemiology', in E.H. Hare and J.K. Wing (eds) *Psychiatric Epidemiology*, London: Oxford University Press.

MECHANIC, D. (1978) *Medical Sociology*, Second Edition. New York: The Free Press.

MERCIER, C. (1890) *Sanity and Insanity*, London: Walter Scott.

MIDELFORT, H.C.E. (1980) 'Madness and Civilization in Early Modern Europe: A Reappraisal of Michel Foucault', in B. Malament (ed.) *After the Reformation: Essays in Honour of A.M. Hexter*, Philadelphia: University of Pennsylvania Press.

MILES, A. (1988) *Women and Mental Illness: The Social Context of Female Neurosis*, Brighton: Wheatsheaf.

MILLER, E. (ed.) (1940) *The Neuroses in War*, London: Macmillan.

MILLER, J.B. (ed.) (1988) *Toward a New Psychology of Women*, Second Edition, Harmondsworth: Penguin.

MILLER, P. and ROSE, N. (1986) *The Power of Psychiatry*, Cambridge: Polity Press.

MILLETT, K. (1972) *Sexual Politics*, London: Abacus.

MITCHELL, J. (1975) *Psychoanalysis and Feminism*, Harmondsworth: Penguin.

MITCHELL, S. and ABBOTT, S. (1987) 'Gender and Symptoms of Depression and Anxiety among Kikuyu Secondary School Students in Kenya', *Social Science and Medicine*, 24: 303–16.

MOLYNEUX, M. (1979) 'Beyond the Domestic Labour Debate', *New Left Review*, 116: 3–27.

MORANTZ, R. (1974) 'The Lady and Her Physician', in M. Hartman and L.W. Banner *Clio's Consciousness Raised*, New York: Harper & Row.

MORGAN, D.H.J. (1985) *The Family: Politics and Social Theory*, London: Routledge & Kegan Paul.

MORGAN, D.M. (1992) *Discovering Men*, London: Routledge & Kegan Paul.

MYERS, C.S. (1915) 'A Contribution to the Study of Shell-Shock', *The Lancet*, February 13: 316–20.

MYERS, S.K., WISEMAN, M.M., TICHSLER, G.L., HOLZER, C.E., LEAF, P.J., ORVASIHEL, H., ANTHONY, J.C., BOYD, J.H., BURKE, J.D., KRAMER, M. and STOLTZMAN, R. (1984) 'Six-month Prevalence of Psychiatric Disorders in Three Communities, 1980 to 1982', *Archives of General Psychiatry*, 41: 959–67.

NATHANSON, C.A. (1977) 'Sex, Illness and Medical Care: A Review of Data, Theory and Method', *Social Science and Medicine*, 11: 13.

NATIONAL INSTITUTE OF MENTAL HEALTH. *Mental Health, United States, 1987*, Washington DC: US Government Printing Office.

NAVARRO, V. (1976) *Medicine Under Capitalism*, New York: Prodist.

NEWMAN, J.P. (1984) 'Sex Differences in Symptoms of Depression: Clinical Disorder Normal Distress?' *Journal of Health and Social Behaviour*, 25: 136–159.

NORTH EAST THAMES REGIONAL HEALTH AUTHORITY (1994) *The Report of the Inquiry into the Care and Treatment of Christopher Clunis*, London: HMSO.

OAKLEY, A. (1972) *Sex, Gender and Society*, London: Temple Smith.

OAKLEY, A. (1976) *Housewife*, Harmondsworth: Penguin.

OAKLEY, A. (1981) *From Here to Maternity: Becoming a Mother*, Harmondsworth: Penguin.

OAKLEY, A. (1982) *Subject Women*, London: Fontana.

OAKLEY, A. (1983) 'Women and Health Policy' in J. Lewis (ed.) *Women's Welfare: Women's Rights*, London: Croom Helm.

OPPENHEIM, S. (1991) *'Shattered Nerves': Doctors, Patients and Depression in Victorian England*, New York: Oxford University Press.

ORBACH, S. (1978) *Fat is a Feminist Issue*, London: Hamlyn.

ORBACH, S. (1984) *Fat is a Feminist Issue 2*, London: Hamlyn.

ORBACH, S. (1986) *Hunger Strike*, London: Faber.

ORBACH, S. (1993) *Hunger Strike*, Second Edition. Harmondsworth: Penguin.

PADESKY, C.A. and HAMMEN, C.L. (1981) 'Sex Differences in Depressive Symptom Expression and Help-Seeking Among College Students', *Sex Roles*, 7: 309–20.

PARRY-JONES, W. (1972) *The Trade in Lunacy: A Study of Private Madhouses in England in the Eighteenth and Nineteenth Centuries*, London: Rouledge & Kegan Paul.

PARSONS, T. (1951) *The Social System*, London: Routledge & Kegan Paul.

PARSONS, T. and BALES, R.F. (1956) *Family: Socialization and Interaction Process*, London: Routledge & Kegan Paul.

PENFOLD, P.S. and WALKER, G.A. (1984) *Women and the Psychiatric Paradox*, Milton Keynes: Open University Press.

PERELBERG, R.J. and MILLER, A.C. (1990) *Gender and Power in Families*, London: Routledge.

PHILLIPS, D.L. (1968) 'Social Class and Psychological Disturbance: The Influence of Positive and Negative Experiences', *Social Psychiatry*, 3: 41–6.

PHILLIPS, D.L. and SEGAL, B.F. (1969) 'Sexual Status and Psychiatric Symptoms', *American Sociological Review*, 34: 58–72.

PHILLIPS, P. (1990) *The Scientific Lady: A Social History of Women's Scientific Interests, 1620–1918*, London: Weidenfeld & Nicolson.

PLUMMER, K. (1975) *Sexual Stigma: An Interactionist Account*, London: Routledge & Kegan Paul.

PLUMWOOD, V. (1989) 'Do We Need a Sex/Gender Distinction? *Radical Philosophy*, 51: 2–11.

PRESIDENT'S COMMISSION ON MENTAL HEALTH, *Task Reports 1978, Volume II, Appendix*, Washington: US Government Printing Office.

PRIOR, L. (1993) *The Social Organisation of Mental Illness*, London: Sage.

RADDEN, J. (1985) *Madness and Reason*, London: George Allen & Unwin.

RAMON, S. (1986) 'The Category of Psychopathy: Its Professional and Social Context in Britain', in P. Miller and N. Rose (eds) *The Power of Psychiatry*, Cambridge: Polity Press.

RAMSAY, K. (1996) 'Emotional Labour and Qualitative Research: How I Learned Not to Laugh or Cry in the Field', in E.S. Lyon and J. Busfield (eds) *Methodological Imaginations*, London: Macmillan.

REED, J. (1992) *Review of Health and Social Services for Mentally Disordered Offenders and Others Requiring Similar Services*, London: HMSO.

REGIER, D.A., BOYD, J.M., BURKE, J.D., RAE, D.S., MYERS, J.K., KRAMER, M., ROBINS, L.N., GEORGE, L.K., KARNO, M. and LOCKE, B.Z. (1988) 'One-Month Prevalence of Mental Disorders in the United States', *Archives of General Psychiatry*, 45: 977–86.

RICH, A. (1976) *Of Women Born: Motherhood as Experience and Institution*, New York: Norton.

RIPA, Y. (1990) *Women and Madness: The Incarceration of Women in Nineteenth-Century France*, Cambridge: Polity Press.

RIVERS, W.H. (1918) 'Preface' to G. Elliot Smith and T.H. Pear, *Shell-Shock and Its Lessons*, Cambridge: Cambridge University Press.

ROBERTS, H. (1985) *The Patient Patients*. London: Pandora.

ROBERTSON, N.C. (1974) 'Relationship between Marital Status and Risk of Psychiatric Referral', *British Journal of Psychiatry*, 124: 191–202.

ROSALDO, M.Z. and LAMPHERE, L. (eds) (1974) *Women, Culture and Society*, Stanford: Stanford University Press.

ROSENBERG, C.E. (1968) *The Trial of Assassin Guiteau: Psychiatry and Law in the Gilded Age*, Chicago: University of Chicago Press.

ROSENHAN, D.L. (1973) 'On Being Sane in Insane Places', *Science*, 179: 250–8.

ROTH, M. and KROLL, J. (1986) *The Reality of Mental Illness*, Cambridge: Cambridge University Press.

ROTHMAN, D.J. (1971) *The Discovery of the Asylum: Social Order and Disorder in the New Republic*, Boston: Little Brown & Co.

ROWBOTHAM, S. (1973) *Hidden from History*, London: Pluto.

ROY, A. (1981) 'Vulnerability Factors and Depression in Men', *British Journal of Psychiatry*, 138: 75–7.

ROYAL COLLEGE OF GENERAL PRACTITIONERS (1986) *Morbidity Statistics from General Practice, 1981–2*, London: HMSO.

RUSSELL, D.E.H. (1986) *The Secret Trauma: Incest in the Lives of Girls and Women*, New York: Basic Books.

RUSSELL, G. (1979) 'Bulimia Nervosa: An Ominous Variant of Anorexia Nervosa', *Psychological Medicine*, 9: 429–48.

SAMSON, C. (1995) 'The Fracturing of Medical Dominance in British Psychiatry?' *Sociology of Health and Illness*, 17: 245–68.

SASSOON, S. (1937) *The Complete Memoirs of George Sherston*, London: Faber & Faber.

SAYCE, L., CRAIG, T.K.J. and BOARDMAN, A.P. (1991) 'The Development of Community Mental Health Centres in the United Kingdom', *Social Psychiatry and Psychiatric Epidemiology*, 26: 14–20.

SAYERS, J. (1982) *Biological Politics*, London: Tavistock.

SCHEFF, T.J. (1966) *Being Mentally Ill*, London: Weidenfeld & Nicolson.

SCHEFF, T.J. (1975) 'On Reason and Sanity: Some Political Implications of Psychiatric Thought', in *Labeling Madness*, Englewood Cliffs: Prentice-Hall.

SCHRAG, P. and DIVOKY, D. (1981) *The Myth of the Hyperactive Child and other Means of Child Control*, Harmondsworth: Penguin.

SCHUTZ, A. (1964) 'The Dimensions of the Social World', in *Collected Papers II: Studies in Social Theory*, The Hague: Nijhoft.

SCOTT, J.W. (1986) 'Gender: A Useful Category of Historical Analysis', *American Historical Review*, 91: 1053–75.

SCULL, A.T. (1975) 'From Madness to Mental Illness: Medical Men as Moral Entrepreneurs', *Archives Européenes de Sociologies*, 16: 218–61.

SCULL, A.T. (1979) *Museums of Madness: The Social Organisation of Insanity in 19th Century England*, London: Allen Lane.

SCULL, A.T. (1984) *Decarceration: Community Treatment and the Deviant: A Radical View*, Second Edition, Cambridge: Polity Press.

SCULL, A.T. (1989) *Social Order/Mental Disorder: Anglo-American Psychiatry in Historical Perspective*, London: Routledge.

SCULL, A.T. (1993) *The Most Solitary of Afflictions: Madness and Society in Britain, 1700–1900*, New Haven: Yale University Press.

SEDWICK, P. (1982) *Psychopolitics*, London: Pluto Press.

SEGAL, H. (1964) *Introduction to the Work of Melanie Klein*, London: Heinemann.

SEGAL, H. (1979) *Klein*, London: Fontana.

SEGAL, L. (1987) *Is the Future Female? Troubled Thoughts on Contemporary Feminism*, London: Virago.

SEGAL, L. (1990) *Slow Motion: Changing Masculinities, Changing Men*, London: Virago.

SELIGMAN, M.E.P. (1975) *Helplessness: On Depression Development and Death*. San Francisco: W.H. Freeman.

SELYE, H. (1956) *The Stress of Life*, New York: McGraw-Hill.

SHOWALTER, E. (1980) 'Victorian Women and Insanity', in A. Scull (ed.) *Madhouses, Mad-Doctors, and Madmen*, London: The Althlone Press.

SHOWALTER, E. (1987) *The Female Malady: Women, Madness and English Culture, 1830–1980*, London: Virago.

SHUTTLEWORTH, S. (1990) 'Female Circulation: Medical Discourse and Popular Advertising in the Mid-Victorian Era', in M. Jacobus, E.F. Keller and S. Shuttleworth (eds) *Body/Politics: Women and the Discourse of Science*, London: Routledge.

SKULTANS, V. (1975) *Madness and Morals: Ideas on Insanity in the Nineteenth Century*, London: Routledge & Kegan Paul.

SKULTANS, V. (1979) *English Madness: Ideas on Insanity, 1580–1890*, London: Routledge & Kegan Paul.

SMART, C. (1976) *Women, Crime and Criminology*, London: Routledge & Kegan Paul.

SMITH, D.E. (1967) 'A Version of Mental Illness', Department of Sociology, University of Essex, Unpublished.

SMITH, D.E. (1975) 'The Statistics on Mental Illness: What They Will Not Tell Us about Women and Why', in D.E. Smith and S.J. David (eds) *Women Look at Psychiatry*, Vancouver: Press Gang.

SMITH, D.E. (1978) ' "K is Mentally Ill": The Anatomy of a Factual Account', *Sociology*, 12: 23–53.

SMITH, D.E. and DAVID, S.J. (eds) (1975) *Women Look at Psychiatry*, Vancouver: Press Gang.

SMITH, R. (1981) *Trial by Medicine: Insanity and Responsibility in Victorian Trials*, Edinburgh: Edinburgh University Press.

SMITH-ROSENBERG, C. and ROSENBERG, C.E. (1973) 'The Female Animal: Medical and Biological Views of Women and Her Role in Nineteenth Century America', *Journal of American History*, 60: 332–56.

SMITH-ROSENBERG, C. (1974) 'Puberty to Menopause: The Cycle of Femininity in Nineteenth Century America', in M. Hartmann and L.W. Banner (eds) *Clio's Consciousness Raised*, New York: Harper & Row.

SPECTOR, M. (1972) 'Legitimating Homosexuality', *Society*, 14: 52–6.

SPITZER, R.M., GIBBON, M., SKODOL, A.E., WILLIAMS, J.B.W. and FIRST, M.B. (1994) *DSM-IV Casebook*, Washington: American Psychiatric Press.

SROLE, L., LANGNER, T.S., MICHAEL, S.T. and OPLER, M.K. (1962) *Mental Health in the Metropolis*, New York: McGraw-Hill.

STACEY, M. (1988) *The Sociology of Health and Healing*, London: Unwin Hyman.

STAFFORD-CLARK, D. and BRIDGES, A.C. (1990) *Psychiatry for Students*, Seventh Edition. London: Unwin Hyman.

STARK, E. and FLITCRAFT, A.H. (1988) 'Women and Children at Risk: A Feminist Perspective on Child Abuse', *International Journal of Health Services*, 18: 99–118.

STOLLER, R. (1968) *Sex and Gender*, New York: Science House.

STONE, M. (1985) 'Shell-shock and the Psychologists', in W.F. Bynum, R. Porter and M. Shepherd (eds) *The Anatomy of Madness*, Vol II, *Institutions and Society*. London: Tavistock.

SUDNOW, D. (1965) 'Normal Crimes: Sociological Features of the Penal Code in a Public Defender Office', *Social Problems*, 12: 255–76.

SURTEES, P.G., DEAN, C., INGHAM, J.G., KREITMAN, N.B., MILLER, P. McC. and SASMIDHARAN, S.P. (1983) 'Psychiatric Disorder in Women from an Edinburgh Community: Associations with Demographic Factors, *British Journal of Psychiatry*, 142: 238–46.

SZASZ, T.S. (1960) 'The Myth of Mental Illness'. *The American Psychologist*, 15: 113–8.

SZASZ, T.S. (1961) *The Myth of Mental Illness*, New York: Hoeber-Harper.

SZASZ, T.S. (1971) *The Manfacture of Madness: A Comparative Study of the Inquisition and the Mental Health Movement*, London: Routledge & Kegan Paul.

SZASZ, T.S. (1981) 'Anti-psychiatry: the Paradigm of the Plundered Mind', in O. Grusky and M. Pollner (eds) *The Sociology of Mental Illness*, New York: Holt, Rinehart & Winston.

TAVRIS, C. (1992) *The Mismeasure of Woman*, New York: Simon & Schuster.

TAYLOR, E.A. (1985) *The Hyperactive Child*, London: Dunitz.

THANE, P. (1978) 'Women and the Poor Law in Victorian and Edwardian Britain', *History Workshop Journal*, 6.

THOMPSON, E.P. (1963) *The Making of the English Working Class*, Harmondsworth: Penguin.

THOMPSON, L. and WALKER, A.J. (1989) 'Gender in Families: Women and Men in Marriage: Work and Parenthood', *Journal of Marriage and the Family*, 51: 845–71.

TOTMAN, R. (1990) *Mind, Stress and Health*, London: Souvenir Press.

TOWNSEND, P. and DAVIDSON, N. (eds) (1988) *Inequalities in Health: The Black Report*, Hamondsworth: Penguin.

TUDOR, W., TUDOR, J.F. and GOVE, W.R. (1977) 'The Effect of Sex Role Differences on the Social Control of Mental Illness', *Journal of Health and Social Behaviour*, 18: 98–112.

TUKE, J.B. (1865) 'On the Statistics of Puerperal Insanity as Observed in the Royal Edinburgh Asylum, Morningside, *Edinburgh Medical Journal*, 19: 1013–28.

TUKE, S. (1813) *Description of The Retreat*, York: W. Alexander.

TURNER, B. (1987) *Medical Power and Social Knowledge*, London: Sage.

TURNER, R.H. (1962) 'Role Taking: Process versus Conformity'. In A.M. Rose (ed.) *Human Behaviour and Social Processes*, London: Routledge & Kegan Paul.

TYNDEL, M. (1974) 'Psychiatric Study of 1000 Alcoholic Patients', *Canadian Psychiatric Association Journal*, 19: 21–4.

UNSWORTH, C. (1987) *The Politics of Mental Health Legislation*, Oxford: Clarendon Press.

USSHER, J. (1991) *Women's Madness: Misogyny or Mental Illness?*, London: Harvester Wheatsheaf.

VAN DEN BRINK, W., MAARTEN, W., KOETER, M., ORMEL, J., DIKSTRA, W., GIEL, R., SLOOFF, C. and WOHLFARTH, T.D. (1989) 'Psychiatric Diagnosis in an Out-patient Population', *Archives of General Psychiatry*, 46: 369–72.

VEITH, I. (1965) *Hysteria: The History of a Disease*, Chicago: University of Chicago Press.

WALBY, S. (1989) 'Theorising Patriarchy', *Sociology*, 23: 214–34.

WALBY, S. (1990) *Theorising Patriarchy*, Oxford: Basil Blackwell.

WALKER, N. (1968) *Crime and Insanity in England, Vol 1: The Historical Perspective*, Edinburgh: Edinburgh University Press.

WARREN, C.A.B. (1987) *Mad-Wives: Schizophrenic Women in the 1950s*, New Brunswick: Rutgers University Press.

WEISSMAN, M.M. and KLERMAN, G.L. (1977) 'Sex Differences and the Epidemiology of Depression'. *Archives of General Psychiatry*, 34: 98–111.

WEISSMAN, M.M. and KLERMAN, G.L. (1985) 'Gender and Depression'. *TINS*, September, 416–20.

WEST, R. (1982) [1918] *The Return of the Soldier*, London: Virago.

WING, J.K., COOPER, J.E. and SARTORIUS, N. (1974) *Description and Classification of Psychiatric Symptoms*, Cambridge: Cambridge University Press.

WINOKUR, G. (1972) 'Family History Studies: VIII. Secondary Depression is Alive and Well, and ...', *Diseases of the Nervous System*, 33: 94–9.

WITTKOWER, E. and SPILLANE, J.P. (1940) 'A Survey of the Literature of Neuroses in War', in E. Miller (ed.) *The Neuroses in War*, London: Macmillan.

WOOD, A.D. (1974) '"The Fashionable Diseases": Women's Complaints and their Treatment in Nineteenth-Century America', in M.S. Hartman and L. Banner (eds) *Clio's Consciousness Raised*, New York: Harper.

WOODIWISS, A. (1993) 'Postmodernity: Only in America? BSA Research Imaginations Conference, University of Essex, April.

WOODWARD, J. (1974) *To Do the Sick No Harm: A Study of the British Voluntary Hospital System to 1875*, London: Routledge & Kegan Paul.

WOOTTON, B. (1959) *Social Science and Social Pathology*, London: Allen & Unwin.

WORLD HEALTH ORGANISATION (1992) *The ICD-10 Classification of Mental and Behavioural Disorders: Cultural Descriptions and Diagnostic Guidelines*, Geneva: World Health Organisation.

WRONG, D.M. (1963) 'The Oversocialised Conception of Man in Modern Sociology', *American Sociological Review*, 26: 184–93.

WYNNE, L.C., RYCKOFF, I., DAY, J. and HIRSCH, S. (1958) 'Pseudo-mutuality in the Family Relations of Schizophremics', *Psychiatry*, 21: 205–20.

YALOM, I., LUNDE, D.T., MOOS, R.H. and HAMBURG, D.A. (1968) '"Postpartum Blues" Syndrome', *Archives of General Psychiatry*, 18: 16–27.

ZELDOW, R. (1978) 'Sex Differences in Psychiatric Evaluation and Treatment: An Empirical Review', *Archives of General Psychiatry*, 35: 89–93.

ZIMMERMAN, M. and CORYELL, W.H. (1990) 'Diagnosing Personality Disorders in the Community', *Archives of General Psychiatry*, 47: 527–31.

Name Index

Subject Index